PRAISE F

'Wise words from an experien[...]
finding very helpful during a period of deep personal [...]

Richard Bonner, Operations Director at Micro Nav Ltd

'It was a wonderful read'

**Gomathi (Krishnan) Vinod, Director at AnCenergy
Technology Services Pvt Ltd**

'An inspirational journey into the world of self-belief and
self-leadership'

Charles McGeoch, Service Operations Manager NTT Ltd

'Whatever cards you've been dealt, this is a superb guide to
playing them well!'

Jim Lawless – Author of *Taming Tigers*

thrive

7 Steps to Successful Self-Leadership

GEORGE WILKINSON

Red Door

Published by RedDoor
www.reddoorpress.co.uk

Every effort has been made to trace copyright holders and to obtain their
permission for the use of copyright material. The author and publisher
apologise for any errors or omissions and would be grateful if notified of any
corrections that should be incorporated in future reprints or editions of this book

Some names and identifying details have been changed to protect
the privacy of individuals.

ISBN 978-1913062-31-6

A CIP catalogue record for this book is available from the British Library

Cover design: Adam Thorpe

Typesetting: Sheerdesignandtypesetting.co.uk

Printed and bound in Denmark by Nørhaven

To Jane, Maria and Lewis
who have taught me more
than they will ever know!

To all those who wish to lead and inspire themselves and others. Who may be out there, right in the thick of it, looking for hope and a clear way ahead.

To build a better tomorrow we must be better than we are today, and we cannot look outside of ourselves for the answer. We must drive forward internally so that one day we will flourish, which we all have the power to do. And that day could be tomorrow – you just never know.

Contents

Introduction   9

Chapter 1:
Achieving Success   19
'Success is truly a personal thing – but make it count.'

Chapter 2:
Perseverance   55
'To persevere and dig deep is sometimes the only way forward.'

Chapter 3:
Emotional Mastery   93
'If we don't master our emotions, they will only ensure that they master us.'

Chapter 4:
Embracing Failure   141
'Failure teaches us lessons; there can be no other way to view it.'

Chapter 5:
Decision-making   179
'A skill that if we improve on, will improve us.'

Chapter 6:
Leadership of Others   235
'In order to lead others, we must first lead ourselves.'

Chapter 7:
Serving Others   283
'Service to others is a privilege, that builds our character.'

Afterword: Build a Better Tomorrow   309

Acknowledgements   311

Notes   313

About the Author   319

Introduction

Life, and work, is not just about survival, getting by, maintaining the minimum – it's about thriving! Living a life that feels more dynamic in nature, moving, growing and alive. Seeing potential and possibility in everything that you do – even the small things in life, and in those quieter moments too. Seeing the possibilities that lie in front of you – believing that you can be and do more and then intentionally driving change. Then, as a result, feeling that excitement, that joy, that pleasure, or being aware of a sense of quiet contentment in your actions – both in your everyday life as well as in your work.

To thrive is never to be a victim to circumstance, or others. It is about always living your life much more on your terms. Living in the moment and breathing new possibility into your life as each second unfolds. And taking these precious moments and consciously transforming them with purpose, thus giving your future self and career – a better opportunity than they had yesterday.

But how on earth do we undertake this? How do we get to a position in which we believe we are putting the best into our activities – and getting the real juice out of them – and into our lives? And doing this to the extent that we can move forward and grow and maintain that momentum?

THE ANSWER – SELF-LEADERSHIP!

To lead yourself in everything that you do, to take conscious ownership of what you do day-to-day – this tool will take you there!

Thrive: 7 Steps to Successful Self-Leadership focuses our attention on seven steps in life that if followed can help to bring about significant transformation in our own leadership potential.

I'm sure we are all familiar with the term leadership, but maybe not self-leadership? Either way, let's define self-leadership, as it is so relevant. Well, self-leadership is about looking into the mirror and taking charge of that person staring back. It's about taking responsibility for your own life and actions, to see it through – to take on the tough times – being accountable for your own choices and actions and aiming – really aiming – to give life your best shot!

It concerns the courage to be vulnerable and make the tough decisions that life will inevitably present you with, even when you don't want to. Self-leadership deals with the knowledge of yourself, maintaining a strong awareness of who you really are and how you affect your own life and the lives of those around you. And when it's called for, to hold the mirror up to yourself to both reflect and influence your mind, to improve your body and soul so that you are able to move beyond who you are today – to become the best you can be in life.

Life can throw a lot at us, and it can be tough, remarkably tough at times. Nonetheless, in any given moment we have choices to make – the choice of what we think about, how we act, feel and speak; and yes, we can change our actions with practice. There are many people we can be in any given point in time: the friend, the hero, the villain, jealous one, the confidante, the decision-maker, the protector, the speaker, the listener, the giver, the courageous one, the lover, the best that we can be. It is up to us how we wish to express ourselves and how we act – and how we respond.

It is not always easy to be our very best – it's a fact. At times, we don't have the energy, the time, the freedom, the patience, the immediate support, or even the know-how. However, we can at least be aware that we have choices in any given situation, and we can aim to be our best, and to make it our goal in life. It won't always be simple to make it work because life, our thoughts, our habits, our emotions, and a host of past experiences, which shape us, will crop up and try to throw us off course. But by leading ourselves, and by adopting responsibility, we can always go further. And I firmly believe that we can all make progress.

If we thrive and work and do well in life, as best we can, then we will always be a better person today than we were yesterday. Doing well in life, as I see it, does not need to be about obtaining vast material possessions. Sometimes to do well is having the ability to get through another day, to be mentally strong when situations are draining, to make the crucial choice, to persevere when times are hard and there are no answers in sight; to listen well, to support others and direct them to success; to attend someone who is sick, to give advice to another that you wished you had been given (but which they might not want to hear).

It all returns to the fundamental maxim – to thrive by growing yourself, so by applying the seven steps explained within seven chapters, you can shine and become the best version of yourself that you can be. It's not about the cards that you are dealt, but how you play your hand. To obtain more happiness, to self-improve, to live a life with more emotional freedom, and to make better choices with the aim of leading a more rewarding life, both at work and at play.

Successful self-leadership is not only fundamental to achieving the improvements mentioned; it also gives you the building blocks with which to lead others. While some could argue that leaders are born and not made, in order to lead others, we must be able to lead ourselves. And so, leadership starts from the inside out: we become a leader, we are not born one. Therefore, the art of self-leadership is a fundamental quality in the leadership of other people. How is it possible for someone to lead another if they still have not mastered the art of leading themselves?

Modern-day leadership walks hand in hand with challenges that include strategic thought, decision-making, diversity of teams, locations and working time zones, automation, company politics and the eternal management of stakeholders.

Today's leaders find themselves in perhaps a more demanding period than at any previous point in the history of working life. Which only emphasises the point that all leaders – and that includes parents – must be able to grow and develop their skills in self-leadership. It's a vital skill, necessary not only to survive in the world of leadership, but also in order to thrive in the role.

This book addresses the subjects of success, perseverance, emotions, failure, decisions, leadership of others, and the ability to serve others. I address these subjects through the seven key steps of self-leadership – which will help to develop a greater potential in us all.

The seven steps have been born out of reflection on my own experiences in my working and personal life, observation and research. I served in the armed forces for seven years. I Left the British Royal Navy shortly after having served in the Gulf War in 1991. This period gave me my first real introduction to really starting to learn about myself and how to push beyond my limits. It also gave me the benefit of working with and to really learn about a whole variety of people from different walks of life.

Later, I spent two decades as a leader and manager in various industries, and close to a decade as a trainer and consultant. My working life has seen me spend time in leadership and strategic roles on several multimillion leading-edge business programmes, which have tested me to the limit at times – and where I've seen the best and also the worst in others.

Although work and life has thrown a lot my way and I've sometimes failed – and ended up with a metaphorical bloody nose and dashed hopes several times over – I've also tasted accomplishments that have grown me, and had some superb achievements in both my career and personal life. An example in my career was when I played a pivotal role in the set-up of an offshore company office. Then, before I could catch my breath, I was asked to lead a cross-company project to success – against all the odds – both of which contributed towards personal recognition from the company CEO of a large corporation. And that one had to be earned through sheer grit!

These successes have led to more tests being thrown my way, where I have worked in several industries, with a whole variety of people. On reflection, my whole career has given me a truly special insight into how I work and also, which is more fascinating to me – the way other people tick.

I have several examples of accomplishments in my personal life, but the ones that stand out the most are my various philanthropic endeavours and organised fundraising events. But probably my proudest achievements from fundraising have come from several physical personal endeavours, which have included marathon running, several long-distance bike rides and a long-distance swim, and throwing myself 15,000 feet out of a perfectly serviceable aircraft. All of which raised several thousand pounds for great charitable causes. Each of these activities loomed large and were daunting to me to begin with – and as I undertook them, they became excellent vehicles for me to learn self-discipline and gain confidence. I definitely grew as a result.

But the biggest lesson that I had to learn was about myself, was how to make use of the seven steps of self-leadership in my own life, and to promote it. After I pursued my business in another direction for a time, after a failed venture with a huge personal commitment, I drove myself into a bad physical state through sheer overwork, one where I prolapsed a disc in my back as a result! It was as I lay in a hospital bed and reflected on the *white hot pain* that had struck my lower back the previous day, when I couldn't even crawl due to the pain – I knew something had to change. Something that was only reinforced when I discovered that I would be left with permanent nerve damage in my back.

It's ironic that adversity can be our biggest teacher in life; it was at this point I knew my life could no longer continue in the same way any longer. As a consequence, I believed that I could help others out there to recognise, and navigate through, the eminently difficult paths that we can end up travelling down. To advise on how we can take control of our lives, or the other forces that influence us – and to make a genuine difference in the world. Hence, this book.

I don't count myself any worse off than anyone else, and I have learned and aimed to grow through these negative experiences to better myself. What is more, my purpose now is to use all of my experience and my research to support you in your path to improve yourself. I genuinely want the very best for you.

Like it or not, you are the driver of your own life. Your life is your responsibility, but you can choose to rest a stack of blame on situations and on other people. Yes, life can throw some hardship in your direction at times, as it does at all of us. But you should always remember that no one ever needs to be beaten by circumstance or setbacks.

If you are to change and improve, the change in you must come from within, no one will hand it to you. The biggest enemy in life can be ourselves, which can leave us frustrated at the best of times. And yet our biggest friend, ally, supporter and saviour can also be ourselves. The trouble is that we sometimes simply don't accept this. We find it difficult to hold up the mirror and realise, with honesty, that we need to grow our character. Therefore, I ask that, while you read the book in its entirety, you pause, stop and self-reflect after each chapter to assess what you can change or introduce into your working and personal life in order to improve your situation.

This book is written in seven chapters, each representing a step that will provide you with insights, techniques and real-life experiences, along with contributions from other authors on their own experiences. It is written in a way that allows you to reflect on your own life after each chapter, and to introduce new ways of thinking, reacting and speaking in your daily working and personal life. By leading yourself more, you will thrive.

Good luck with the book. My aim is that it provides you with seven steps with which to improve all areas of your life. We only have one life to live. Be the best you can be.

The relationship between the 7 steps where emotions are fundamental to everything.

Chapter 1

Achieving Success

'It is not the mountains we conquer but ourselves'

Sir Edmund Hillary

The definition of success is 'the accomplishment of an aim or purpose', and history is full of success stories of one kind or another. In this modern age you only need surf the internet for a short period before someone's definition of success is staring you in the face. However, success can be the achievement of any aim or any purpose that could appear insignificant to some, while others it will greatly please; success is relative to the given situation.

Success can occur in any area of our lives, including work, relationships, sports, hobbies, business deals, and the raising of healthy and happy children. Success for some can be as simple an act as remembering your wedding anniversary or being a good neighbour. It does not necessarily need to be bound to a rag to riches story, fame, or the next big college drop-out entrepreneur who floats their company on the stock market within a few years of starting out. Maybe you are already enough, and don't need anything new to make you feel more successful. Maybe success to you is a feeling of security, a friendship, a love and continuing great relationship that you already enjoy. Success is truly a personal thing.

There are several aspects to success that must be understood, or at least reflected upon, before we look at success with respect to self-leadership. Although achieving success is what we are aiming for – it can present us with several challenges along the way. Well, no surprise there then. But, typically, these challenges can all be overcome if we approach things in the right way. Then again, it doesn't always have to be *exactly the right way*, it can be any way – a way – to help us move forward, because we can always learn and improve as we progress. We really can.

So, before we dive into this subject a little deeper, let's reflect on some of the mechanics related to success to show that it's not some magic black art, there is a science behind it. There are things that we need to know and there are things that we have to master. And sometimes it's actually all about reflecting or knowing what we really want that counts, as opposed to 'thinking' it's what we want. That, my friend, knowing what we 'actually' want, can make all the difference between success and failure in a whole variety of circumstances. Anyway, let's crack on.

SUCCESS AND OUR MINDSET

If you are looking outside of yourself thinking that it's the world you need to conquer in respect to any success, then you could not be more wrong. It's all about you, and this is the lesson we all have to painfully learn, especially when it comes to any substantial achievement in life. An accomplishment out of the norm, a feat or goal that you have to strive for that takes you out of your comfort zone, will demand your thoughts, actions, self-discipline, patience, and faith that it will all come together. It will also require the essential ability in you to believe in yourself when the path is uphill and there is no end in sight, and also to be able to find comfort in small pieces of happiness in times of hardship; something which is nicely spelled out in Rudyard Kipling's poem 'If'.

In these types of situations, where you are being stretched, rather than playing out life's daily routines, the battleground of success is firmly in the mind. Get this fact and then believe it, and you are more than halfway towards to achieving your goals.

A great example are topflight tennis players, where they state that playing another top seed in the latter part of a tournament is not just about the physical game. The real game that they are playing is in the mind. They first need to win the battle in their own heads – before they can go on to win the physical one. When you watch their pacing, their temperament, their self-control – it's all part of a game of the mind.

Many moons ago while at school and Naval college, I used to swim competitively, and before any race I undertook the nerves would fly. The butterflies would be circling inside, flying in no formation whatsoever. It all got worse, with odd glances and smart comments in the dressing room and the warm-up laps. It all started to crack away at my confidence. However, we were all in the same boat, even the swimmers that were truly stronger than me felt the same edginess before their race meets. But this never struck me at the time. If I met those swimmers in the street, we were equal, but before a race, well, most of them were all invincible – in my head.

Some of us had rituals that we would not deviate from before we competed. One of my rituals was that I had to pack my swim bag and have the same equipment in it, even if I knew some items were never needed. They had to be packed! Others wore the same top or had an odd physical routine. But all of it was part of building some form of personal endorsement that we were kind enough to turn up and that things were going to be okay. We weren't going to collapse in a heap and sink like a brick or make a horrendous turn at the edge of the pool – like an idiot.

None of these thoughts was anything to do with our physical strength or stamina; all of this was in the mind, deep in our thoughts. It didn't matter that the average competitor was probably committed to a gruelling training schedule that ran into the order of fifteen to eighteen hours a week – before and after school and college. We were fitter than the vast majority of our age. And in the right frame of mind, with the right mindset, there was virtually nothing in between first and last in terms of time, but maybe a few seconds. A good state of mind on the day – could win you the race against stronger swimmers, whose mindsets were in the wrong place. Each one of us was in a state of peak fitness! But no one gave a single thought to that fact.

Then if you did do well in a race, you never looked back! You were full of endorphins and euphoria, and you never gave your needful rituals or your lucky blue top a second conscious thought. They were ignored. That was until the next time. And that is when they all came back for the next race, as a strange but comforting habit, to support our thoughts, to aid our mindset, to help boost our self-confidence, to help control our ridiculous and crippling mental saboteurs. And if we did this, we felt better, and we believed we performed better.

And that is where self-leadership comes into its own, because it's within the brain that the battles of success are won and lost – in the mind. There is a famous quote from Henry Ford – 'Whether you think you can, or think you can't – you're right' – which emphasises how much attitude determines success or failure. If you think this is a misleading statement, and you are under the illusion that it's all about something out there, something or someone outside of you, it is not. And I could not be more serious about this point.

To succeed – mindset is everything

Moreover, whilst others can and will contribute towards many of your successes in life, and sometimes frustratingly, annoyingly get in the way of it, it's not about them. Success depends on you. Your head, heart, thoughts, emotions, your quirks and habits, your likes and dislikes, all of which make up you.

We need to understand that success is in our head and not outside of it – it's an interpretation of reality, a perception, a set of events or a situation that you wish to create or co-create. So, when things do come together to your satisfaction, then this interpretation of your reality can be deciphered as a success. We must come to terms with the knowledge that no one has ever strived for and achieved anything in life without first winning the battle of the mind.

Though, typically, unless you are a top athlete or company CEO, successful business owner or similar, and are conditioned to fully understand and live this insight, you won't realise this until you have achieved something of real significance.

So, if a fantastic feat does come together in your life, something that you have stretched and strived for, then that is absolutely wonderful, and I'm sure you feel the self-growth inside as a result. However, first things first: understand and appreciate that success is in your head, because if you get this point, know this truth, then you will be able to unlock some of the self-leadership potential that is resident within you when you need it. Also, it will help you build the ability to become more self-aware and self-reflect. To learn the lessons when things don't go your way, which in life can and will happen, even though some of those lessons can be tough to take when they do come about.

> 'If I have the belief that I can do it, I shall surely acquire the capacity to do it even if I may not have it at the beginning.'

Mahatma Gandhi

ARE YOU A DABBLER, OR ARE YOU SERIOUS?

Many of us play around with life at times. We tinker, dabble, do a bit of this and that – we experiment. We may take up a hobby for a period until something else comes along and then drop it, and then on occasions only go back to resuming our old hobby. Does this resonate?

I firmly know and believe that to undertake the above modus operandi is perfectly acceptable – when you are fully conscious and self-aware of what you are doing. Life has many twists and turns, and toying with life's activities is all about exploring, learning and knowing what you want from its rich tapestry; it's part of building your self-knowledge and, yes, often merely to amuse yourself. We've all dabbled in various activities from a young age when we began to explore the world around us; it's part of growing and learning, so why should we stop as adults?

When you dabble or experiment (whatever word works for you) there may also be an element of trying to understand what you are good at or what you are not so good at, or better expressed – appreciating your limits. Accept that this is all okay, life is not always about striving to be your best all of the time and there are times when we do indeed need to lighten up a little. To drop the pretentious nonsense that we always have to be strict or severe with ourselves and determined to be our best – every damn day of every week. Sometimes – we want to have fun – switch off, and hey – do something for the sheer hell of it.

But be careful here – you need to know the difference between experimenting and being serious. Where are you? On what side of the fence are you sat? You need to know and become fully self-aware of where you are positioned. To be honest I have been guilty in the past of investing money and time into what could have become an expensive hobby, where I *thought* I could grow an interest, which was to make a passive income through affiliate marketing. But it began to take up all of my spare time until I brutally woke up through my own growing self-awareness that I was literally wasting my time. I eventually detected deep down that I wasn't actually that interested in the whole affair.

My goal was to raise an additional income – but with no genuine interest in what I was doing, what was the damn point of spending all my time spare time *playing with something*, that I simply had no enthusiasm for?! Now, the few may have made real money out of this activity, as a sole income, and good for them, but it just wasn't for me.

And this is the point: you need to have love – or at the very least have a genuine vested interest – in what you do, otherwise where are you taking your life? What have you got going forward to look back on?

So, you really ought to reflect on whether you are investing in something that you believe deep down you will not be committed to – unless you see it solely as an interest or hobby. Therefore be fully aware of your stance here. Appreciate that you only have so much energy to spend in this life – so spend it well, my friend.

Look, I believe the majority of us in life have been guilty of deluding ourselves at times, and we fall into the trap and get ourselves involved in something that we know will not captivate our interest or love. But part of us 'thinks' we can. Part of us wants us to commit to something that deep down inside – we simply feel or know will get us nowhere.

But it can feel a tricky path-balancing act – that's for sure.

So, the point here is to establish your position, whether you are serious. Do you wish to dabble, experiment or grow your experience and not focus on something specific? And if you do wish to be deliberate about your vision of success, then engage. If you are in doubt as to your true position, seek the support of a mentor or coach, or trusted friend, to help you to know the difference, someone that can help you observe your situation, as if you were independent of it – before taking the next step, which is where the rubber hits the road – the honesty test.

BE HONEST WITH YOURSELF

There are two simple but powerful questions you must ask yourself to assess whether you are absolutely serious about your project.

Self-reflect on your goal, and without thinking too deeply, first consider: 'Can I achieve my goal?' Do you have a plausible and achievable goal that you can fully commit to? Second, ask yourself: 'Do I want to achieve my goal?' Do you have a genuine interest in your goal and do you feel genuinely passionate about it, even if obstacles are thrown in your path – time constraints/family ties/ long evenings working/financial sacrifices?

Now find a quiet place where you feel comfortable and ask yourself the questions again – ask your gut. Feel the sensations within.

This honesty assessment is a quick and straightforward self-reflection on how you feel intuitively, within your body. You are then asking your heart and not your head. If this assessment turns out to be positive, even if you don't yet know the exact steps to take you need to achieve what you wish, you are part way to achieving your goals already, even the tough ones.

An honesty assessment is not about fooling yourself, it's about having a natural inner feeling that you can achieve what you wish to even if you can't yet see the full picture. By asking for a sincere (heart) answer, rather than a head answer, you are drawing on your inner friend, 'you', when you need support most. This is where your intentions lie, deep inside, and if you can tap into these a whole new world can open up for you.

It's important to carry out this assessment on a regular basis, and to never fall into the trap of lying to yourself while doing this. If you maintain this honesty with yourself in how serious you are and take corrective action when things do not feel right, it will be hard for you to go wrong.

One excellent reason for doing this exercise is that if you can tap into that part of you where a passion stirs, then this can be the very fuel, inside of you, for what you want to achieve. A passion for something can move mountains in that it can move all sorts of obstacles out of your way to create what you want. And if you are honest with yourself and feel that you have a passion for something, then you have tapped into that special incredible force within. One that can help inspire and self-direct you – and make the most difficult of challenges feasible and the seemingly impossible possible.

And this is true for a great many people today that have searched within for what really counts and are honest with themselves in the process. On occasion, being honest with yourself can be tough, but a lot of good can come out of it if you stand tall and pluck up the courage and move forward to where your heart wishes to lead.

'Self-awareness involves deep personal honesty.
It comes from asking and answering the hard questions.'

Stephen Covey

MAINTAIN SELF-AWARENESS BUT PUSH FOR SUCCESS

If you passed the honesty test, and you consider your situation a little more, how do you feel about your goal now? This is a time for inner reflection, which is likely to leave you feeling excited, eager, maybe with an edge of trepidation. Do you have a sense of inner drive and vigour? Do you sense that you have a self-belief in what you can achieve and succeed with your skills and expertise? Or on the contrary, do you currently feel like a cog in a wheel, not totally in control. And are you aware of your shortfalls, and how will you make up for them?

Many different sensations will be pulsing through your body and mind when assessing how you perceive yourself in the process of trying to achieve what it is you wish to be successful at. This inner reflection is close to the first exercise but requires you to pay close attention to how you feel when you visualise yourself in the process as you acquire your goal.

Feeling scared or worried about the unknown are natural sensa-tions, and these will fade with time as you create momentum. If you feel overwhelmed, it can be a sign that you have taken on too much, and need to seek some degree of support or even take a step back and make an assessment of what you have taken on, with a view to reconsidering your approach. Either way, maintain a healthy self-awareness at all times, and pay close attention to your heart and not your head when it comes to what you 'want' to do as opposed to what you think you 'should do', as there is a clear difference.

Here, one significant aspect to be addressed is the subject of failure. For us to fully get to grips with our challenge, we must face the prospect of failure squarely in the face. We perceive failure as our biggest headache, our demon, and our own worst enemy. It is typically the thought we hate the most, but it should be the thing we learn to embrace. That doesn't mean we should want to fail and it doesn't mean we shouldn't plan to avoid failure; it just means that we should not be afraid to fail, because it will happen from time to time.

What it comes down to is the question of what we look to conquer or achieve when it comes to success. Where is the fight, what is the battle? By this I mean we need to ask ourselves: Is it the battle out there, in the objective world? Is it the tangible, practical things that we can touch, feel and see, and that we must use as we try to pull our plan together to make progress? The meetings, the materials, the seemingly endless time and tiresome effort that we expend for us to get our thing off the ground? Or is the battle in our mind? Is it in our conscious self-perception of what we believe we can or cannot do or achieve? Do the problems or the obstacles that stand in our way on the outside, actually lie within?

Well, it's an illusion that the issue is always out there somewhere in the objective world. So, my response to these questions is – it's both! Both genuinely make a difference when we are up against a challenge. If we don't or can't possess the materials or practical elements to achieve, then it stands to reason that we can only prog-ress so far. If I don't have the correct materials, the tools, I haven't got the right uninterrupted space to write my book, I don't have a meeting venue booked with the right people in attendance to present my business proposition successfully, and so on, then how I can be successful? So yes, if we don't have or can't acquire the practical and objective parts, the tools that contribute towards our ability to achieve most things, then there are genuine issues we need to overcome.

But when we have both elements to address the mindset and the practical aspects, if we have enough emotional drive and belief in ourselves, then we can achieve almost anything, even when the objective and practical parts of our puzzle are few and far between, and we can't see a way through. Therefore, the heart must be leading on this one, at the forefront of the battle, otherwise there is no point moving forward, as the head will only get so far without the heart. The heart will make all the difference. It will conquer many obstacles along the way and make all the difference in a time of crisis or massive indecision.

That is where we need honesty and determination to become the driving force; we need to flip the conscious switch inside our heads that fill us up with hope and self-confidence so that we are able to stride forward and make progress. Even if we need to turn our goals into smaller and more manageable tasks – to make progress in small baby steps. If the heart is absolutely committed, there isn't much in life that can stop you.

A BATTLE OF WILL OVER CIRCUMSTANCE

There has been research out there to show that you don't have to be overly talented physically or mentally to succeed in a variety of cases. In my own experience I have seen the less gifted, astute at a given task or physically adept, manage to muscle through virtually any task, given the time and the tools to do so. This is down to people who adopt a laser-like focus, the desire, and the ability to strive on.

An example of this is when I served in the Navy and was part of a difficult week-long intensive training course with the British Army, during one hot summer. This was so that we could qualify to become part of a Quick Reaction Force to defend against enemy threat, such as terrorism, back on ship. Essentially, we were training in some of the Army's tactics, but we were not soldiers, at the end of day, and as a result we had to work extra hard to learn and employ their methods.

Then over the last three days and nights of training we were out in the field. Here we performed various training drills, explosive training, armed and unarmed combat sessions with them during the day, and overnight the camp was split into three groups. With each group being on a two-hourly rota, which consisted of patrolling, guarding the camp and painfully trying to sleep in bivouacs with no sides, which meant they were open to the elements. And one night it rained – and hard! Now, being from Scotland I practically grew up in the rain, but this was not my idea of fun. So, in all, there was a maximum limit of two hours sleep you could grab in any one night. Not ideal.

When dawn broke on the last day, we were all exhausted, but we tried to maintain our best composure to fight back the fatigue – even though it was emotionally difficult. Suddenly, at about 6 a.m. that morning, just as we rounded our gear up after a rubbish breakfast, the staff attempted to invade the camp! All part of their devilish plan. There then ensued a three-hour-long pretend battle, made to feel real, with a thirty-plus strong team of armed protesters who challenged our camp, which we had to defend. Most of us had to use riot shields, which were being hit with baseball bats and the like, as they attempted to force their way into camp.

In addition was the fact that they attacked us so early in the morning, which made it all the more a mental and physical challenge. And because of the lack of sleep bloody hard; I personally had not slept for over three days due to the humidity and heavy rain. However, everyone pulled their weight, even though we were not by far the most gifted and definitely not the smartest of would-be soldiers; *after all, we were not soldiers.*

I personally knew some of the guys well and was aware that like me they were just about keeping their heads together through this physically challenging and noisy affair, especially with the lack of sleep! I at one point had to drop to the deck where I stood, which happened to be in a deep muddy puddle, and guard against another attack. I was armed with a rifle and lay as still as I could, but after five or so minutes I fell asleep and only awoke after I sucked muddy water up my nose. I was left gasping air in hard through my mouth, as I thought I was drowning! Which is one way to wake up on a wet Friday morning.

Either way, we were all determined not to fail; we were all emotionally driven, focused and displayed some real signs of grit to get through this demanding battle, of course, successfully. We were self-aware of our situation and our shortcomings and made up for these through our tenacity and aspiration to succeed.

I'm glad to say it all kind of went well, we all got through the course in one piece. However, I must admit, when we clambered onto the train home later that evening, through sheer fatigue we would have had trouble fighting off a mosquito. However, the point here is that this simple example demonstrates that having an awareness of our abilities was paramount, but the overriding belief that mind over matter could win over in a time of importance was what got us through.

Maintaining self-awareness is key to knowing your abilities, how you are feeling and maintaining your relationship with your experiences. It also helps you know emotionally how to best to interact when challenges that are thrown your way, and whether you lack the natural talents to deal with them, in a given situation. But don't let a lack of abilities that you feel you may suffer from prevent you from hitting your goals. Our ability not to give in and push through with sheer grit and determination can make all the difference between success and failure. If you believe in yourself and push through the obstacles with audacity and a good strategy you will succeed.

'Success is not final; failure is not fatal: it is the courage to continue that counts.'

Winston Churchill

OUR BIGGEST ENEMY

Much more significant than any self-doubt in our abilities that we may suffer from, and which may call on us to use grit to push forward – is fear. Fear is, by far, the biggest enemy that we face when we are not already successful at what we do or knowing what we want to achieve.

Like most, I have personally feared many things in my life, but like most, in almost every case my fears have never actually transpired to be anything real. And most people that I have worked or consulted with over the years are in the same position – our fears very rarely play out. Even so, they feel so real when they occur and can almost swallow you up if you allow them to – so don't.

People fear a whole host of things: failure, the unknown, being judged, fear of themselves and even fear of success. Yes, people will even fear success, because success then means more work and potential life changes for us. Then there is the possibility of feeling even more fear than before we succeeded. When our mindset is in a state of scarcity, or we feel overwhelmed at the prospect of what we aim towards or embark upon – then fear can creep in if we allow it to.

If fear of success does strike, this is an odd fear. It is not like a common fear we feel when we are afraid, because we become torn inside. Internally when we embark on a course of action or new project part of us yearns to be successful, yet if we fear success, we fear the change it will make to our lives. Life will somehow become new, different, maybe even a little weird. Essentially, you are entering into unchartered territory. And people will resist change – even though constant change in life is inevitable.

When we are torn in this situation, it's between that sense of the known, the comfort of the now, our daily routines that we are familiar with – and all the unknowns and changes that will arise if we venture forward. When we may face the potential precipice, which can give rise in parts of our psyche to thoughts that we would much rather stuff deep under the carpet.

When we are trying to succeed at anything, we will typically feel some fear, but once we can see past fears such as fear of failure – which is our ego standing in our way – the fear of success will become a fear to commit. To put your name to a project, to agree to it, to live it, to breathe it, to own it, to make it part of our being, and when we aim to succeed, then we will need to commit, and typically that means work – and usually hard work.

Yes, you've got it, when we fear success deep down we don't know if we have it in us to commit! And in terms of self-reflection, this can mean that we may even begin to fear ourselves. We may start to curse the very moment where the original idea of the thing we are aiming towards arose. We may begin to consider the whole task of success as a frustrating chore.

And here may come a time on your journey towards your goal where you think back to the original thought behind your would-be successful idea and want to view it as preposterous. Whilst you create every obstacle known to man not to achieve it. With excuses such as – it will cost too much, I haven't got the time, I don't know enough about the subject, or I don't understand how to market it, and so on. Also, besides, I now have two children to care for daily, or I'm not clever enough, or I'm another year closer to retirement than I was last year, so what's the ruddy point anyway?

So maybe being a parent or not having a MENSA recognition, or retirement will save us from the extra hassle – but is that really what we want to happen? Think about it – surely things shouldn't get that bad?

However, to get back to the real point, inherently if we fear the commitment, then what is happening is that we realise that things will change for us. The world, as we know it will change. We will have to be honest with ourselves. We will have to show our underbellies and face the world with all of our imperfections. We will have to know things that we may not understand now; we will have to sweat it out, and life will change in some way.

So, if you wish to succeed – genuinely succeed – then get used to the change it will create, as it's a natural offset of the action you need to take to hit your goal. Lean into the change, this will help reduce any fear you feel.

Alternatively, you aim to achieve what some may view as impossible, but your body and soul are not entirely on board. You are busting a gut to obtain it, then your forced self-commitment will make you drunk with its overpowering vapours, and they won't smell sweet, as this will mean you will be trying to hit a target you will never reach, and this is the last thing anyone needs – least of all you. In this instance – stop trying. To be brutally honest, lay down your tools, dust yourself off and choose to take on your fight with something else another day. As I'm afraid this particular goal, my friend, is not for you.

The magic ingredient

So, what's the answer? What is the ingredient that will make you welcome the fear, all of the concern, and most importantly, the commitment? The answer is love. Love is the answer. You must want what you strive for, and your heart, body and soul must be entirely behind it. When you have this, it really is the time when you can ask the question out loud: 'What would I do if I were not afraid?' And have the answer! The bigger your successful idea is, the bigger your want must be, and you must fall in love with what you want to do. No science in the world will alter this fact.

You can create all the best plans in the world, have all the financial backing, have the best accountant at your side, and the regular set of loyal fans, which when you are starting out on an idea is probably your immediate family. However, you will get nowhere fast if you don't follow your heart. Which brings us back to our starting point – to ask your heart for the answer.

If you consistently stay in your headspace alone – in your ever-circling thoughts – you will never accomplish anything because you will always return to survival mode. And when you are in this mental state, you will merely overthink things, you will stay in the here and now, and will always conjure up excuses that appear logical for why you can't achieve. But when you harness your heart, you are more emotionally guided; your emotions are probably the most significant and most natural cause of inner energy and momentum that you have. When you are internally invested in what you plan to do, it can create such a significant momentum forward. It will empower you, increase resilience and unlock your natural intuitive guidance to make better choices.

And one thing to note is that the fear that you feel when not doing what you aim to do is more significant than the fear that you will feel when you take action. Perhaps this is what our ancestors would have called 'faith' in centuries past.

Intrinsic motivation

Daniel H. Pink's book *Drive* (Pink, 2009) addresses the subject of motivation in order to achieve, and touches on the topic of intrinsic, or internal, motivation – that internal drive we all have to find the 'want' that will drive us forward when we undertake our course of action, because we have a desire to do it. Daniel points out the difference between Intrinsic Motivation and reward-based outcomes, e.g. money, which is an extrinsic, or external, motivator. Intrinsic motivation has been proven to have a more successful result – humans will achieve more if they 'want' do to something they enjoy and feel the internal emotional rewards, because they actualise their potential while doing so.

However, to follow your heart without a plan, or without any structure or practical element behind it, will only get you so far, and should be avoided. To proceed in this vein would not create any useful traction whatsoever. But even then, if for any reason you do become successful but are not emotionally invested in what you are achieving, then you will soon become bored or even disillusioned, as the outcome will become predictable. Believe it or not, the world is full of dull, shallow millionaires, who cry out for some rich abundance in their lives. Some millionaires are poor; all they have is money. That is not a place anyone consciously chooses to be, but some end up there because they concentrate on the financial aspect of success without paying any interest in their passion or what motivates them. I saw a recent post from a gentleman on an entrepreneurial Facebook group complaining about this specific topic. He has 'enough money' using his words, through renting property, a business he dislikes, and is now left miserable.

By contrast, to follow your heart with a direction, focus and inner yearning can create so much motivation that it can move mountains and will be far more fulfilling than being successful at something – just because you can be.

*'The reason that I can't find the enemy
is that I have yet to look within myself.'*

Craig D. Lounsbrough

SUCCESS AND SELF-SABOTAGE

For centuries philosophers have contemplated the ancient Greek saying, 'Gnōthi seauton', or 'Know thyself', and many have written on what the self is – and isn't. Personally, the theory that the person is an individual that changes and adjusts depending upon the situation sits well with me. So, deep down we have a core character from where we act. This core character adapts and serves depending upon circumstances that we find ourselves in, and whom we come into contact with. Hence, we are one person at home, another at work and another at play; the self has to continually adapt to the circumstances at hand. We also become different people at different stages in our lives.

The subconscious mind plays a massive part in how we react in certain situations, and when this happens we can lose part of our self-control or self-direction. In these moments, we tend to act less from the conscious and rational mind and begin to make less mindful choices. Instead, we revert to an emotional response, sometimes wildly so, and this can cause conflict with our logical thought patterns and our intentions. So, for example, in a demanding business meeting when faced with a complex decision, you may revert to a standard response and say that you will think about it later because it makes you feel better in the moment – and may never have the problem fully resolved.

Alternatively, you may even start to feel awkward and flustered or upset and not arrive at any useful answer whatsoever. In these moments, our subconscious mind muscles its way into the situation, and we begin to self-sabotage what could have been a great decision made consciously.

Self-sabotage in action

I've seen self-sabotage in action several times, but one of the most memorable was in one of my first corporate jobs working on a large defence project, to upgrade a computer-based naval training system. Jim, one of our team members who was close to retirement but was not totally ready to go yet, could be a vocal and head-strong individual. But overall the organisation loved him; he was a remarkably valuable talent, he was accomplished in his field, and an intelligent man. And he was actually a great person to be around. Even so he was known to bang the drum for things, and on this relatively new project we were still learning lessons, there was room for improvement. Now I can be assertive at times – but you should still know when to keep your mouth shut.

However, there was one particular issue that Jim became so passionate about, a deep-seated procedural issue which prevented our team from doing their best. But one that annoyed us, as it became accepted as the norm. The solution, however, was a radical change to the way the project was being run, and it would be an expensive fix. But the topic did make its way to the agenda of a strategy meeting, so there was an appetite to listen. I happened to agree with Jim on this point, it made radical sense, therefore, when the topic came up and Jim spoke, I backed up his case.

However, about twenty minutes into the conversation, which took on a healthy debate, it appeared that a stronger case would have to be made, maybe at a later date. I recognised this point and backed down, my thoughts turned to the fact that more evidence was required and so on. Jim on the other hand did not think of it as a delayed success; instead he self-sabotaged. He did not make the conscious decision to try a different tack or simply draw his case to a close for the time being but got hot-headed and really vocal with it! The meeting was then, quite rightly, drawn to an abrupt halt.

Then, oh dear, disappointingly he could not let things rest there. The next day in a coffee break, he found and ranted to a senior member of the company and explained that if things did not change, he would take the matter even higher. But he had just spoken to the wrong person and within days Jim was forced to move on to another company project. He then became so disillusioned and dissatisfied with the forced move that he took early retirement within a few short months. We had lost such a valuable talent from the business, and all through the fact that he lost his self-control, and some deep-seated ghost within him could not be mastered. A sad loss, of someone we missed deeply.

Apart from these moments being potential career changers, or perhaps character-building, they are at the very least annoying, and at most prevent you from taking any strides forward to resolve these more challenging decisions or occasions and put them to bed.

Self-sabotage, in a nutshell, is a behaviour that we can all play out when there is a disparity between how we feel on the inside due to a situation that occurs in the outside world. For example, you have an aim in mind: a diet, a promotion at work, a successful business meeting, a house move, the start of a new relationship, or even to end a difficult one, then for some reason, as you move forward with purpose – or at some point in the process – you don't feel right about it, you don't feel comfortable.

It might be something that you may not even be able to put your finger on or doesn't sit right with you; you could also become overemotional. In these moments anyone of us can become doubtful, passive, angry, scared, or overly controlling and we may begin to feel stressed. We may even lash out verbally or even physically.

Typically, your mind will more than likely emotionally chatter away to itself about why you can't be involved in your intention, or why you are not good enough to even try. It may even scream at you in a somewhat more fearful and indignant way at the thought of doing what you want. It may also have a more parental soothing voice, to gently let you know that it's okay not to try, persuading you to give up as it's all just too much bother, but these are our saboteurs in action. The saboteurs are the internal enemies. They are a set of automatic and habitual mind patterns, each with its voice, beliefs and assumptions that work against your best interest[1].

Now, these somewhat stronger emotions that we have whenever we think about what we wish to achieve can be long-standing, so we know what we want to do but we can't help but feel negative about it, which results in sabotage that was always waiting to happen. Maybe it is a more fleeting sensation in the heat of the moment, which instantly jeopardises the situation and leaves us having to overreact or carry out habitual acts to avoid the circumstances. For example, if we avoid the difficult decision because it makes us feel uncomfortable. This, to be honest, is not always a bad thing, to put a tough problem on the shelf for another day, as let's face the fact that we don't always feel in the mood or can't always cope with difficult issues that feel overly demanding in the moment.

However, if to put the problem off becomes a habit, then that's a classic case of self-sabotage; so, we never address those challenges, that deep down (or maybe not even that deep down) we know we can solve.

Self-sabotage results in many different things, such as never reaching health goals, career goals, relationship goals, and struggling with decision-making. Deep down you may not even feel worthy of any of these. Therefore, your subconscious will stand in the way and try to prevent you from achieving them. It will do this through various means, which will result in thoughts such as, 'I'm not good enough' or 'I'll stand out from the crowd if I achieve what I wish to,' or it will ask the question, 'What if the success doesn't last'? It may even set you on an emotional outburst. All of these thoughts can lead to all sorts of varied behaviours, which include procrastination, overeating, alcohol or drug abuse, negative decision-making, or overcontrolling behaviours.

Self-sabotage in action, once more

When I was in the forces, on one ship I served on I reported to Stuart the chief of our department, where we both maintained a radar for a strategic missile system; so an important job for the most part. Stuart was a great guy to work for, but by Jove could he drink a great deal of alcohol, even during the day and when on duty; I was genuinely amazed that he got away with it. I doubted Stuart was an alcoholic; however, he wasn't far off being one. I didn't realise it at the time, but in reflection the amounts he drank were due to his self-sabotaging behaviour. I know this from some of the conversations we had that there was something wrong with how he perceived himself in his new position, and mostly he was sabotaging his self-made success.

He had recently been promoted to a relatively new position through years of hard work and had now agreed to take over the maintenance of a complex system which was new to him. Also, even though he had had the necessary training to do the job, he remarked on several occasions that he still felt out of his depth.

However, when we worked together, Stuart had a great work ethic; he was knowledgeable, amazingly fair and was a really likeable character, sober or not. While at work I used to have to cover for him a fair amount, and made several excuses for where he was, which he knew I was not happy with. When I couldn't cover for him, or if there were an issue with the system that I couldn't solve on my own, I would have to extract him from his bed, which could easily be at 2 o'clock in the afternoon. Don't take me wrong – he always stayed around and took charge if there was a significant issue with his system, and aimed to resolve it, and he never neglected any of his essential duties; then again, he had no choice but to carry them out. However, if he could, he'd make his excuses and slink off out of the way. His absences always sounded plausible when he returned.

So, there was Stuart, an influential, well-educated chap, who had been a responsible person up until this point, but now lived in a world of denial that prevented him at the time from being that responsible person again. What was going on in his head? Well, it was likely that he assumed others thought he wasn't good enough to carry out his new position, or he himself even imagined he wasn't good enough, or maybe he wasn't entirely willing to commit to learning on the job in order to become the expert he needed to be. Or it may have been due to the fact that he'd hit a glass ceiling. Mentally he had reached a point in his career where he didn't feel worthy of his new rank? All classic self-sabotaging thought processes. Whatever it was, the consequences were not good.

Perhaps I should have said something to someone – but I didn't. In the armed forces, you know your position, and you stick to it. And not to do so could have had the world tumbling down around my ears and not his. But someone must have said something to him at this point because he began to clean up his act, which was an absolute relief for me.

Thankfully, Stuart appeared to win the battle against his self-sabotaging behaviour – despite his inner demons trying to jeopardise and destroy the career he had spent so long building. Demons which did not feed off anything more than ill-founded doubts.

Can we stop self-sabotage?

These automatic and habitual mind patterns appear to be against us and can at times be powerful brakes applied to our potential success, but can we take a stand against our self-sabotaging behaviours? You bet we can! However, I honestly believe that we can never stop sabotaging ourselves fully unless we change the way we perceive ourselves. It is vital to maintain a healthy self-awareness of our thoughts, our actions and their consequences.

When we do take a stand against our poor behaviours and change, it can be easy to slip into our old behavioural patterns. Change will be short-lived and superficial unless we honestly change inside. We seek to look at ourselves and the world differently, being more mindful of our thoughts and actions, so that our character, our spirit and our outlook all change for the better. That requires a change in belief. Here are three steps, or stages, that will put you in a great position and avoid self-sabotage. When you read through these, truly reflect what they mean to you and what conscious future actions you can take in order to embody them. Try to remember your self-sabotage will try to stop you succeeding. But don't let it.

Step 1 – Stay Conscious and Rise Above

Most of us suffer when we operate in a constant *doing mode*, and when we are in this state we find it hard to think of an alternative path. I think that most of us at some stage have fallen into this trap, where we flit from one thing to another – never taking stock of our situation. We become busy being busy.

An acquaintance of mine, Simon, was always so busy he would rarely get anything finished at work without someone else stepping in to support or delegate the task. I'm sure most of us have come across a similar individual. He would typically have around five or six jobs on the go at the same time. He also had demands outside of work – hobbies, being on several committees of various kinds, acting as a parent governor at a local school.

Simon carried a little extra weight, and instead of focusing on losing that, he kept his demanding lifestyle without thinking. And he appeared to be taking on more as time went on. His eventual downfall was that he very badly prolapsed a disc in his back, which required operating on and several weeks away from his office. He was forced to reflect on his behaviours and change his ways after his admittance to me that he had become – *a very busy fool*.

One way to address this busyness is to consciously slow yourself down and become more mindful, to self-reflect when in action and more especially at rest, and come to appreciate that the mind doesn't just think. It can simply be aware, and mindful.

For example, when you have the opportunity, be seated and spend some time on your own and become more conscious of your body. Feel the entire weight of your body as you sit in your seat, feel your breath as it enters and leaves your nose or mouth. Allow your mind to become aware – aware of your surroundings, your entire body, your emotions, the more fleeting sensations you feel – and you will begin to perceive beyond all of the influencing factors of your self-saboteurs that cloud your judgement. The level of heightened awareness beyond these influences is pure awareness.

'Pure awareness transcends thinking. It allows you to step outside the chattering negative self-talk and your reactive impulses and emotions. It allows you to look at the world once again with open eyes. And when you do, a sense of wonder and quiet contentment begins to appear.' (Mark Williams N.D.) As we experience this level of awareness, which takes regular practice to become a habit, we can become more conscious of our next moves and develop the ability to consciously choose them. Our choices become more focused, more selective and more acutely correct.

Step 2 – Take Action and Stay Aware of Your Progress

Another superb way to keep your self-saboteurs at bay is to take action. Cool, wicked, joyful, enjoyable, but sometimes demanding – action. Give yourself permission to be out there and be involved. Activity reduces fear and increases your power, your influence. Scared of public speaking? Then allow yourself to speak publicly. Afraid of hospitals? Then go and volunteer at one? Fearful to apply for that promotion at work? Then apply. Just do it – get out there and give it a go. Unless you have a recognised medical condition and you don't intend to put yourself or anyone else in some form of grave danger – take action!

Early in my career, like a lot of people, I used to dislike public speaking due to nerves. I realised that I could not live and thrive in the workplace without getting over this fear. So, I then joined the Toastmasters organisation, a friendly environment in which to really learn the craft of speaking in public. And to be frank, in the beginning I felt that I failed many times. However, I set high standards for myself.

Then, only eighteen months after joining, I was presenting to an audience of close to one hundred, at a business conference in the Netherlands. Something that I would have thought absolutely ridiculous before I chose to throw myself into action and master my nervousness. At the beginning I had my back turned to them whilst I received support from a technical assistant. Then, when I turned, the room had suddenly jumped from about ten people to well over ninety – and a wave of nerves swept over me. But the talk went well, and I felt elated. And a result I have delivered many since that event.

Nothing is so refreshing for the soul than to become involved, and even if you do fail at times, it's okay. It's okay not to do so well at things when you start – as this is how we learn. But to take action is crucial and will put to bed any black and white thoughts you may have that tell you you'll automatically fail. Alternatively, it will busy you too much to listen to any mental saboteurs that attempt to take hold and gently tell you that you are not good enough to succeed and why you should sit things out. Well, just start! Look, if there is one thing you take from this book that will help you move forward and lead more in your life, it's to start to make progress. Take action, and see the results reveal themselves.

But a word of warning: when our goals are too complicated or too grand then we can succumb to failure, and self-sabotage will find an easier foothold in the direction of giving it all up. Make your goals smaller, more achievable and group them together and then reward yourself with small incentives when you have achieved them; even a warm cup of coffee on a cold day can be a nice reward.

By the way, this is not extrinsic motivation, doing a task purely for the reward. A little pat on the back, even from yourself, is a helpful self-motivator to keep yourself going.

The human psyche has a certain number of invisible barriers. Everyone has them to some extent, it's just that some more successful people have a knack of moving through them, or looking past them. Typically, these invisible barriers are crossed or shattered through action. In these moments when you give yourself the permission to take action and cross these boundaries, you can see them disappear from your mind as you develop internally, as your soul leaps forward in personal growth.

However, a word of caution, – don't expect immediate results in everything you do. To aim to rid yourself of negative thoughts and self-sabotaging behaviour takes character change and personal growth – and these take time. Please don't believe in any quick fixes – because they don't work.

And please, please don't give up at the first sign of a hiccup. Commit to moving through the invisible barriers by being conscious of your progress and small achievements – and before you know it you will be able to look back at the distance you have come – and the personal growth you have achieved – with immense pride!

Step 3 – Practice Self-empathy

We addressed self-empathy earlier in this chapter, but I wish to revisit it and take a slightly different spin on the topic, to say that typically we are conditioned to be critical of our mistakes and where we go wrong. We are much tougher than we know on ourselves when we are wide of the mark than we are on our colleagues or family – it's a weird twist on things! However, if a colleague at work, even someone that you know on a more personal level, makes a mistake, if you care about them then you will show some degree of compassion and understanding. So then why do we beat ourselves up when we fail?

Our inner voice is our worst critic. Therefore, you should practice self-empathy on a more regular basis.

To practice self-empathy during periods of self-sabotage is to treat yourself with kindness. It allows you to dust yourself off when you are emotionally low, to recover and be ready to go back out there and make some headway towards your success. To get back out there in amongst it all. One significant part of self-empathy is the act of self-compassion – to care and comfort yourself while you reflect on how you feel.

Some see self-empathy as a weakness, but it's plainly the opposite. To give yourself empathy, to listen to your feelings and unmet needs with self-compassion and understanding is an immensely productive aid to self-recovery. To cut ourselves some slack and not to take ourselves too seriously can be just what the doctor ordered, and to go through a period of self-empathy is to develop inner strength. Moreover, self-compassion isn't dependent on external circumstances; it's always available – especially when you fall flat on your face! Research indicates that in comparison to self-esteem, self-compassion is associated with greater emotional resilience, more accurate self-concepts, more caring relationship behaviour, as well as less narcissism and reactive anger[2].

What is happening with being empathetic to yourself in tough times is essential healing of internal wounds, which will only strengthen your relationship with the outside world. This relationship with the external world may be a barrier that needs to be built at times of personal need or to develop your character for future exchanges or potential conflict. That could be your relationship with the world at large or your people relationships, whether your colleagues in the workplace or personal ones.

Alternatively, it may be a help in building a bridge for you to engage more with others and life's challenges. So, in both of these instances, your stage of self-empathy could almost be seen as 'taking a breather' from the active engagement in life to take stock. While in this state you fully realise that you need to step into the thick of things at some point, but it's currently time to take a temporary step back and allow yourself a period of psychological recovery, which is a good thing. It genuinely is.

It is worthy to note that the practice of self-empathy can make you easier to work and live with – useful to note from your colleagues' perspectives. When we replace all the harsh self-criticism with more caring, and compassionate understanding, this naturally makes it easier for us to understand and relate to others. So, don't be hard on yourself at the end of the day if you genuinely feel you've had it tough. It does no one any good, least of all you. Feel the self-love and recuperate.

WE ARE AMAZING BEINGS – SO TAKE ADVANTAGE

If we reflect, we humans, or Homo sapiens, are such complex animals and can be traced back some 315,000 years, and we are really incredible thinking machines that have taken so long in evolutionary terms to reach the stage that we are at today. With this in mind, to merely drift in life would seem such an incredible waste. So, if you can be independent and have full or near full physical or mental abilities, step out there and attempt to gain some traction in your life, make some success. Because I can assure you there will be thousands out there in the world that are dealing with their challenges who I'm sure would dearly love to have your talents.

We should always take the advantage of the marvellous human systems that we have in place today – not just for the reason that we are human, but because if you consider it, what is the point in our existence at all if not to gain experience and get all the juice out of this life that we can.

There is, I believe, an exception to this where we should actively choose to take a far more laid-back approach and take a step back from life's trials. A good example of this is when we need to reflect on changes in life or to come to terms with those more challenging and more painful events that can appear when we least expect them. There are short periods in everyone's life when we feel the need to switch off – to take a step back. I mean, even top athletes have rest days!

When you need to self-reflect after the loss of a loved one or someone close to you or to deal with a life-changing event, you are unlikely to demand anything of any real significance in your life. Moreover, you may want to drift, to go with the flow, to recuperate and to come to terms with the loss or whatever change has taken place. In these more difficult times that do come our way, to feel a good degree of self-empathy can be such a great healer.

To continually beat yourself up when you don't accomplish things and try to power on, but recognise that you are doing this to yourself, is a real talent and not a weakness. You would never chastise a child, in your right mind, that had suffered a bad dream or who had fallen off their bike. You would console them and encourage them to continue whilst you gave them advice for their future benefit. You wouldn't scold or punish them for trying, and demand that they should 'get on with it'. Therefore, why should you treat yourself any differently?

Nevertheless, this is not an opportunity for a pity party piece to fill us with excuses for not aiming to achieve and a justification to feel sorry for ourselves when our day is not going to plan. No, the point being raised here is that life, at times, can be difficult. Yes, sometimes things don't go to plan and we come up against obstacles or the unexpected; it can be painfully frustrating and this can make us feel dejected even dismal. Let's at least recognise and acknowledge this.

In a state of self-empathy, trying to accomplish anything not related to how we get by in life and our recovery should rightly take a back seat. Sometimes not to ask much of yourself will be the right thing to do. Nevertheless, you know you can't carry on like this for ever. There will come the point where you must regain a level of control and direction, to re-engage and step back into the swing of life. It may be tough to manoeuvre yourself back into the flow of things, and to have to face life's challenges, to go out to work, to deal with the complexities of when we meet others, and sometimes this transition should be a gradual one.

Success during these more difficult times will be to decide that you need to commit to being your old self again, whilst you take the baby steps that are required for you to get you back to where you need to be... to live your life in full once again, while you stay self-aware of your progress. But all of this is a success.

I opened this chapter stating that success is not necessarily some grandiose achievement; sometimes, success is to get back on your feet after a setback. After any kind of setback, embrace any move forward in the right direction and take a step towards where you want to be, irrespective of what success in your heart is for you, and you are bound to make the progress towards what you want – and also what you need. But ensure you make full use of the body you are in with its skills, talents and also its potential. There is so much that we can achieve when we put our minds to it – so get out there and do it! Be the change in life you wish to see.

'You will never be free until you free yourself
from the prison of your own false thoughts.'

Philip Arnold

NOW, OVER TO YOU

So, what is the success you want/desire in your life? I'm sure you have something in mind. If it doesn't come to mind, self-reflect and discover within. Write down your wishes, goal or goals that you would love to become successful. Brainstorm – have that difficult conversation with a partner about what you want. Self-lead. Do not use the excuse that you don't like writing lists, or you will start tomorrow. Lead yourself and take action. And don't keep thoughts running around your head of what you perceive success to be – express it, do it now. In fact, don't carry on with this book until you have done so.

Have you taken the steps to record what success is to you? I have already mentioned that success is not necessarily about making an enormous amount of money or becoming an extraordinary successful entrepreneur. For some, these are not the paths to take in order to bring happiness to our lives. Being a good parent is success in itself, especially if our children have additional needs in some way.

Always remember, you are the one that has to live with yourself, and success is always personal and relative. However, we should set standards for ourselves, and these standards should be high enough that we grow and strive to improve. To be better in some way than we were yesterday, even if this is a marginal improvement. We can use yesterday's building blocks for today, and so on. Then, when we face setbacks, as we all will, we become stronger emotionally. Remember, transformation is an ongoing process – success does not happen overnight.

Our bodies and minds were not made perfectly. Self-sabotage is an unconscious action formed from a variety of reasons but that we have to make conscious in order to overcome them. If you then take positive and concrete action you will begin to awaken those parts of you that can make more successful and informed decisions.

You are likely to need to grow your character to succeed in both, so work on your emotions and be as physically fit as you can be for the challenges ahead. Live life more consciously in the moment and lead your way to successful goals; even if you don't hit them exactly, you will become a better person during the journey – it's guaranteed.

PERSONAL CONTRIBUTION
BILL WEBSTER: IT CONSULTANT

Practice Makes Perfect

I'm an IT consultant with a busy family life and for many years public speaking always held numerous terrors for me. Why wouldn't it? Any time I'd had to speak to an audience – at family events and giving presentations at work – I felt strongly that people would be judging me for what I said and how my speech was delivered. So success in this area of my experience had always been a struggle for me, and one struggle I wanted to successfully overcome.

All of the doubt was simply my own imagination running wild. Rationally, I knew this. But of course, rational thought has little bearing on the ability to suppress that familiar feeling of panic whilst standing in front of an audience, feeling like a lamb to the slaughter.

For some reason, before I even had children, I became preoccupied by the notion that, in the future, I might be called on to give a speech on my imaginary daughter's wedding day. The idea of this filled me with pride and dread in equal measure. Even worse though, was the scenario which replayed in my mind: I gave the speech, I made a terrible job of it, and ruined her special day. My family did not yet exist, but I had already created this outcome in my head.

I decided that I must tackle my fears once and for all. I joined a club whose activities included regular toast-giving and responding. I convinced myself that practice makes perfect – but did I really believe that I could succeed?

I soon had my first chance to find out. I stood in front of an audience of perhaps fifty people. I remember the atmosphere of expectation... all eyes on me, everyone waiting for me to say something. Heart thumping and voice shaking, I began. In that moment, I was filled with fear, I felt panicky, sick – I basically self-sabotaged.

The dread persisted despite me occasionally managing to get a laugh from some members of the audience. I simply didn't believe that I could speak well. I felt I had no place addressing these people. There was no way I could feign credibility. It was simply embarrassing.

After what seemed like a lifetime – which was probably about five minutes – I nervously mumbled the final part of my speech and then thanked the small audience for their kind attention. I raised my wine glass in a toast to their health, but immediately regretted it because my hand, and therefore the glass, shook wildly due to the adrenaline hit. I wanted the ground to swallow me up. Applause came, but I believed this was through politeness only. I scurried back towards my seat, willing the spectacle to be over.

An elderly gentleman grasped my forearm in passing. He leaned in slightly as I paused, bracing myself for his inevitable criticism.

'You're amongst friends.'

I doubt he could have known the impact of those words. He was right, of course – every member of the audience had, in fact, been rooting for me all along. After that night, I forced myself to accept other opportunities to speak publicly. I started to believe that frequent practice would eventually pay off; that I might one day even come to enjoy public speaking.

Several years later, enjoyment is something I do occasionally experience while speaking publicly – as through practice and main-taining a determination to succeed, I have overcome my fears. More often, it is enough that I simply feel in control whilst doing it. I am more able to engage with an audience, and much less inclined to find myself standing in front of them heart-in-throat, like the proverbial rabbit caught in the headlights. I am also convinced that I improve, somewhat, with each attempt – even to the point of enjoyment.

In my humble experience people can tend to focus on the negative; it's a defence mechanism which helps us learn and survive. I try to remember this to keep my own self-defeating thoughts in check. Maintaining a sense of self-belief is integral to any success, however unnatural it may feel to attempt it.

It is important to remember that there is a fine line between confidence and arrogance. They are not the same quality and they do not emanate from the same source. Self-belief is well within my grasp now and the years of practice make it feel more achievable.

To this day, my loudest critic remains the nagging voice in my head when looking for my own successes. The trick is to realise that nobody is forcing me to pay any attention to it. Self-doubt only survives if fuelled. I make every effort to starve it, confident that it will eventually fade away.

I did go on to have a daughter. She's now six, so assuming she does get married someday, I'll still have ample time to prepare for that long-feared Father of the Bride speech! I expect to pay tribute to the strong, self-assured woman we are striving to raise. In the meantime, I want to instil in her the same sense of self-belief, when trying to succeed, that I have myself fought to acquire; to help her to appreciate the person she has become, that she might better recognise her many strengths and achievements. If I can convince her of these things, I feel that an important part of my work will be done. I believe that I can.

Chapter 2

Perseverance

*'If you can't fly then run, if you can't run then walk,
if you can't walk then crawl, but whatever you do you
have to keep moving forward.'*

Martin Luther King, Jr.

Through gritted teeth, I was not giving in. I was dragging a large blue floor mat across the gymnasium floor for the last time on my final test day of basic training, having joined the Royal Navy several weeks earlier. The day was called 'Mad Monday'. My twenty-four other troop mates and I had been up most of the night preparing our kit for inspection and several other things we had to prepare for that day. There were assault course runs, two of them as I remember, a kit inspection, a parade ground test, written tests and last of all, a final brutal gym test.

After weeks of physical and mental training, and then this last intense day with so much packed into it, I was gasping for breath, and could hardly think, run or collect my thoughts. However, if we passed our challenges, then this madness would be over; at least for now. Somehow, I had managed to pass everything up to this point, but I knew I was tinkering right on the edge of failing, and if I put one foot wrong – I was out. However, I was fully determined not to go back home, to the life I had left, the one I had made my mind up to leave four years earlier at the age of fourteen, no matter what. Life was not easy back home, so I needed to create a brand-new direction for myself.

However, there was one catch: I felt dreadfully sick. I had been ill for some days and by this point my symptoms were growing worse. They had gone from a simple cold to something more serious, but I had no idea just what. Others in my troop, who were suffering as I was, had ended up in the naval base's small hospital, coined as the sickbay, two days earlier. I was given the opportunity to do the same at the time, but I chose not to go. I pretended to be better than I felt and continued to persevere, refusing to give in! I was not being back classed, moved back to a later week's basic training intake, or worse still being kicked out of the Navy. That was my biggest fear!

So, with my bloody-minded head on, I decided to continue. Except, this gym mat felt like a ton weight at the time, but with my legs aching and my lungs wheezing I carried on! I had of course been ill before in life, I believe I had suffered all the common ailments as a child, but I had never felt quite like this; my lungs were wheezing, and I had pain in my chest. I mean, I felt terrible! At this point, the day was taking its toll on me. But I had one goal in mind now, to get to the end of it, to the end of this agonising trial. It was sheer bloody grit that had got me to this point in the day, and the only thing that kept my momentum going was the thought of failing; that to me at this time would have been an utter disaster.

I was so focused on the end goal, that somehow, with virtually no energy left in the tank, I had installed a belief into my system that I could still make it. So, I carried on.

When I completed my final turn of the gymnasium, still dragging this large blue concrete-filled gut-buster of a mat, I stood at the end of the line, sweating from every pore in my body. My legs were trembling, my hands shaking, and my head felt like I was in another world. I just wanted to lie down in a corner and be left alone to die, or at least pass out and be left alone. Still, that was never going to happen. All I had to do was to stay upright for a short while longer, and as far as I was concerned, I was through, and could then go to bed early and sleep. Sleep for hours and try to shake this ruddy illness off.

When the gym test was over, which I just got through by the skin of my teeth I may add, we showered, changed and ended up in a classroom, to be informed as to whether we had passed our basic training or not. By this time, most of my shaking had stopped, but I felt weak and wanted to sleep. Our petty officer was about to announce the overall results of our training thus far, as he stood behind a lectern at front of the classroom and told an unfunny joke to try and lighten the atmosphere. No one was in the mood to humour him, though, as everyone was on tenter-hooks to hear their results.

Then, after no one laughed at his silly joke, he went on to read our results aloud, by name and then the outcome: '...Smith, pass, Peterson, pass' and so on. Then when it came to my name, '....Wilkinson.... pass... sickbay, now! You two over there escort him, and make sure he's okay,' our petty officer said, pointing to two of my troop mates who had been given their results already.

I was sprawled over the desk where I was sat, somewhere between a dream state and awake, but they somehow managed to pick me up, and escorted me to the sickbay. By this time my body was squeezed dry all of its adrenaline, and I could hardly walk. If I was asked to run around any gym at this point, mat or no mat, I would have gladly crawled out of the camp gates and ended the whole damn affair. The only mood I was now in was to give in.

A few hours later that evening, while in the sickbay, I collapsed. Afterwards I was diagnosed with pneumonia, and suffered a fever with a temperature of 102°F, but at least I could sleep, and that I did for almost twenty-four hours. Not the best way to start my naval career, but ultimately, I had persevered with gritted teeth and sheer bloody-minded determination.

GOALS AND MOMENTUM

The Oxford English Dictionary defines perseverance as 'the quality of continuing to try to achieve a particular aim despite difficulties', and perseverance is a fascinating and necessary characteristic to uphold when things become demanding. Perseverance, to me, is one prime human attribute that brings about the most in our self-leadership skills.

It's the very nature of having the staying power in any given task, project or personal endeavour that can bring out some of the most amazing qualities in us. Those difficult times that test our metal in things we do, and also the ones that we don't want to do, can be callous.

To persevere with some of the things we face in life will require, amongst others, self-control, self-discipline, excellent relationship skills, energy, and bags of it, and at times a great deal of creativity. To stick a task out, say a work project, to the point where even you, or others, would typically throw up your arms and surrender, can easily transfer through to the difference between success and failure.

Some of the more significant challenges and complexities we face in life must be conjoined with courage and a huge dose of mental toughness to overcome the severest of tests. These more trying moments will have you either reaching deep down inside yourself or from the ether, or even from the universe at large to see yourself through. Reaching out in some way to look for the fuel, the inspiration, the guidance and the momentum to keep going and prevent things coming to an early close.

Still, why do it, why persevere in the first place?

The answer to that question can only really come down to the fact that we have put ourselves in a position where we firmly believe there is a need to achieve, or we put ourselves in this position as we perceive there is no other choice. Then, once we are there, we make a choice, consciously or unconsciously, at some level, choose to stick it out, to see past the hurdles, and hopefully arrive at our destination with a good outcome. Besides, to persevere your way to success, if we can put the triumph of success to one side, is one of the most significant character-building and soul-searching exercises you will ever do. One which only goes to act as a stepping stone for future challenges in which you find yourself involved.

Ultimately, perseverance is a tough character builder, and will help build resolve into the spirit of the self-leader.

YOUR MOTIVATION TO ACHIEVE

The one key factor in achievement is to have a big enough motivator in the first place to set you off in the direction of success. Without motivation you have not want or need inside of you. Motivation drives our habits, reactions, desires, emotions and the targets we set for ourselves. And motivation is, by far, one of the biggest influencers on behaviour that you will ever meet. Take, for example, a seriously ill child who is in urgent need of medical attention; even in the middle of the night, just that situation alone would influence you greatly to take immediate action and seek medical advice. Nothing else will matter to you. Your complete attention will alter all of your behaviours, where you will focus on the direction of pursuing help, and nothing else will drive your every action.

If we look at the motivation needed to achieve something of significance for yourself, if you have a burning desire to do something, to aspire to be someone, something that drives an excitement, a spark, an inner determination inside of you, you will have then created that motivation; that driving force towards a target or goal. Which, if this drive is large enough, inspiring enough, there isn't much around that will stop you. The next step will be goal setting, which is, by far, the most practical self-directed step to accomplishment.

Goal setting creates that first move towards direct action and building momentum, but in the real world many people will shy away from goals as they can scare them. I mean, even committing to a goal, which you don't reach, even if you told no one about it, can hinder you from making future goals as well as affecting your self-confidence.

More than this, if we have hastily shared our goals with someone else, then to a greater or lesser degree, we will be held accountable. In this instance, you can feel somewhat vulnerable, especially if you miss your goal or come around to the conclusion that you won't achieve it and have to explain this. Therefore, goal setting should be considered as a more serious step in hitting your ambitions and targets. And we should be careful who we tell, too. It's good to be accountable – as there are people that will rarely achieve targets unless they are held to account, frankly. But you want to be held accountable to the right people. A mentor, coach or a trusted business partner or colleague is ideal.

Create goals consciously

When it comes to goal setting, we should be aware that we pick up many goals from others, from society, the media and advertising; and some of these are simply nonsense. These days we are faced with an inordinate amount of information and influencing factors that programme our minds. Therefore, it's important to stay self-conscious of the goals that you set for yourself and ensure that you genuinely wish to own and achieve them. Otherwise you can fall into the trap of trying to hit someone else's goals, which could be pointless or even detrimental to your own life's journey.

Goals that you set yourself should either come from the heart or touch your heart. If your goals do neither then they will not inspire or motivate you, and the likelihood is they are not your goals, but someone else's.

Goals and personal growth

In addition to inspiring you and sustaining your motivation, goals are mandatory things to work towards, as they not only create something to achieve, something of value, but they also keep you growing. Also, growth is a human need. If you're not growing, you're dying. If a relationship is not growing, if a business is not growing, if you're not growing, it doesn't matter how much money you have in the bank, how many friends you have, how many people love you – you're not going to experience real fulfilment[3]. So, as a self-leadership philosophy, growth is a must and having a definite aim or goal in mind to obtain that growth is healthy.

Working towards a goal creates a degree of feedback on progress. When people work on a task, they compare their current performance with the goal. Self-evaluations of progress strengthen self-efficacy and sustain motivation. A perceived discrepancy between present performance and the goal may create dissatisfaction, which can enhance the effort. Although dissatisfaction can lead to quitting, this will not happen if people believe they can succeed, for example by changing their strategy or seeking assistance[4]. Then, if they do achieve their goal, this only goes to strengthen their self-belief and they will select new, and potentially more challenging, goals, leading them to new ventures and aspirations.

Goals, me?... Seriously

One of the biggest obstacles to setting a goal is that people think it's boring, dull or pointless, and they can never bring themselves to consider it mentally, let alone write them down. Nevertheless, goal setting fundamentally does work! It's a technique used by professional athletes and successful businesspeople alike. I've used goal setting personally and seen it put to great use in working environments in terms of team goals. On a personal level, goals give you something to aim towards; even if you do not end up meeting them precisely, you will have no doubt grown as a result.

Besides, we all have goals; it may just be that they are not written down or even thought through. However, in this instance they are unconscious and are typically survival or mundane goals: getting to work, surviving another day, purchasing the groceries for the evening meal, waking up tomorrow on time, going back to work again.

On the contrary, conscious goal setting done well does work and is fundamental to maintaining growth and making progress. Goals can and will move you forward in life and your career if used well. Usain Bolt, the eight-time Olympic gold medallist, and widely considered to be the greatest sprinter of all time, puts his setting of goals and their achievement as key to his success. He sets harder and harder goals for himself, continually striving for them, and puts goal setting down to what keeps him going in his career. At the launch of his new autobiography *Faster Than Lightning* (HarperSport, 2013) in London, the world's fastest man said: 'If you want to be the best, or you want to strive for more, you've got to set goals in life.'[5] Goals give you something to reach for, to stretch for, and this stretch will help create a different you.

> *'One way to keep momentum going is
> to have constantly greater goals.'*
>
> Michael Korda

ACHIEVABLE GOALS

Goals will not work unless they are achievable, and that is a fact – you must be able to achieve them. There is absolutely no point trying to make something happen that is not attainable. No matter how much we dig in – goals that are not achievable are merely impossible to hit. By this I mean physically impossible. Usain Bolt, although he was the world's fastest man, would not have been able to halve his personal best for 100 metres. Now, that's the kind of impossible goal I am referring to here.

On the other hand, stretch goals are good! These goals help us push ourselves to new limits which lead to personal growth. When I used to swim competitively, we used to set stretch goals that would involve us targeting new personal bests for the year-end, which we knew were not impossible but were difficult to reach. Then we would aim to hit them, pushing ourselves more intensely on a daily basis, but working on the foundation skills such as leg-kick or breathing for long periods. Not anything new, but deeply practising the fundamentals with complete focus, to empower and enrich our technique, to improve our results over the long term. Essentially, getting the foundations right. The basics simply must be in place in order for you to stretch your current targets, because if they are not – you don't stand a chance of hitting your goals.

Stretch goals and targets are used in the workplace with the same philosophy. They are not meant to be impossible to hit, but do serve to create a high-performance culture and motivation that pushes an individual or team to go above and beyond to hit a project milestone. You may have found yourself in similar situations in the working environment, where you have been encouraged or even told that you or your team need to meet a difficult target? But stretch goals or targets only work if the motivation is there in the first place, and teams believe in what they are doing! This means that they bought into the target through negotiation. Then, as well as hitting the target if they succeed, which is an accomplishment in itself, on a personal level, the individual or team can enjoy a real feeling of achievement and even elation.

On the contrary, stretch targets don't work if they break people's spirits, and will reduce motivation and momentum significantly if they are not introduced correctly, or are used too often or for too long. In spite of this well-known understanding, some organisations or projects will become so caught up in such an absolute frenzy to hit milestones that they are likely to forget about their more precious commodity – their staff. And a happy workforce is crucial, as we all know.

If you are faced with the position of a stretch target as an individual, try and ensure that you are involved in the negotiation and agree to the milestone in the first place. If you don't have any emotional commitment, then you won't be bought into the task in hand with – no matter how hard you try and persevere.

BREAKING GOALS DOWN LEADS TO SUCCESS

The only way to succeed at any meaningful or serious goal is to break it down, otherwise you could be faced with something that is too cumbersome and impossible to achieve and where you are likely to resign yourself to failure. Goals can be broken down into the following hierarchy. These are:

- Low-level goals
- Mid-level goals
- Top-level goals

Breaking these goals down is especially important when it comes to the need for you to persevere to complete a mission of some kind. And then beyond goals there are aspirations. Yes, these are the things that you wish to achieve, but which are not measurable and objective, things that you are not working towards, that you aspire to be or to want to have but are not serious about.

A career aspiration, for example, is not a goal, and besides, aspirations can sometimes change with the wind. Children are great at aspiring to be all sorts when they are growing up, and that's fine, they are still learning and exploring. But then again, let's face it, many adults are too.

Low-level goals

Low-level goals, or what I like to call quick-wins, are the immediate or concrete stepping stones for you to work on towards your mid-level goals. These goals can be broken down to such an extent that they cover specific day-to-day activities, such as I need to phone my client back before midday, or I need to complete that section of my report. These items are often added to daily to-do lists and set the foundation for your mid-level goals.

Your low-level goals must align with your mid-level and top-level goals. There must be logic and consistency at each stage, therefore, the reason for phoning the client or the reason for completing the report is all a means to an end to achieving your subsequent goals. When I goal set, I always ensure that I sense check my low-level goals when I'm carrying them out; if for any reason, I can't see how they are progressing me towards my next level of goals, or they *don't feel right* – I have a rethink. Essentially, I am continually evaluating my goal planning as I work.

Mid-level goals

A mid-term goal is the second of two stepping stones to get you to your longer-term target. Goals set at this level should be a breakdown of the top-level goal and can exist in different sizes and durations. And whilst the top-level goal may be more abstract or be more generalised (I'll come back to this later) the mid-level goal will still need to be more defined and specific. One example could be, if your top-level goal is to complete a year-long college course, here your mid-term goals will be focused on successfully completing the course subjects or modules. Another example could be where you identify a top-level goal to increase your company turnover by 25 per cent over the following two years. Then in this instance the mid-term goals could focus on improved marketing, reaching out to existing customers or the offer of product promotions.

Again, as for low-level goals, whatever your mid-term goals are, they must align with your top-level goals.

Top-level goals

If you are working towards a fixed target, a goal that is not a means to any other result, then class it as a top-level goal. It is the end result, the final destination in itself. Termed by some psychologists as the *Ultimate Concern*. This goal will become your compass that gives substance and meaning to all other goals to get you to that target. This level of goal will typically be more abstract and less detailed in nature, for example, a top-level goal could be to have a successful business or become a successful author. The reason being, is that these goals are typically at the top much longer in duration in terms of what you are aiming towards. And so, in some instances there is bound to a degree of *greyness* about the specifics. Also, the greyer the goal is, the more you need to ensure you are review them on a regular basis, to ensure you are headed in the direction you want to.

On the other hand, top-level goals are always context specific, so could be somewhat more clear-cut. For example, if your goal was that you wanted to graduate from university, this is a straightforward example of a top-level goal that is more definite in nature. Either way, it is the end point. When you have achieved this goal, you have then met the original need or desire.

One point to note on top-level goals with respect to persever-ance is that you need to be stubborn and self-motivated in order to achieve these. There will be a need to keep your goal top in your mind, when you tackle your daily tasks to keep you focused and motivated. Therefore, to feel a passion for your *Ultimate Concern* will aid your momentum during the hardship in those tougher days, to help you to achieve it. Where there is passion – there is perseverance.

Individual goals and their duration

When *actively engaged* on any goal, regardless of level, generally I would not advise having a single goal of a period over three months in duration. And when I say actively engaged, I mean where there is any level of meticulous planning involved. Now, this may initially sound like a short period to you, but in the context of genuinely persevering towards a target you are focused on – it's essential.

You see when we persevere to any detailed plan and stick with something, we are typically in a primary state of focus, and the like-lihood is that we are head down and somewhat oblivious to what is occurring around us. And when in this mode of focus we are adding time, cost and effort into the equation. In addition to this, when we persevere on a given goal, we will always have to deal with difficulty, by nature of the definition. Therefore, to remain flexible to external forces, whether these be financial, environmental, health or resource related, ensure that you keep your goal focus relatively short in duration, so you can adapt if required.

Also, coping with pressure for long periods is tough; and there are no two ways around that. Besides, when we press on towards a goal, the kind of qualities we display are: concentration, determi-nation, dedication, and you also have to maintain your momentum, and deal with difficulty. Try leading yourself towards a goal for a period of six months or even two years without that feeling of success; even if you believe that you are truly headed in the right direction, it can be hard – very hard. The majority of us are likely to want to throw our hats into the ring.

If you have classed something as a mid-level goal that is longer in duration than three months, say the college subjects I used in my earlier example, then create more than one mid-level goal from its related top-level goal. In this simple example, create additional mid-level goals (which may be of different size and duration) by breaking down the subject you are learning into exams that you need to sit, or assignments to be conducted. Low-level goals can then be further derived. But as always, make this idea of a maximum duration for your goals context specific, when applying to your own situation.

Every achievement you accomplish can give you that much-needed boost, and will help ensure you are headed in the right direction. Likewise, if you continually having to move a goal out, as in you are always having to chase success, you will naturally start to become despondent. And we don't want that – we want the reverse! We want success.

All of these examples are down to the fact that the more difficult a goal is to achieve and the less tangible progress you make, the more you may miss the opportunity to pivot and change plans, and the more difficulty you will have in maintaining a self-belief that you can achieve it. There will be a natural inward reflection of how tough, awkward or even how absurd the goal is; it's a given. Consequently, where there is detailed planning and effort required, these longer-term objectives must be broken down to lead you step by step towards your overall target.

Short-term results can influence long-term targets

The outcome of short-term results, and by this I mean the outcome to low- and mid-level goals (and potentially unforeseen curveballs), will typically influence how you set and work towards your longer-term targets. And therefore, the whole goal setting process must be seen as relatively fluid. The reason for this fluidity is because a lot can change in a relatively short space of time, and you need to work through these changes, and possibly reprioritise your goals.

Doing this will also help maintain your self-confidence and self-belief that you can hit your longer-term targets. You see, life changes, people change, things become blocked or altered, you may be injured, the proverbial can hit the bloody fan, your goal may be wrong, your approach may even be incorrect and may need to be altered.

In addition to the above, be aware that merely the outcome of your short-term results may create a change of heart or circumstance, which may impact or influence your top-level goals, especially in terms of their timeline. However, to stay focused and passionate on your longer-

Ultimate Concern, will help with these fluctuations when they occur.

As I write this passage, Sir Andy Murray, the world's former number-one men's singles tennis player, is progressing back into single-tournament tennis, after being fitted with a metal hip. An absolutely remarkable feat if he achieves it. After his surgery he was at the mercy of his recovery and dealing with how he would manage to persevere to meet his mid-level goals of recuperation, and the gruelling training he and his team would put him through, the reason why he made no public statement about getting back to singles tennis.

During 2019, since his operation he progressed enough to play doubles matches, winning one of them at the Queen's tournament in London. So, while he made no definitive plans for a return to singles immediately after his operation, he at some point during his comeback must have made it his top-level goal to play singles again. Even so, he was still happy to play doubles in the US Open in August of the same year.

However, Andy then decided to switch his attention back to a singles comeback after losing to older brother Jamie in the Cincinnati Masters quarter-finals, a tournament that is played before the

US Open. Stating 'doubles is done for me for the time being'[6]. Therefore, irrespective of how Andy fairs in his return to competitive singles tennis, this is a prime example whereby the outcome of short-terms results can have a real impact on longer-term targets.

Create meaningful goals

The correct strategy when it comes to goal setting and their achievement is to create meaningful goals you believe in from top to bottom, i.e. breaking down top-level goals into relevant and viable mid-term ones that you can work through, and then down to the essential tasks of achievement or low-level ones or quick-wins, which as stated earlier, they are often added to daily to-do lists. And when you strike off a quick-win that you have achieved, especially one that takes you on the march towards a top-level goal, nothing gives you better satisfaction.

Goal progress keeps momentum moving you forward towards your overall aim; without momentum and continued motivation your top-level goals are dead in the water. Therefore to see yourself achieving and making progress you retain your self-belief and focus, which gives you that much needed boost to meet your larger goals.

When you are down in the belly of perseverance, and things are getting the better of you, the achievement of the smallest of gains and your self-acknowledgement of their success really can make all the difference. A successful training session, that vital email, an awkward conversation with the boss, a long overnight drive, plodding another mile round a half-marathon route or scoring off another day of hospital treatment. All of these are achievements in their own right; regardless of what they are, here the most significant factor is what they mean to you. If they mean a great deal to you, then they will carry you towards your top-level goals, and help you in your perseverance towards them tremendously.

MEETING THE GOALS OF AN ORGANISATION

One of the biggest struggles that can try your will in any given area of life is achieving someone else's goals, and the place where you will find the most examples of this is in the workplace. Here, you have to meet someone else's goals every day, make them your own and believe in them enough to get behind them; and be emotionally invested in them sufficiently for the process to work. That process being whereby you are handed tasks to meet goals in the form of milestones, objectives and targets, and then you adopt the attitude of wanting to make them work. On the other hand, if you then take them too seriously to the extent where you become too emotionally involved, your health can begin to suffer, through stress, anxiety or even depression.

This process does have its place, however, in helping the industry to function and to benefit the employee, or the self-employed. To make another's goals your own, however, you need to ensure that you are leading yourself to a successful outcome for both parties, you and them. No one wants you to become ill through employment, least of all you!

But if you can achieve a balance between what the organisation wants and what you want, then a harmony can co-exist. Although some organisations don't create a big enough 'why' so that their workers fully appreciate the reasons they are trying to hit company targets. In this instance, this lack of company vision and communication will help ensure workers don't strive to hit their own organisation's goals. These organisations will cry out that they exist to make a profit, but that's not a company's purpose. A company exists to provide a product or service to the community or the world at large, whatever the scale. If you can't, at some emotional level, believe in that product or service – then you will never be bought into the company's goals. It's not rocket science.

Invested in a company's goals

Hopefully the product or service provided by a company will be something of real value, which means that if the company had never existed, or went bust, it would be sorely missed, and not just be perceived to exist in order to retain a turnover. However, if there is a lack of clear purpose in a company, this inadequate drive, as stated, will trickle down to the foot soldiers, and they will find it hard to motivate themselves, as there is no damn good reason for them to do anything much but make an appearance and get paid.

The bottom line is: if an employee in an organisation, can't be bought in at some emotional level to believe in that product or service – then they will never be bought into the company's goals. And in this situation – what is boosting the morale of the workforce?

On occasion, in most fields of industry, things do become complicated in the workplace through several factors, including competition, transformation and demand. Primarily these are required to grow an organisation and develop its function. It's not a surprise then that not all targets or goals that an organisation works towards manage to keep their staff engaged. In a recent poll conducted by Gallup, entitled 'State of the Global Workplace', that covered 155 countries, it reported quite an interesting statistic: worldwide employee engagement is just 15 per cent. Two-thirds are not engaged, and 18 per cent are actively disengaged[7].

There are, of course, a whole number of ways that this can be addressed from within, i.e. employers resolving these issues, through excellent management and leadership, investing in the correct training, and the provision of meaningful work and realistic objectives. Then again, this approach is only going to stretch so far; after all, the company is there to maintain its various targets, and not just look after the employees' best interests. For that reason, some of the responsibility lies with the workforce to get behind the company goals, at their level.

Now, being remunerated at the end of the month will help your motivation as money does provide a degree of this; however, even those who highlight the motivational effects of money accept that pay alone is not sufficient[8]. Therefore, you need to find another motivator in meeting the company's goal, and this is particularly important when you have to strive and persevere to reach the most difficult of targets, these being the targets of your organisation.

There are the times when you need balance what the organisation wants and also take your benefits out of the role, as opposed to solely accepting the situation for what it is. What I mean by this is actively seeking your benefits and learning experiences from the tasks you are engaged in, for example people skills, communication skills, expertise, travel experience, life experience, negotiation skills. So, you aim to learn skills, whatever they may be, from the task in hand. Skills that you may never have thought of or had any intention of learning.

Whatever personal benefits you may take, you have to find an intrinsic motivator (see page 36) from within the organisation's goals in what you do. Intrinsic motivation is also a stronger predictor of job performance than extrinsic motivation – so it is feasible to expect higher financial rewards to inhibit not only intrinsic motivation but also job performance. The more people focus on their salaries, the less they will focus on satisfying their intellectual curiosity, learning new skills, or having fun, and those are the very things that make people perform best[9].

It all boils down to this: to keep or help make an organisation successful you need to believe in their goals and become emotionally attached to them. If you have no emotional investment whatsoever in the goals of an organisation you won't help them to meet them; it's fairly straightforward. Then, when you have to dig in and persevere in helping your organisation hit its goals, you both stand a much better chance of success.

'If a man knows not to which port he sails, no wind is favourable.'

Seneca the Younger

PERSEVERING WHEN GIVEN NO CHOICE

There are the periods in life when we have no choice but to push on, to drive through any obstacles that may stand in our way, to persevere and be counted. Periods of difficulty not of our choosing, but which appear at times to be our fate. These are the spells in life when it would seem that Lady Luck, for us, has got up and left. However, I'm sure you will agree that your life never used to have as many hardships.

When you remember back to when you were a small child, I hope that, as for the vast majority of us, you found that things always seemed to go well. By this I mean, we were provided food and drink regularly enough, clothed, we were loved, and we had somewhere to sleep; our major decisions were all but made for us. Life was, well, much simpler. Those were the days!

At some point, something happened – we grew up, we naturally took on more responsibility, and then things began to change for us.

And now, no longer does it all go our way, no longer are things landing on our laps, with everything done either for us or around us. Sometimes, it seems almost the opposite. And there are even times, and I'm sure you will agree, when it would appear that things are against us.

Whilst not trying to sound too melodramatic here – and I'm not – you have to admit there are days, weeks or even longer when for a whole variety of reasons things can be tough and, somehow, we are left to cope with it all. The loss of a job, the death of a loved one, a more severe or chronic illness, a turbulent time in your business, being bullied, going through a painful divorce, the list goes on.

In these periods, these more challenging times, when we have brought a situation down on ourselves inadvertently, or one has landed on our lap, like a bolt out of the blue, irrespective of how they've arrived, it does not feel right. Then when faced with difficult or even distressing situations, we are typically winded for a period, or hurt, or even both.

The more sudden the difficulty we face and the more turbulent, the more significant the effect it can have on our system. Even so, we don't need to stay in this space. There are tactics that we can use as tools to guide us out of these times, to guide us back to safety and security.

Create choice in times of hardship

In these more trying times one simple but effective tactic we have at our disposal is choice – and choice matters. Choice can make all the difference in the world to the outcome, so we ought to choose well. So, if you feel fully up against things – *create choice* – make the options visible. Do not stay where you are, in fact, simply refuse to. And no matter if we have made the correct choice or not, we have to appreciate that if we want to face our difficulties, to solve a problem, or deal with what we have to face head on, while this will take us down a path of hopeful resolution we should be prepared for some occasional hardship.

If you encounter these conditions for long enough, in striving to resolve them and looking for that way through, then you will enter into a phase where you need to persevere in order to see the light at the end of the tunnel. Real human difficulty is not pretty and can take you to some demanding places, both mentally and emotionally, and at times we don't always feel prepared for it. In fact, you can say that when life's real challenges take any one of us unawares, no one feels ready. Even so, push forward if you believe you are right.

And whilst you choose to face up to the real challenge of pushing through and improving your situation, you will no doubt, at times, feel vulnerable and lost, like a victim. To persevere, to fight and see things through, when you think you cannot go on, or are running low on energy and can see no clear path ahead, is arguably the most courageous thing a human being can do. And we all have a choice to be daring. You have the power of choice to move yourself forward and persevere down the path that you believe will lead you to safety and security; so be that gusty, brave soul.

Self-acceptance of your situation

Pure perseverance in the face of long and drawn-out difficulties in life can be downright painful, but the quicker you self-accept your situation, a self-appraisal of your current situation, your limits and capabilities, the better. To fight against, reject or dismiss your condition when things are not going your way will only bring about the likelihood of more chaos. Hence it is admittance through genuine self-acceptance that will kick-start a healing process within you, and this can only lead to better things. While I've never personally been a member, this acceptance is similar to the first of the twelve-step process of Alcoholics Anonymous, which forms the basis of their recovery programme.

This first step states: 'We admitted we were powerless over alcohol and that our lives had become unmanageable.' Taking this first step and admitting you have a drinking problem can be difficult and scary, but it is the foundation of all positive change[10].

Consequently, self-acceptance of any difficult situation is a must, irrespective of how it makes you feel in the moment, because to lead yourself out of difficulty you need to reflect and ask the question, 'Where am I?' Trying to navigate yourself from a challenging period without knowing exactly where you are is a little like trying to navigate your way around a foreign city in which you are lost. Unless you know your precise location and then accept this is where you are, you can't plan your route out of there! This understanding is the first key, and sometimes a courageous step in taking responsibility for your given circumstance; responsibility being an essential principle in self-leadership.

Self-acceptance and more especially sharing your situation can make you feel vulnerable, there is no getting away from this, but if you can share with someone who can genuinely empathise with your plight then it's the correct course of action to take. There is no heroism in locking up something that is destroying your health or getting the better of you emotionally. However, it's also true that sharing your plight, for some, can be one of the hardest things you will do when you feel trapped or cornered by a predicament; but just hearing your own words and admitting you have an issue can help enormously in the most difficult of circumstances. For you to process the acceptance of a problematic condition, even the most extreme, is the first step to healing. At least when you have accepted your situation, you can take constructive steps to recovery, even if you find yourself having to live with a new you, due to some life-changing circumstances. Perseverance and passion for aiding recovery can follow, but self-acceptance must be the first step.

'Accept – then act. Whatever the present moment contains, accept it as if you had chosen it. Always work with it not against it... This will miraculously transform your whole life.'

Eckhart Tolle

ARE YOU PLAYING THE VICTIM?

There is an excellent line in the movie *Jerry Maguire*, when Jerry's mentor, Dicky Fox, gives Jerry, played by Tom Cruise, a superb piece of advice, 'Roll with the punches, tomorrow is another day'. That, I believe, is such a terrific mantra when we are in the thick of it and are trying to manage a difficult time. You need to roll with the punches and concentrate on the longer game, the bigger picture, because even if we have been stopped in our tracks today, we always have tomorrow. In this thought holds hope, faith and belief that things will improve, that we will reach our aim and not play out as the victim of our current circumstance.

These three elements alone can carry us through hardship and challenging times and keep us moving forward, to persevere when things appear all too much. Also, I use the word 'appear' here deliberately, as assumption and belief can play a large part in how we view things. Belief, as I use the word, is all about moving forward and consciously working through your difficulties, not allowing them to master you or even influence you to the extent that they alter your expected outcome, your vision, or even stop you in your tracks.

In times of really bloody hardship in my own life, I think to others that have persevered through adversity and triumphed in one way or another, and one such individual is Tim Hague the author of the book *Perseverance: The Seven Skills You Need to Survive, Thrive, and Accomplish More Than You Ever Imagined* (Viking, 2018).

In his book, Tim tells the story of being diagnosed with Parkinson's disease, at just forty-six years of age. This condition soon ended his career as a healthcare professional, but three years later he still managed to win the inaugural *Amazing Race Canada*, with his son Tim Jr. A reality-TV event, the race is a gruelling 23,000 kilometres across the country, essentially a travelling scavenger hunt.

In the book, Tim tells the story where he discovered that he was suffering from a real issue when a tremor in his toe turned into a foot tremor. Up until that point, he had been keeping this from his wife, but when the tremor wound up in his thigh, he couldn't keep his secret any longer, and broke down and explained everything to her. Then later, upon receiving a diagnosis, he was naturally depressed to find his condition was Parkinson's disease.

The journey he tells of being diagnosed with the condition is touching. He writes, 'I wanted to believe that it would somehow go away, that the doctors would be proved wrong, or that I could set it on a shelf and ignore it'[11]. He goes on to explain the disease as 'his best friend whom he hates', how some days he feels that he can't deal with it, but needs to live with his condition every single day. Where some days he's continually shaking, or when even if he's not, he thinks about when the shaking will come back.

However, there is a brighter side to Tim's story in that he goes on to recount, as a result of his wife's passion for the race, initially televised in the US, she actively encourages him to apply. And although he was initially reluctant to be involved, eventually, after jumping through several hoops, he amazingly found himself on the starting line. However, the race was not kind to him; he suffered setback after setback, partly due to his condition, and at times all he wanted was to be sent home by disqualification. Although incredibly, as a result of his utter diligence and attention to detail, he ended up winning the final round, and as such, winning the entire race.

The contest made Tim Hague an instant celebrity, and he's now a Parkinson's activist and sought-after speaker on the subject in North America. What I love about his story of the race and the way he aims to deal with his Parkinson's is his utter perseverance to fight on and take each day as it comes. Tim's constant 'war' with his condition, as he puts it, and his motivation to keep going and persevere in the face of his challenges is admirable. Then to take his difficulties and turn them into a mission of supporting others with the condition is the mark of a man that rolls with the punches of today and believes in what the sunrise of tomorrow may bring.

Victims can't lead

Self-leadership can come in many guises, and one of these is the ability to maintain focus on your aim, once you have discovered what your goal is. Being dealt a hand where you feel you have been given no choice or feel that life has been unfair can seem unjustified and cruel. However, this is the view of a victim, and you can't lead anyone, let alone yourself, whilst in victim mode. If you feel that you are the target of your difficulty, it will not help one bit, and you must then turn this around to create strength in your corner.

With power, you can generate fuel and courage to become motivated to move forward to reach a better place. Choose to look forward not back for the answers, as the past does not provide the driving force for where you are going or solve problems.

I've experienced the victim mindset in a big way in the past but had to self-lead myself through to eventually discover a positive outcome. Off and on since a child, I have suffered from a chronic atopic eczema. Fundamentally, a chronic skin condition that causes excessively dry skin from which you can't escape, only alleviate, the symptoms.

Now, if this is bad, it affects your emotions, but when it is terrible, like most chronic conditions it can make you feel trapped – a victim. Dry, itchy, red, swollen or cracked skin is far from good. When it's bad, it can be an absolute misery to suffer from. My symptoms had been off and on for years. Even so, I was allowed to join the Royal Navy after being assessed by a dermatologist, as my symptoms at the time were hard to see. It almost looked as though the condition had gone for good.

Then five years later, and out of the blue, my skin condition returned with a vengeance. I was on leave on a camping trip with my fiancé, and it got so bad that my face became swollen, so swollen I had trouble opening my puffed eyelids. I ended up in the hospital.

Long story short, the Navy tolerated my condition. Only because I swore I could manage things and the type of work I was doing at the time wouldn't worsen the condition. Then three years after I left the services, my symptoms spiralled out of control. My maintenance schedule, which had grown into the use of creams, steroid ointments, antihistamines, and breath-holding cold baths once or twice per day to further calm the itching, even in the winter, was no longer cutting the mustard. I'd have a few weeks of relief only to be followed by itchy, swollen and red skin. Then – and out of the blue – my symptoms spiked and became unbearable.

My dermatologist was aghast at how bad my symptoms had become, and I ended up being re-admitted to hospital within hours.

At the end of second week in the hospital, I felt pretty low. I waited for the dermatologist to come around and discharge me – but I was beaten. I was promised by a GP when I was in my early teens that this condition would be gone by the time I was eighteen, and here I was, in my early thirties, in hospital again. I believed I couldn't escape; I felt depressed – like a victim. It's at these points in life, when you are in this mindset that you cannot drive yourself forward; therefore, you cannot lead for toffee.

Here, you need leverage! Something that will put momentum back into your system. You can either build in that leverage, that big enough reason to get back on with things, or the trigger, the stimulus, can come from without. From someone or something else.

My leverage came when the doctor arrived. He explained that some of the collagen in my skin was breaking down due to using so much steroid ointment use. He explained that if I didn't stop its use, then the eczema would become a lot worse.

You may be able to relate to this, where you hit a point in suffering with a difficult situation, where something happens, an event takes place that makes you self-reflect and become more self-aware of your current situation – and the realisation engulfs you, as you realise – enough is enough.

Well, in my story, this is how I felt. Enough was enough. And although, it was deeply heart-breaking news to hear at the time, later, when I picked myself up and snapped out of the pathetic low, I was in, I realised it was just the message I needed to hear. I then went on a search determined to find a cure, even though I was told by every qualified specialist I came across that there wasn't one!

I went on to try just about everything that did not involve applying potent creams to my skin: herbal creams, herbal pastes, several washing powder changes, random diet experiments and spiritual healing. I even successfully pleaded with dermatologists at the Royal Free Hospital in London to include me on a six-month trial of a new Chinese herbal treatment. It did have monthly blood tests, through fears, it could crystallise the liver, which added to the cost. However, I did not care one jot at the time – I was desperate! But even that failed to work. Was I doomed?

Then, after I persevered for what felt like a long eighteen months – with still with no joy – I found my lifeline through homeopathy. A simple no-side-effect treatment where practitioners use highly diluted substances to charge the body to heal itself. That excellent and simple practice and a diet change altered my life for the better. And this whole experience taught me that living in victim mode never wins; you simply must find leverage – a big enough reason – to break free to seek an opportunity to succeed. Find this advantage – and success is yours for the taking.

TOMORROW COULD BE YOUR DAY

Perseverance at times, is not fun, c'mon let's face it, but to stick with something and maintain momentum, you cannot under any circumstances, feel defeated. If you ever feel this way, move yourself out of that mode of thinking – and quick. Create a goal, a self-initiated goal, one that you believe will see you through your struggle. Then stay consciously focused and self-directed on that goal; breaking it down into mid-level goals and quick-wins as appropriate. If you let others or the influences of external events dictate to you, or gently try to persuade you to take their route, you will be taken off course.

Now, a caveat to this will be if others are trying to guide or help you and are correct. Not to listen to great advice is a thing of fools.

But on this note, I say again, if you do make a mistake, remember to roll with the punches, as tomorrow is another day.

Errors will be made, but we should learn from them, and keep going in the right direction with a laser-guided focus, while keeping your senses alert to what is happening around you. This approach should see you hit your goal, maybe not when you expect to hit it, but just when the time is right.

'Your next morning is your more important morning.
Tomorrow is your day!'

Sir Alex Ferguson

THE INNER GAME

When we were younger, we hoped that we could make a difference in the world and we could be someone. We wanted to be all sorts. I can remember changing my mind about career aspirations several times when I was a young boy. I even wanted to be an astronaut at one time and took a deep interest in space. Still, we all had some image of that someone we wanted to be as children. Someone that counted, someone who could paint, be loved, make money, serve, care for others, and many more.

It's somewhat ironic then to find that as we grow and mature into adults, we are likely to have found ourselves in an almost different place from where we thought we'd be as a child. With this fact in mind, with the endless bombardment of the media with its advertising, the news, the struggles and politics of the average working environment, we all suffer heavily from distracting factors. We then have to ask ourselves how do we keep going? How do we remain on track to accomplish anything?

I've already addressed the fact that motivation is needed to help you sustain direction, and that momentum will keep you in motion. Goals are great as they will provide something tangible to aim towards, and passion is required in order to keep the flame alight inside of you.

Even so, there is another aspect that can move the human spirit in the realms of perseverance much further. One that can provide you with all of the reasons to rise each morning and continue with your endeavours, however frustrating, tiring or challenging they can feel at times. And this is – *purpose*.

Finding your purpose

Purpose is what gives you enjoyment and meaning in what you do, or what you wish to do. It can be focused on the contribution that you want to make to society, which will also benefit your personal growth. It should not be driven by others and not be driven by society's current values or what others think you should be doing with your life.

Purpose is above all else life's most significant driver, and the bigger the purpose the bigger your drive and the more you'll have of the all-encompassing dynamic energy needed to push you that extra mile, to keep you going when others have fallen by the wayside. Purpose in its purest, innocent and most authentic form can move mountains for you as it creates such an inner drive and energy that attracts change.

In her book *Living with Joy*, Sanaya Roman states, 'When you look at life purpose, ask your soul and yourself, "Am I doing this for me, for my highest good, or am I doing it to please others, to live up to their image of me?"' [12] In this instance, you need to ask if you are fulfilling a need to be recognised or to receive acknowledgement. Or is it because there is an internal need, an inner drive, that gives you joy, and that fits with who you are?

There is an issue, however, in that while most of us may think we have a purpose, actually we don't. In many instances most people are on autopilot, going through life one day after another, being endlessly busy, and never questioning what they are doing.

Take the time to reflect for a few minutes and consider what is your purpose in life, and in your career, and then contemplate the answers. Maybe you only have one purpose, in that your job is your purpose in life, but some of us will separate work and life into two distinct parts. Note that these are not meant to be difficult questions to acknowledge, and there should be an instinctive understanding of each if you have worked your purpose out.

On the other hand, one of the biggest drivers that will inspire a purpose in just about everyone who walks this beautiful planet is doing something for another person over and above themselves. Creating and having a purpose of helping or supporting another can inspire you to create one of the biggest drives to humankind possible, as we will do more for another that we love than we will for ourselves.

If you ever find yourself in a position of striving for someone else, or even a group or community, you will naturally want to achieve more, to persevere. You will want to dig in more, and make a success of any situation you are striving to complete.

A shining example of inner purpose

One of the most notable characters of a recent generation is Nelson Mandela, who pushed this aspect of retaining an inner purpose in the face of adversity to the limit, because he believed he could make a difference to the apartheid regime in South Africa. Mandela, a graduate in Law, was a South African political activist who spent over twenty-seven years in three prisons for his opposition to apartheid; he was later released in 1990. He then said these years of incarceration in jail were a period of great learning, even if painful. However, when released, devoid of self-pity, he reached out to the same people who had jailed him to preach 'true reconciliation'.

Mandela later went on to jointly win the Nobel Peace Prize, with F.W. de Klerk, in 1993, for his work to help end racial segregation in South Africa; and later became the country's President in 1994. Nelson Mandela is one of the most admired political leaders of the twentieth and twenty-first century for his vision to forgive and forge a new 'rainbow' nation[13]. Plus here was a man whose inner drive while in prison would be committed to working towards peace, which he actively did when he was released. He had a clear inner purpose and vision for the change he could bring about when he was set free. Simply, a shining example of human inner purpose and what can be achieved as a result.

'Challenges arise to make us aware of our inner purpose.'

Deepak Chopra

ACHIEVING FLOW

With some tasks come our ability to choose how we feel and how we respond to certain situations in life. We can decide how to behave, but many people will react to conditions rather than imposing some degree of self-control over a situation they find themselves in. For example, they react charged with emotion, rather than responding more calmly.

The ability to apply reasonable degree of control over our behaviour is needed when times are challenging, and we need to persevere, otherwise things can descend into an emotional chaos. We all know individuals that can transform hopeless situations into challenges just through the force of their personalities. This ability to persevere despite obstacles and setbacks is the quality people most admire in others, and justly so; it is probably the most important trait not only for succeeding in life, but for enjoying it as well[14].

If we are then able to apply emotional management over our responses it makes the challenges of perseverance easier when things are getting complicated, or too challenging.

Let's face it, to persevere, to last out, especially for an extended period, can be tiring and energy sapping. You and me both know this as we've all been there at least one time, we've all gone that extra mile at one point in our lives. And to keep yourself focused in one direction you need that inner drive, that purpose, that burning momentum.

But now and again we all need to give ourselves some time off to rest and recuperate. To lay off things for a period. And that is perfectly normal. Because if we weren't going to do this once in a while, if we were going to keep charging forward instead, then it could be fatal to the challenge that we would be aspiring to achieve; let alone to our health.

On the contrary, when we do have reasonable emotional control over our pursuit and the difficulties that can arise with it, and if we have a passion for our quest, we can enter a state called *flow*.

In a state of flow, your conscious mind is optimised and achieves a state called 'transient hypofrontality'. And when the brain is in this state, it means that for a while, under certain conditions, there is a slowing of its prefrontal cortex, which allows other parts of the brain to become more predominant. Hence the reason why when you are in a state of flow hours can pass you by in what appears like minutes. This phenomenon is because the part of the brain that is associated with a sense of time is now switched off.

When in flow the challenge disappears

Flow is a state of mind that we can adopt when we are in the process of pursuing an activity where we become lost in the task. Except flow is not momentum. Flow is a blissful state of mind that is a by-product of perusing an interest that you love and manage to achieve with 100 per cent focus. You may know this as being 'in the zone', or 'runners high', and it is typically attributed to a state of mind found in top athletes or even those that are creative. But this is a state of being that any of us can achieve, and I'm sure most of us have experienced it at one time or another.

You notice when recovering from flow because you become so lost in the pleasure of carrying out your venture that when you stand back from it, you can be struck with surprise at the progress you have made. Thoughts, intentions, feelings, and all the senses are focused on the same goal. Experience is in harmony. And when the flow episode is over, one feels more 'together' than before, not only internally but also with respect to other people and to the world in general[15]. Hence why this state can also be enjoyed through activities such as meditation or even when you daydream.

In this state of mind, what was once considered a state of perseverance no longer becomes a challenge, the difficulty or struggle disappears; the love for the pursuit changes your whole focus. Then, if you also have a purpose for what you are doing, this is when the internal emotions typically associated with perseverance turn on their heads, and you then stride towards success with much more ease. Your inner purpose literally becomes abundant with energy, and perseverance, for you, becomes a thing of the past.

NOW, OVER TO YOU

If you took some time to reflect and consider what you are currently persevering with in life, there is a chance you may not think of anything. You may regard that you tolerate a few things? Nonetheless, if you are actively engaged and involved in something to the degree that you wish to influence it or see it through to a successful fruition, then perseverance is involved on some level.

So, please take a short while to really reflect on what you believe you are persevering with. It could be your health, diet, finances, a child's challenging behaviour, developing a business, your boss, tackling a complicated relationship, shift-work or even a project you are engaged in carrying out. There is a chance there are several ongoing projects happening together, and there is typically always something, less or more significant, taking place.

Reflect on what has happened up until now with the task you are persevering with. How do you feel about it, and what you believe is the outcome you want to achieve? Are you happy to see things through to successful fruition?

These questions are to gauge your level of commitment, and only you can answer them. But if there is hope and a more deep-seated need to continue, then there are a few items that I have covered in this chapter that you will need to hold close.

Establish your goals and break them down if need be. Remember that you may need to stretch your reach to achieve these goals; no harm there. Though, make sure your goals are achievable. And never play the victim of circumstance, always aim to stay in control, create choice and options, and allow yourself to make progress, find a way forward.

If you can take things one step further and generate a passion while you are persevering towards reaching your goals, it will pay dividends. Tasks become a delight to do, and you can get so much done in such a short space of time, as work becomes less of a chore and more of a joy. If you feel you need to persevere and stick things out, ensure that you believe in the outcome, and if so the right result will transpire.

PERSONAL CONTRIBUTION
DIANE & MEGAN: HEALTHCARE PROFESSIONALS

Inner Strength

My name is Diane and I am a healthcare professional. My youngest daughter Megan has anorexia. This extract is a short summary of our journey over the last twelve years. I would describe it as stressful but as avoiding the illness is not an option, it has been a journey that as her mother I would not change, and will not until Megan is back. I hope our story can be considered as insightful and positive.

I have always believed in my daughter and I have always believed that my beautiful, clever, funny daughter was hidden inside her tiny frame and would one day find the strength and courage to answer the question, 'What does Megan want?'

Being told that your child has an eating disorder is a message that takes considerable time to absorb and fully comprehend. Emotions vary from disbelief and desperation to feeling completely out of control, and all are overwhelming. Fear of losing your child is present every day.

This mental health illness remains relatively unknown within general medical practice and attitudes are unsympathetic and disbelieving towards those affected. I have had to listen to numerous clinicians in GP surgeries and doctors in Casualty say, 'Go home and just eat.' Such attitudes and the lack of knowledge serve to further demoralise the individual and entrench the illness deeper. Services are limited in every county, with long waiting times and few in-patient services. Family support and education are limited and the illness damages not only the individual but whole families too. Anorexia has the highest mortality rate of all mental health illnesses.

I was determined to educate myself in every aspect of the illness and explore fully national guidelines and services available to ensure that I could act as my daughter's advocate when she was unable to speak up or even be heard. It takes courage to speak up, and developing a determination to challenge and demand the right level of clinical and psychological support at critical times is crucial to keep your child alive. These critical times occur every twelve to eighteen months, with admissions combined with hospital and specialist eating disorders units lasting anything from six to twelve months in duration. During the lead-up to these admissions and often during the admissions my child fought against me, turning away from me, perceiving me as the enemy.

My whole position internally was to remain consistent and to persevere in supporting my child when all seemed so lost and hopeless. Signing section papers against her will was painful but necessary to keep her alive. The time in between admissions is still spent tip toeing around the illness and supporting her even though her main aim is always to avoid eating.

Twelve years on and we are faced with yet another relapse, but this time Megan is showing perseverance in a positive way, for the first time ever answering me when I ask, 'What does Megan want?' Here is her open and honest response never discussed before with anyone.

Battling an eating disorder is a million emotions and challenges every day but I would feel confident to say that one thing that every person needs to have as a weapon in fighting back is self-perseverance. Trying to hold on tightly and remember that this doesn't have to last forever and if you want to free yourself you can. No day is ever the same but when you've found that goal you want to achieve, you have to keep that target in your sight at all times even if you have to realign your thoughts or if it's just a glimmer in the distance – keep the fire lit.

Anorexia knocks you down and it knocks you down damn hard sometimes. I found that when I've fallen there are three options and I've experienced them all, and actually they are all okay: 1) Sometimes when the voice tells you to give in when you fall, you jump back up, brush yourself off and say, 'No, I'm keeping going.' 2) Other times you have to take a moment and get back up slowly and acknowledge the way you feel before reacting. 3) And sometimes it's just okay to lay there and allow help to get you back standing again. I've had all three reactions at different times in my journey and that's okay. You may have noticed I've said that it's okay a fair few times because I'm a great believer that it'll be okay in the end and if it's not okay it's not the end.

Right now, it's hard to believe that there will be a time when total freedom from the mental beast will present itself because life isn't predictable. I know I will be faced with more difficulties that will make me want to succumb to feeling unworthy, but treating every day as a new start and remembering that without bad times we wouldn't know what good times are... I will always persevere and keep my passion to survive, alive.

Chapter 3

Emotional Mastery

'What we feel is a choice.'

Piyush Shrivastav

It was back in July in 1995 when my heavily pregnant wife was admitted to the local maternity hospital due to the fact that she was ten days overdue. She had a potentially serious condition called pre-eclampsia at this stage, but we didn't know this at that time. She was fairly swollen around her ankles and her face was puffed, which are some of the telltale signs of this condition, but we thought this was due to the relatively hot weather at the time. Nonetheless, her bag was packed and she was now admitted to hospital.

For two days while they were attempting to induce the birth, I took time off work to be with her. By the second morning, when nothing much had happened, I decided to do the weekly shop. I picked up my father-in-law, Ian, to help me as my head was all over the place, due to anxiety, lack of sleep and little nourishment. But, to be perfectly honest it was still totally chaotic; I was running on adrenalin and now feeling darn tired by this point.

I had no plan here, and was randomly grabbing things from the shelves. But playing in my mind was the fact that this was our first baby. Is this how it's meant to go? Am I meant to be doing this? Are all anxious fathers-to-be meant to be running through a supermarket at speed, with their expectant wives cooped up on a maternity ward miles away? Little did I know things were about to get much worse...

We arrived back at my house to hear the telephone ringing, just as I slid my key in the door. My mother-in-law explained my wife had phoned her and was in a terrible state. Her consultant had decided they had gotten the birth date wrong and she was to be sent home. She stated that she had never heard my wife sound like this – inconsolable and lost. But at that moment, clarity dawned, and I suddenly knew exactly what I needed to do.

I made my decision consciously, and as I recall this was a fully rational one to avert this situation. It was a choice of leaving her until I was fully ready to go or leave that instant to go to her aid and aim to overturn the consultant's decision. There was no other feasible option open to me, so I had to act quickly.

The plan that came to me in a moment was to use strong emotion to alter the consultant's stupid-sounding decision. You could consider it naïve – but I believed I had no other option. However, what I was not prepared for was the growing emotion in me that would begin to overpower my rational thought and was about to teach me in no uncertain terms the potent power of our emotions.

'Anybody can become angry – that is easy, but to be angry with the right person and to the right degree and at the right time and for the right purpose, and in the right way – that is not within everybody's power and is not easy.'

Aristotle

I had made up my mind that I needed to lick this consultant's stupid idea into shape! After all, my wife was admitted some ten days overdue and had been in hospital for a further two days, yet they were now stating she needed to go home? The situation seemed completely outrageous. I arrived at the hospital some time later determined, angry – but controlled – and demanded to see my wife's consultant. I'd never been in such a situation before, so although I was angry, I was also unusually scared.

At this point my emotions were now running rife. They had grown a life of their own and my head was swimming due to the situation we had been put in, with all kinds of thoughts spinning through my mind. It was at this point that I realised my emotions were completely taking over. And this is exactly the power our emotions can have, they can essentially take you over, and thinking becomes less rational and thought through. And my thoughts were just doing that.

I went into the consultant's room to try and understand his thinking. My communication method was assertive bordering on aggressive. He needed to see that I wasn't going to back down in gaining a rational explanation. I also needed him to take responsibility for my wife's situation. He explained to me that on re-examining the three-month scan he had decided the baby wasn't actually due yet. But he now claimed she wasn't twelve days overdue – but five – and was to be discharged for a week.

What I tried to do was use my anger to attempt to disarm him, as this was ridiculous. I challenged him on this course of action strongly. I asked if he had even taken her emotional state into account and why had they not explained the date difference when the scan was taken – why wait until now?

To me the consultant had some bizarre hidden agenda up his sleeve, and I just couldn't get my head around his responses. I almost lost my temper completely, which is way out of character for me. But why wasn't he listening to me? Why was he not making any sense? He was locked into rationalising his decision-making, explaining that pregnancy and birth wasn't an exact science.

I had to think fast and adapt my approach. So, I then tried to appeal to his better nature. But after some fifteen minutes of an anger-fuelled debate, he explained his word was final and he wanted to hear no more. My shoulders dropped and I gazed across the room and caught the eyes of the ward sister who was standing behind him, and her look told me that my challenge to this man was fruitless – we were on our own!

I left not caring that this man had years of medical training and years of experience. To me he was just a man who'd got my wife's case all wrong. I went back to her bed and found a nurse there packing her bag. I emptied it and enlightened her under no uncertain terms that my wife wasn't leaving the hospital until she'd had the baby.

Seeing the situation as futile, the nurse then left, and I gazed out of the window into a crisp blue Friday midday sky. I knew I had to calm down, but I felt sick and overwhelmed. I searched my mind for an answer, but none came. I knew the self-leader in me was there trying to assemble order out of this chaos. I also knew that even though I was in a totally foreign situation, I had to get my thoughts and emotions under some level of control. I also realised I was completely enveloped by feelings, and really didn't believe that they could be so powerful; it was a potent lesson in their influence. Emotions were coursing through me like bitter waves. And I felt helpless, utterly helpless. If you have been in the position yourself, where you feel hopeless, it is at this point something must pull you out of this position, it has to. You simply can't stay there.

In my case it was triggered by the ward sister rushing in and explaining that my wife had suffered some sort of episode, and that the baby was showing signs of distress. She then quietly told me it was my right to change consultants, and that I should do so right away. She also added: 'I didn't tell you that!'

This was the answer I'd been searching for. I now really needed to temper the emotional monster, take hold of this news and cut my way through this tangled emotional path I was on; collect my thoughts and have the self-belief that I could see this situation through. If I now couldn't manage myself fully, then things could end up going badly wrong, and I knew it. I managed to corner the consultant once more and, in a controlled and confident way, requested a change of consultant, informing him I knew it was my right. He paused, thoughtfully and then agreed to it.

It was nearly six hours later when my wife managed to be seen by the new consultant. By this time it was about 7 p.m. He appeared completely different from the other idiot, charming, amiable but both concerned and genuinely interested in my wife's situation. He performed an ultrasound scan and took a good long look at the results – and appeared fairly concerned. He reported after his inspection that the baby had to come out and he chose a more aggressive method of inducement, with a possibility of a Caesarean section. The reason being: the placenta was breaking down!

He reassured my wife as best he could, then turned to me and said something that will stay with me always. He looked at me square in the eyes and said calmly, 'You did the right thing today. There is no way your wife should have gone home.' I replied, 'Are you saying the other consultant got it wrong?' To which he responded, 'I didn't say that, I said YOU did the RIGHT THING!'

Just over thirty hours later my daughter Maria was born, and after they had drained her mouth and throat of fluid, she cried for the first time. Pure emotional relief is an understatement.

EMOTIONS CAN SIMPLY TAKE OVER

Emotions are profoundly influential – they are powerful things. And by this, I mean they are a massive influence on our lives and our actions. My personal story above displays this. The influence and power of emotions are more powerful than the average individual going about their daily business will ever realise, or even be interested enough to acknowledge. This is simply due to the fact that they don't see emotions as something that can be studied or examined and have never explored their power or their influence; they're just there, and they always have been.

We live, and deal with, emotions every day – they are embedded in our physiology, so why should we study them or even consider them? Even so, we do need to understand them more in order to allow us to manage them better and so that they can act on our behalf, rather than of their own accord.

As a self-leader, someone who has an active interest in their goals and their pursuits, in order to thrive, we must at least recognise the power of emotions. We need to appreciate their influence in order to both live with them and also to grow and manage them. We need to do this because we wish to be the best that we can be, and due to the fact that emotions drive a lot in our lives. Our thoughts influence our emotions, our emotions in turn influence our actions and behaviours, which then in turn give rise to our results. Our results in life are what matter, our results are our reality.

Here, we will not study emotions in depth, but we will to a degree explore them and their influence, and consider their impact on us. We will also look at how we can aim to take better control of or master them in a fashion that suits us as an individual, as ultimately, emotions are a personal thing and no one really knows our own emotions better than ourselves. But learning more about them and some techniques that will improve our abilities to manage them, is necessary, as their influence can be all encompassing – they can both serve us and deny our goals and our abilities in life.

So, how do we define emotions?

Emotions – well, what are they? According to the Oxford English Dictionary the definition of emotion is: 'A strong feeling deriving from one's circumstances, mood, or relationships with others'[16].

Emotions are powerful social signals deeply embedded in the limbic system of the brain. Input is received through our senses, it passes through the limbic system and then on to the rational brain.

Our emotions send us quick, powerful, physical messages that allow us to respond to our environment. They also enable us to communicate voluntarily or involuntarily; which is an important point to note in the subject of self-leadership, when we are trying to control our actions and our destiny.

Our emotional parts of the brain have developed over millions of years of evolution. From these emotional parts evolved the thinking brain or 'neocortex'. The fact that the thinking brain grew from the emotional reveals much about the relationship of thought to feeling; an emotional brain existed long before a rational one[17].

Therefore, emotions are part of us, and are components of our thinking and the way that we act, react and respond to situations and events; we cannot escape them as they are part of our physiology. They can also take control of our lives and our actions, which is something we need to be consciously aware of. As the limbic areas of the brain are so powerful, they can have us act almost irrationally, or at least cause us an emotional episode before we even know what on earth is going on.

In his book, *Emotional Intelligence: Why it Can Matter More Than IQ*, (Goleman, 1996) Daniel Goleman writes about the subject of 'emotional hijacking', where he gives examples of where emotions can literally hijack our rational actions. Here Daniel proceeds to describe examples of where people have carried out acts that have resulted in a range of disastrous consequences, ranging from the profoundly awkward, right the way to murder – even before those poor people were fully aware of what was going on; where their emotional brain has simply 'hijacked' their rational brain.

Now, I'm sure most of us have had occurrences, less dire, where we've had an emotional outburst in the heat of the moment and have said something that we really didn't mean because in that moment our emotional brain 'took over'! But we are then left picking up the pieces for hours, days or even weeks afterwards, as the rational side of our brain wonders where the hell that ugly comment came from.

Nonetheless, there is a flip side where the same 'emotional hijacking' part of our brain also has a positive side, where the primitive emotional parts of the brain will sometimes spring us into action milliseconds before our thinking or rational brains have had time to understand exactly what is going on

An example of this could be the time when I was fifteen, when my family and I were on holiday, and I was carrying my one-year-old brother in my arms whilst climbing over a wooden stile. Just as I got both legs over, still holding onto the wooden frame, momentarily only holding him with one arm, he pushed away from me with both hands. He certainly would have landed badly if not fatally on the hard surface below had not my reactions kicked in – adrenalin filled my system and my whole body dropped and safely caught him in mid-air, before my rational brain even knew what was happening.

Now, I realise that my own life wasn't at stake, but that of one of my close family members was, and potentially my instantaneous reactions saved his life. Due to our *'emotional hardwiring'* we are saved in these types of events, which are based in our evolutionary past when our brain fired off an emotional signal in a split second to allow us to escape our ancestral predators.

So, our emotions can take over the brain and can dominate the situation for better or for worse, and the daily challenge of dealing with emotions is critical to the human condition because our brains are hardwired to give emotions the upper hand. Our emotional brain can also play an important role in more everyday events, as they can fill us with both positive and negative emotions. These feelings can influence us in many ways, which can be both our biggest tormentor but also our absolute saviour in life. Let's dive into these two elements in more detail.

*'Negative emotions are like unwelcome guests,
just because they show up on our doorstep doesn't
mean they have a right to stay.'*

Deepak Chopra

THE POWER OF MORE NEGATIVE EMOTIONS

Emotions like anxiety or anger are associated with tendencies to act in specific ways, that is: the flight or fight response. These kinds of emotions are resident within us because of our ancestral past, and are primitive in their nature but can influence us immensely. Therefore, if your body begins to lock-up because of an emotional situation, you can be caught like a rabbit in the headlights, and then your body will not allow you to act or respond in a rational way to the situation at hand.

An example could be that you are attending an important meeting and a colleague is explaining something that doesn't sit well with you, it could be bad news? It could be that they are revealing something that is undermining your plan or your strategy for the project you are working on; something that you have fought vehemently for, for the past six months. And now a number of others present are looking at you a little confused, as if they are beginning to realise that you have done something wrong. You are now being made out to be a bit of a failure, or at least, you are now feeling a bit of a failure.

In this kind of situation, the limbic component of your brain, or your sympathetic nervous system, is likely to kick in and your emotions will be in overdrive. More than likely you will start to brood or ponder over the problem, so your attention and your focus will not be in the room; instead you will start to focus internally, and go deep into thought to consider your own situation. So, there in the room the conversation could be vibrant, and you may have several opportunities to defend your corner, or at least make enquiry. But whilst words are being spoken you simply cannot process them and, sadly, in this condition will not have the ability to defend yourself.

By this point you are more than likely perspiring, your gut could be turning over because you are probably feeling anxious. The chemistry in your body has touched or influenced several of your bodily organs and at this point you will feel stunned. The space around you will feel detached, even slightly surreal, and your world is now internal as you are in *fright mode*. This is hardly the place for anyone to take a level of control over a situation or even to lead themselves out of a difficult position, and frankly, not really a great place to be in.

This is a simple example of the power of negative emotions that are deeply embedded in our brains and through it I have tried to emphasise their impact over us in the body. More destructive negative emotions can have big effect on us and make us feel depressed or, worse, suicidal, and if left to fester can end up with us potentially taking destructive action against ourselves or even others; never mind the numerous studies of the effects on our health that negative emotions have on us[18].

As indicated above, one thing that we should bear in mind is that negative emotions can tunnel our vision and prevent us focusing, or even correctly perceiving and appreciating the events that are happening around us.

For example, if you are overly anxious or very angry about something, there is no way that you are going to want to appreciate a complex situation around you that requires a cool head. Your body chemistry is incredibly powerful and will prevent this from happening; it will narrow your focus, your attention will be skewed, and you will act in an acutely primitive way – and be of no use to man or beast.

So, all in all we need to remain conscious and aware of the undesirable effects of negative emotions and the havoc that they can play on us and others. Simple self-control in these situations is not always the answer and can sometimes be difficult and impractical to implement. And to distract ourselves with a hobby or something of interest to us like going for a walk can sometimes provide a practical solution.

However, on a brighter note, we will look at ways to help master and support our emotions a little later on. At this point I am simply trying to highlight their influence and the power that our emotions can have over us. Therefore, be aware of them. We will do this by looking at the counter part of negative emotions, and we will revel in the power of positive emotions – which is exactly what we want and we are all looking for: to be flooded with the juices of constructive emotions.

The beneficial effect of negative emotions

On the flip side, it's useful to point out that even though negative emotions can be destructive, some do have a beneficial effect and can actually play a role in the healing process. One example could be the anger that I displayed towards the consultant in my wife's pregnancy situation. Whilst I'm sure that like all of us I don't like to become angry – in certain situations, controlled anger may be the correct emotion to express in order to force a point, and at the time of my story, in the opening of the chapter, I felt it right to point out the apparent sense of injustice in my wife's situation.

Anger of course must not get out of control and should only be used for beneficial effect. For example, it can be argued that anger can be a motivational force. In the realm of self-leadership to be angry at yourself can help to spur you on and to try harder in a given situation, where deep down you know you have the ability to power through – but for some reason your motivation has dropped.

When I was in the armed forces taking part in assault-course runs, you would often hear runners shouting at themselves *forcibly* – to spur themselves forward when they felt they were lagging behind. They were using the power of their emotions to generate more action.

Using anger as a self-motivational force on the assault course is just one place that it can be used beneficially. Shouting at yourself in the office would be frowned upon, I'm sure, but used appropriately in the right setting, it's a powerful tool. So, you should go ahead and try it when you can, that affirming boost will definitely help move you along.

Another example is grief. We can have a tendency to battle on with busy lives and sometimes don't give ourselves or those around us enough consideration. When grief of a loved one hits us hard, however, it can help us to slow down and reflect in order to put our lives into perspective through wisdom, as part of the grieving process. This self-reflection if used wisely, allows us to prioritise things in our own lives and can also make us realise or help us highlight what is important to us, which may be our health, our affairs, or a mixture of the two.

> *'Positive and negative emotions cannot occupy the mind at the same time.'*
>
> Napoleon Hill

THE POWER OF MORE POSITIVE EMOTIONS

Whilst it's probably true in life that not enough is said about positive emotions, and too much is focus is given to negative emotions and their impact, above I have pointed out the power that negative emotions can have on us; they really can be impactful. Positive and constructive emotions, on the other hand, can play a really important and strategic role in our lives if we welcome them and harness their energy, and in order to lead ourselves, we need to appreciate this importance, even though there is less media focus on this fantastic natural phenomenon. Here, I'm not trying to understand all of the different aspects or even the types of positive emotions – the list would be endless. Rather I'm trying to encapsulate the immense power positive emotions have.

Altogether, positive emotions are incredible things. They are the driving force behind a lot of what we do and achieve in life, and they can propel us into places that we never thought we could ever go – or even existed for us. If we can grab hold of that incredible understanding, those good thoughts, that propulsion, that positive emotions can provide us with, then as people we really can achieve a great deal in life.

Some of the great positive emotions such as optimism and happiness allow us to feel simply wonderful in life. They allow us to be creative, they inspire us and they also inspire those around us, because positive emotions fuel our optimism, which can be deeply infectious. I am sure that we've all been in a position where we are just bursting to get going and full of energy and vitality, where we feel we can achieve so much in life, and whilst in this state we know we are infecting those around us with our positivity.

Positive emotions can also help ourselves increase our social skills. If we are exuberant and happy when around others because of our optimism, it can allow us to jump over small social obstacles and hurdles, even with strangers. These emotions allow us to be far franker and more honest with others as they improve our social connectedness.

An emotional platform

Positive emotions can normally be really difficult to just – conjure up. Due to our conditioning we can't create them out of thin air or when we are feeling acutely sad, depressed or even anxious; it's impossible to turn them on. It's not easy to turn those feelings around one hundred and eighty degrees and create some real zealous positivity that gets our juices going. But we can do this much more easily when we have achieved a stable enough emotional platform; if we can do this, we are then in a more powerful place to choose how we feel.

By gaining greater emotional stability or by building our emotional foundations, we can change how we feel, we can push forward in difficult situations and grab hold of any of those positive emotions that we have deep inside of us at any one moment and expand and almost zone into them. To allow that emotion we have inside of us to gradually flourish and blossom and dominate our original state, and envelop us in all its glory.

Therefore, take this into the workplace or another situation you may be in when you have goals to meet and also actions to complete. Positivity coupled with motivation helps us to achieve those goals and actions, with far more ease and vigour than if we were trying to achieve them whilst being unhappy. To recognise the beneficial effects positive emotions have on us is deeply advantageous because we can use them to our benefit. For example, if we tackle a task with dynamic exuberance or even look to make more mundane tasks interesting and attempt to raise our motivation, the chances are that we will have the task done a whole lot quicker and with much greater ease, as in this state we become more solution oriented.

Our targets can be reached or surpassed, always looking to get our work done and moving on to the next thing with more energy and interest. In addition to better task accomplishments there has been a good amount of research done on the advantages that positive emotions have on our physical and mental well-being. Amongst other benefits they offer a buffer against depressive symptoms and help people recover from stress, which alone plays great dividends to our health and achievement of our targets.

So again, emotions are profoundly influential and powerful things. They have a major influence on our everyday lives, influencing our decision-making and allowing or preventing us from make progress. We need to appreciate the many aspects of self-leadership that can be impacted by emotions so that we can make some headway in getting to grips with both understanding and managing what they can influence. See the diagram right, which shows some of the aspects of our world that are affected by emotions. You will be able to see that they are incredibly influential.

FACTORS INFLUENCED BY EMOTION

Health
Appetite
Diet
Sleep
Energy levels
Stress levels
Self-confidence
Self-motivation

World view
Behaviour
Memory
Reasoning
Problem solving
Decision-Making
Concentration
Resilience

*'If you don't manage your emotions,
then your emotions will manage you'.*

Deborah Rozman

EMOTIONAL FOUNDATIONS

As emotions are such an influencing factor in our lives and actions, it makes sense to maintain an element of control over them and provide ourselves with a good amount of emotional management. In order to do this, we simply must have stability; we must create a more harmonious environment around us, and within us.

That can start with becoming selective of who we surround ourselves with, by being aware of those that are trying to negatively influence us, and taking active steps to prevent this. Making moves to ensure that we have more adequate and harmonious living and working environments, even if this is just simple change for the better, is important. Also taking active steps to harmonise our emotions by creating a good emotional stability and foundations, which are so impactful.

Good emotional foundations are the bedrock in our daily lives, they allow us to get by and interact with others and deal with the situations around us with greater stability and ease. View them as you would the foundations of your house: they underpin the walls, the rooms, the roof, your furniture, your family, the home memories made within, and then you. If we need to develop something in our lives in order to create some strength, balance or organised basis – it's our emotions. It's these that affect our thinking, and if we can't think well, we are going nowhere fast. And to build a foundation for our emotional well-being will help towards this point.

As self-leaders, we cannot overlook these foundational aspects, we must appreciate them and realise their powerful benefit to our lives. I have personally seen both colleagues and clients at work create emotional sabotage because they don't appreciate or realise the primary importance of emotions and the part they play.

One past colleague had worked on an item for several months but kept arguing with another over petty school-ground issues, due to some intellectual power play. Both had an 'I'm better than you attitude', but the particular colleague in question would not let things drop easily. One day things got out of hand and it became physical and had to be broken up by another member of staff.

Now, this was hugely disappointing as both members of staff were equally brilliant at their roles, but one got so emotionally charged that he grabbed the other by the scruff of the neck, and as a result lost his place on the project. The place where he had spent the previous six years of his working life and had become such an expert it would have guaranteed several more years' worth of work. This only goes to demonstrate emotions do play a massive influence in our lives and we therefore must address the more foundational aspects of them.

Before I introduce these emotional foundations, I must say that it will not be possible for everyone to carry out the physical aspects of the exercises, due to a physical impairment or other reasons. The most important thing is to do what you can.

There are five aspects to these:

- Sleep
- Mental awareness
- Mental diet
- Physical exercise
- Physical diet

Sleep

This is obviously something that we must all do; we must sleep. Have you ever gone without it for an extended period? Or even experienced broken sleep for several nights in a row due to the fact that you have an inability to flush out the stresses of the day or are worried over something? This could be broken nights due to your crying infant? If so, you will know what it means to feel the emotional effect on you. It feels downright horrible. Brain imaging using functional MRI scanning has been conducted which revealed why sleep deprivation can lead to irrational emotional responses[19]. A lack of sleep causes our mood to dip; we lose focus and then self-control.

When you sleep, your brain literally recharges, removing toxic proteins that accumulate during the day as by-products of neuronal activity. This ensures that you wake up alert and clear-headed. Your energy, attention and memory are all reduced when you don't get enough sleep[20]. Lack of sleep affects your energy, attention and focus then you will be less self-aware and have less self-control, two of the primary ingredients of self-leadership.

Mental awareness

This is about a subject area that focuses the mind on a different level of awareness or consciousness. It's an important subject that, to those who are new to it, may appear as Eastern 'soft skills'. But no! Here we are talking about abilities or techniques that take the awareness to a different level of thought in order to tackle the difficulties of life, or to make those difficulties easier; to give us a fighting chance and allow clarity of thought to shine through.

There are several techniques out there that will do this to some measure and it really is up to you to see what works for you, but it's your duty to take responsibility for your mental awareness, to make a conscious effort to support practices that will benefit your mental health, which in turn will impact your emotional health and beyond, and therefore will benefit your daily thoughts and actions.

One practice to increase your mental awareness is yoga, meaning 'union'. The union being referred to is between the body and mind and inner self (self-leader). The inner self, in modern parlance, is the control centre. The intention of yoga is to unite these three aspects of ourselves. By consciously connecting all three we become increasingly self-aware, giving us greater perception and understanding of who we are and why our emotions affect us in the way that they do. We are more connected to our control centre. Hatha yoga focuses on the physical approach; all physical forms of yoga being types of hatha yoga. Another branch of yoga is meditation, which is a mental approach to uniting with our inner self.

Hatha yoga does have a direct effect on stilling the mind. The use of focused self-awareness on our bodies, its movement and how we are feeling, whilst stretching and also relaxing the body, will have a direct impact on the mind.

If you are under stress your breathing and heart rate will increase, so by acting purposefully using yoga techniques to slow these down, this will eradicate stress and send you towards a more relaxed and less stressed thinking process. I used to practice hatha yoga during my work lunch breaks and then go back to work in a profoundly restful and calm state and full of mental clarity, ready to take on the rest of the day.

However, the technique that I wish to expand more on is: Transcendental Meditation or TM for short, which I practice and have found enormous benefit from. This technique, which has been deeply researched over the years, has an impact on our physiology and in turn will have a great many positive aspects for the self-leader. TM was popularised in the West in the 1960s (although its origins are timeless) and is a simple, natural, effortless mental technique practised whilst sitting comfortably with the eyes closed for fifteen to twenty minutes twice a day. A great book to start where you can find more on this topic is: *Transcendence: Healing and Transformation Through Transcendental Meditation* by Norman E. Rosenthal. (Tarcherperigee, 2012)

The technique allows the active, thinking mind to transcend its internal noise and quieten down to a state where the mind is settled, yet alert – while the body benefits from deep rest and relaxation[21]. This can provide a profoundly quiet and rested state of mind which in the wakeful active state will provide many physiological benefits, such as: security, high self-esteem, easiness with others and inner orientation. Research shows that people practising the Transcendental Meditation technique feel more positive emotions and have a higher level of psychological well-being[22].

This technique, when practised regularly over a period of time, can develop subtle changes in perception, allowing us to have a deeper sense of self-awareness, quietening all the mental noise that rattles around in our heads – helping to stabilise emotional turmoil. David Lynch, the acclaimed film-maker, in his book, *Catching the Big Fish: Meditation, Consciousness and Creativity*, (Lynch, 2007) wrote: 'When I first started meditating, I was filled with anxieties and fears. I felt a sense of depression and anger. I often took this anger out on my first wife. After I had been meditating for about two weeks, she came to me and said, "What's going on?"[23] He was then quiet for a moment and enquired as to what she meant. She then exclaimed that his anger had gone! He later reflected, not even realising that it had lifted.

Mental diet

An ex-colleague once informed me that after his father passed away, he had to stop listening to a certain radio news channel whilst driving – even though he had been an avid listener to it for several years. This was because it began to make him thoroughly miserable; and the bizarre thing was he had never realised this beforehand. As a result, he didn't listen to that news channel again for some time – rather he just listened to music! When he tuned back in to the channel some six months later it still had almost the same effect on him, so from that point onwards he could only listen to it on an occasional basis. Before his father's passing, he felt informed by the news, but wasn't consciously aware of the flow of negatively and irrelevant information that came across.

It seems bizarre for someone in their late forties to realise, for the first time, that a popular national radio station was making him feel so down in the dumps. It took him to be in a grief-stricken state due to the loss of his father to appreciate the effect that external influences, like the news, had on him. The strange thing to him was that he had never been aware of it before, and the conversation I was having with him started on the subject of his dear old dad – and not his mental diet. But even some years after, this was the one thing that stuck out in his memory.

What my ex-colleague was referring to was the mental noise and nonsense that fills our heads every day if we let it. It's everywhere out there; it's in the media, on social media, television and the radio, and you don't need to look that hard for it to be bombarded by its noise.

Mostly this is negative, misleading, irrelevant and overrated news. It affects you, skewing your views and opinions, it persuades and influences you, and on occasion can make you feel unhappy or even depressed.

Nonetheless, there is, of course, a lot of good that can be provided through all these mediums – and they do have their place, I'm not knocking them completely. But these sources do bombard us with a lot of material and not all of it's good for us – we need to decide what is suitable for our health. On most occasions it's not until we are re-sensitised to negative news and meaningless information, like my ex-colleague was, that we are able to become self-aware of the harmful impact. Research has taken place showing the positive effect leaving social media alone has on us after one week of going cold turkey.

But you don't need research to see the difference it can make on you when you make the decision to go without – you simply feel the positive effects.

The struggle is that it has, for some, become part of our daily routine to be 'plugged in' to this mental chatter. A number of us will feel that unless we are scrolling through social media on a frequent basis or watching the television, we are really missing out on something, and don't feel socially included. And of course, there is the influencing power of the media. News organisations assert that their information gives you a competitive advantage. Many fall for this. Some get anxious when they are cut off from the flow of news. In reality, news consumption is a competitive disadvantage. The less news you consume, the bigger the advantage you have. If news really helped people advance, journalists would be at the top of the income pyramid. They aren't – quite the opposite[24].

Another powerful influencer is advertising. It's absolutely everywhere. Practically it serves a purpose, it is needed to inform us of what is available to purchase, but it also influences us: our emotions and our actions. To an extent it takes away our free will and also our responsibility for making our own buying choices. The force shaping world opinion and consumer buying habits is the same force that shapes all of our actions. It's up to you and me to take control of this force and decide on our own actions consciously, because if we don't direct our thoughts, we'll fall under the influence of those who would condition us to behave in the way they desire[25].

To become more self-aware and to take more self-control in order to make genuine conscious choices and purchase what we need, what motivates us and what will genuinely move us forward, is what this purchasing game should be about. Not buying because we've been influenced.

A prime principle of self-leadership is to lead yourself and not for others to influence your day or even your direction, unless it's for the better good of all. But we have to admit this is not an easy escape. We should live our days under our own influence as best we can, unless of course we need to be influenced or informed by others in a useful way. This comes with experience and some self-assessment of the usefulness of what we hear and see. But to simply listen or watch until we genuinely feel we've had enough, or we know we are being influenced in a way that we are not happy with, is a great start. And then – do something useful about it: don't just sit back and let things skew your emotions and your thoughts take over.

Physical exercise

I can completely relate to John Douillard's book *Mind, Body & Sport*, (Douillard, 1994) in which he reported that when in India he asked some scholars what the purpose of exercise was according to Vedic texts. They reported that exercise has three main functions, see below. Where I will expand on each area in more detail.

1. To rejuvenate the body and mind
2. To remove stress
3. To develop mind-body coordination

Rejuvenation: This being the feeling that you should experience after exercise, you should feel refreshed and enlivened. I used to run marathon distances and needless to say – I'm not a born runner – I still remember how difficult it was to start running. I'd start off, run for a mile and just want to stop every sixty seconds or so. Then after several training sessions, and months later, with a lot of perseverance, I managed to slot into a groove where I was out running four to five times a week. I still recall how it felt to say that 'I'm out stretching my legs', where stretching my legs consisted of about a six- or seven-mile run. And when I finished my run, I would feel alive and alert. I don't run these days as I later picked up a back injury, but I still manage to find the same sensation through a good gym workout or a strenuous cycle ride.

Exercise, carried out in harmony with your abilities and physical condition, provides feelings of rejuvenation and being alive.

Stress reduction: Being active promotes mental well-being. Regular exercise allows us to think more clearly and make better life decisions, and reduces stress and anxiety, as it changes chemicals in the brain. Some scientists think that being active can improve well-being because it brings about a sense of greater self-esteem, self-control and the ability to rise to a challenge[26]. When faced with difficult lingering decisions or difficult situations in work or in your personal life, the escape and rejuvenation of exercise can give you a whole different perspective on your circumstances. Problems won't necessarily go away, but your change of perspective will reduce your feelings of stress and anxiety over situations where you can add greater clarity.

Near where I live, my local leisure centre works with medical practitioners across a relatively wide geography to them on a general practitioner referral scheme. This is where a patient's GP will refer them to the centre for a variety of different medical problems. The scheme will introduce them in a managed and progressive way to an exercise programme to help with their ailments. A number of the 'primary reasons' why they are referred is for conditions such as obesity, diabetes and even cancer; and in several cases they will have 'secondary issues' such as mental health problems lurking behind their main issue.

Sadly, the leisure centre has reported that they have seen a growing number of younger people suffering with these sorts of mental health issues, in addition to those existing patients that are typically middle-aged. Nonetheless, this is a very popular scheme, where physical activity is proven to have an immensely positive and beneficial impact on those with a variety of both physical and mental issues.

For those of us that do manage to exercise on a regular basis, if for any reason we stop due to holiday, sickness or work pressures, then we do start to pine for the exercise, and this alone can affect us emotionally. When you see and feel the benefits that exercise has on us both physically and mentally, missed exercise sessions can be difficult. The emotional high, that feeling of rejuvenation that comes with a degree of cardiovascular impact on the body, makes the world of difference to your outlook on life. It gets you raring to go, as the GP referral scheme mentioned above recognises. It can be just the support you need in order to break the patterns induced by a chronically overstressed body. So, if you can get out there and exercise – do it, the benefits for you are superb.

Mind-body coordination: When the first two purposes of exercise have been accomplished – when the system has been rejuvenated and freed from stress – the stage is automatically set for improved mind-body coordination. Whilst most of us don't necessarily need accurate mind-body coordination in our daily lives, such as top athletes, just the fact of having your mind and body working in harmony, communicating with each other and not saturated with stress will dramatically help. Stress and fatigue in the mind-body system break down coordination. The stressed body simply can't respond as quickly and effectively to the commands of the mind. And unless the mind is calm and stress-free, it may not pick up signals from the body.

In a more rejuvenated and less stressed state your responses to situations will be all the more accurate and accomplished when your mind and body are communicating more closely.

Physical diet

As the saying goes: 'We are what we eat', and this is true. For eating the right things cannot only improve our lives, it can also improve our moods, and therefore influence the way we think, act and behave. I'm sure that the caffeine drinkers amongst us have felt the effects of too much caffeine on our behaviour. I know I've been guilty of this in the past, and when I gave it up it also played havoc on my system. I felt I had flu for about two weeks.

It's reported that a Mediterranean-style diet is the best thing for our health overall. Eating a well-balanced diet, with the right amount of protein, carbohydrates, fats, containing a good source of vitamins and minerals, provides us with the right types of fuel and can prevent or manage medical conditions such as diabetes. But what about the effect on our moods and behaviour? Well there has been a lot of research conducted that shows there is a link, and whilst a whole chapter can be dedicated to this subject, I will signpost a few essential aspects in order to summarise the effects food can have on our behaviours.

Low blood sugar affects mood – so you should be trying to keep your blood sugar levels in the normal range through diet, even if you are not diabetic. Apart from the fact that chronically high or too low blood sugar can have a knock-on effect with physical complications in the body, if not managed, both high and low blood sugar can have an effect on your overall mood.

There are a multitude of emotional impacts of having high and low blood sugar levels. For example, high levels of blood sugar can lead to feelings of lethargy, irritability or even depression. This is without the added complication of being diabetic and suffering abnormal blood sugar variations. Eating at regular intervals and choosing foods that release energy slowly will help to keep your sugar levels steady. An important point is that the brain's neurons can't store energy; they need a constant supply. Therefore, a steady blood sugar level can help to regulate our behaviour.

Food allergies or intolerances can also have an emotional impact. As I mentioned in the previous chapter, I used to suffer from chronic atopic eczema, it was so bad I was admitted to hospital on several occasions. As I said, eventually I found the 'cure' through a homeopath. As well as being prescribed homeopathic remedies, through him I came to discover that I was allergic to certain additives, preservatives – and everything that came from a cow. How on earth I became allergic to cows, I don't know – but it had a major impact on my diet.

I had to reduce the normal foodstuff in my diet by roughly a third, and I had to maintain this for several years, but about four months into my treatment I was symptom-free, so I was informed I needed to stick with the diet. Not suffering from chronic, itchy eczema changed my life drastically and my moods immensely.

Food allergies can be at the very least irritating and a lot more severe for some. Some symptoms of food allergies can include: itching, hives, dizziness, swollen or runny eyes, chronic fatigue syndrome, mood swings, depression and even anaphylactic shock.

These more severe allergies or intolerances have a major impact on a larger degree of the population than we realise, and it's our responsibility, if we suffer, to take a degree of control over any allergies or intolerances to food we may have; or any that can make things miserable, for that matter. They can be difficult to live with, always having to maintain a strict diet, scrutinising food packaging and recipes, always having to be careful when eating out.

I know it's hard – I've been there! However, if you have an allergy and are unsure exactly what triggers it, a food allergy and intolerance test could be the solution to provide you with a way forward to tackle the symptoms, or at least manage them. In my particular situation,

I had absolutely no idea that I was suffering with a food allergy but was absolutely astonished and grateful at the overall result.

Turning our attention to what the body should be getting, your brain needs essential fatty acids (EFAs), or a source of 'good fat': omega-3 EFA and omega-6 EFA to keep it working well. When some people think of eating fat, they can turn a little green, but these fats are essential; we need them to survive, and they must be included in our diet as they cannot be manufactured in our bodies. There are other types of fatty acids, but those are non-essential to human health.

Omega-6 EFAs are probably best known for the role they play in supporting physical conditions such as allergies and dry skin. Omega-3 on the other hand provides a whole host of benefits and are important for all-round good health, such as promoting a healthy heart, maintaining healthy vision and keeping joints flexible. It has also been linked to the maintenance of good memory and the treatment of depression. All of which will have either a direct or indirect impact on our emotions and our feelings.

The last point to raise here is hydration. I didn't fully realise until I spoke to a friend of mine, and a keen triathlete, about the amount of water we need to take in just to keep our kidneys in shape. You see he had been suffering with kidney stones at the time and had some them removed from one kidney but was still suffering with the other. Due to the fact that he was prone to them, he had to drink up to 4 litres of liquid per a day.

The European Food Safety Authority issued a report stating we should be drinking up to 2 litres of fluids per day for a man and 1.6 litres per day for a woman, which includes drinking water. This makes sense as the body is 60 per cent water. Hydration aids concentration and clear thought, which has direct impact on our actions. Therefore, as well as being fundamental to us, it also plays an important role in allowing us to carry out our daily routine with some effectiveness.

The link with food and our emotional balance is in providing the right essential nutrients in order to help to sustain a healthy life.

Research also suggests that low levels of vitamins, mineral deficiencies, and a low intake of fatty acids and omega-3s can contribute to altered moods and mimic various mental health issues[27]. So the right thing to do is to take responsibility for our diet, which will have a lot of direct physical benefits, as well as supporting our emotional health.

It's only fair to point out that those with specific medical conditions, and if you have concerns about your diet, should seek professional nutritional advice. Then, with a healthy physical diet, together with these other elements, which have been introduced will provide your emotions with a stable foundation, hence the term 'Emotional Foundations'.

EMOTIONAL FOUNDATIONS

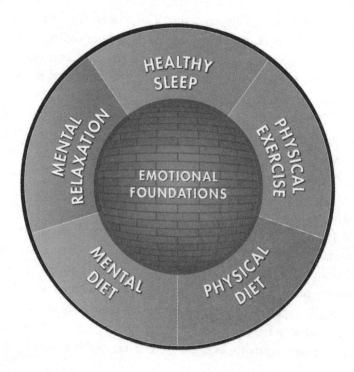

'IQ and technical skills are important, but Emotional Intelligence is the sine qua non of leadership'

Daniel Goleman

SO, WHAT IS EMOTIONAL INTELLIGENCE?

Up until now, we've looked at emotions and their impact, and how to help create some firm foundations to support our emotional health. And I firmly believe we can't grow our next topic, 'emotional intelligence', within us to any great extent unless we have built decent emotional foundations to support them. This is because we are doing ourselves a massive service if we can genuinely learn to help keep ourselves fit, well and aware enough, with reference to our environment, in order to provide an emotional stability. And this emotional bedrock, will then help us to raise our emotional awareness. However, just when you thought that might be it, there is even more than that we can learn and do on this topic of 'emotional mastery'.

I'm sure we've all heard of Intelligence Quotient, or IQ. A score that can be derived from taking a test in order to measure your intelligence. Well, there is also the concept of EQ, or Emotional Quotient, a measure for how emotionally intelligent we are. Now, this is a topic that more are becoming aware of, but EQ is not nearly as common a term as IQ. Only a few short years ago I gave a talk on the topic to an audience in Brussels, to around sixty people, and then gave the same talk to about one hundred in Edinburgh. Yes, these were mostly a technical audience, but no one in either room had even heard of the subject, even though there were several senior managers and business leaders in both of these locations. But little did these audiences know, that a good EQ can boost their chances of success in their personal and professional lives.

So, what is emotional intelligence and why should we be aware of it? Well, it has been argued that IQ, the conventional way of measuring intelligence, does not necessarily relate to how successful we are in life. Some people can be classed as particularly bright and do well academically, but they are not successful people in terms of their social skills or even their self-organisation. They have achieved highly in the classroom but have difficulty in managing their own lives and find it challenging when relating to others. This is not to say that those with a high IQ don't have a high EQ, rather a high IQ does not equate to success.

Emotional intelligence is a term first used by Wayne Payne in 1985. My favourite model is to be found in Goleman, Boyatzis and McKee's *Primal Leadership: Learning to Lead with Emotional Intelligence* (Goleman, Boyatzis, Mckee, 2004). Here, four elements are introduced that are needed to achieve personal and social competence, which are described below. Unlike IQ, EQ is not an inherent fixed attribute. The required qualities of awareness (knowledge and understating) and management (appropriate action) can be learned and they also develop with age.

Take the comparison between a ten-year-old boy and the same person when he's grown into a forty-year-old man. Naturally, the older we become the more emotionally mature we are. However, we can also practise and work at that emotional maturity and therefore grow our EQ. By this I mean taking positive action to develop our bad or negative emotional traits by learning from past mistakes and taking the time to reflect on our own negative behaviour. If you find yourself making the same mistakes in life, the meetings that you chair always go horribly wrong, or you always end up in an argument with even mildly difficult people – then it's most likely not them who's at fault. You will need to develop your emotional intelligence. Without appreciation and an understanding of our own emotions, and handling these successfully, we have no self-leadership.

The benefits of both investing time to mature our emotional intelligence will yield more significant results in our self-leadership in several different ways. It allows us to enjoy greater social interaction. It improves our ability to mix within various social circles and play an active part in more demanding social exchanges, which are commonplace with more challenging roles. It also allows us to learn about ourselves with greater speed. To be less accepting of what we dislike about our behaviours, so naturally drive more refined action into our day.

In addition to this, a key to greater self-leadership is good self-management, which allows us greater freedom to make better choices. This freedom will occur if we are inherently in the right place at the right time through improved self-discipline. What can also follow, through an improved emotional quotient, is the ability to enhance our relationships with others. Which provides the opportunity to learn and improve the management of our interactions.

All of these elements add up to a greater clarity over your behaviour, thoughts and feelings to make a better you, which will only help to develop your character for better growth continually.

COMPONENTS OF EMOTIONAL INTELLIGENCE (EI)

Self-awareness

Self-awareness is the ability to determine how you understand what you do well and less well, and why you take the actions you take. Those that have a good self-awareness are attuned with their own feelings, they are genuine to themselves and won't lie or pretend about their own emotions. By being self-aware, we should be true to ourselves, we should understand where we are headed in life and be in touch with what we want. Our goals and aspirations should be clear to us, even if they are still in the development phase.

But I know that sometimes we don't know where we are headed, and this gives rise to developing our self-awareness, which can be started by taking time out to self-reflect. A simple example here can be our ability to taking the time out to reflect on our behaviour due to past events to improve our future actions. As we saw earlier in the chapter, I'm sure we've all encountered times when we've not behaved quite how we would have wanted to.

A former ex-colleague, Daniel, whom I served alongside on ship, used to lose his temper far too quickly on the odd occasion. These childish tantrums became worse when he got blind drunk – which he did on at times when we were in port. He made quite an unpopular character of himself at times. But annoyingly, he would never take the time to reflect on his behaviour – even when it was pointed out to him by those on the receiving end. Now, emotional outbursts may have been a family trait, because, during one of his leave periods, a family argument between his brother and his mother ensued. And this, I'm afraid, resulted in physical violence, where his mother bore the brunt of his brother's temper. Daniel, who was present at the time, was too drunk to step in to the extent where he could completely stop it.

Now this event, dreadful though it was, gave enough leverage for Daniel to seriously reflect on his behaviour, which he explained to me one day. And from that point forward, he both stopped drinking alcohol, and began to regulate his anger more consciously when he was sober. The whole incident was a truly sad state of affairs, by the sound of it. Still, as a direct result, Daniel became a calmer person.

This story brings home that difficult, offensive or even downright bloody obstinate behaviour in themselves simply will not be tolerated by those who lead themselves – if they are in the serious process of trying to improve! But sometimes they do need a lever, an incident, that kick-starts a period of self-reflection.

Even thoughtless remarks will fall under the category of self-improvement. The self-leader will look to improve on all of these and more, through a quest to be as good as they can be. In addition, we need to carry out an element of self-reflection whilst taking action. This does not mean becoming self-obsessed by our actions, but rather becoming self-aware, more like a kind of moral compass. Inherently we know when we are not on track, and if we don't, then we are not paying enough attention to our thoughts and actions.

I'm sure that most of you have been in the situation where you are about to say something that simply won't go down well, and you catch it just before it leaves your lips. Or are in a meeting where you are not sticking to the facts, you may be clouding the subject as you are feeling emotionally strung out at the time, or even wish to impress others. Observing this behaviour and modifying it to the situation or environment that you are in, as in the first example, is self-awareness and reflection in action.

There are far more significant situations that we can find ourselves in where becoming self-aware becomes vitally important. We are all going to hit obstacles in life where we are thrown into the unknown, or we are thrown into the deep end. This could be an unwelcome job role due to an internal reshuffle, or it may be the death of a loved one. All can be downright difficult, but from a practical perspective we all need to move through them.

First and foremost, in these situations, we have to become our own friend and learn to appreciate our thoughts and emotions as they arise. You will definitely have times when your emotions will run high, even wild. You need to understand that you are going to have emotions that will catch you unawares, but they are happening for practical reasons inside you. Learn to ride and observe these emotions. They will dissipate; they won't last for ever even though they sometimes feel that they will never end. Again, be your best friend, the emotional hijacking will go and you will recover.

Practically, find your way through the situation by taking small steps and learning from your behaviour, learn from the way that you are acting and the results you are getting from your actions. Even small actions have results. Short discussion topics in a meeting, little actions when starting a new job, small passages that you may be writing for a long overdue report, small steps that you are taking on the death of a loved one. Whatever it is, act but pay attention to your behaviour.

Ask yourself some questions:

- How do your results feel?
- Are you acting in line with your gut instinct?
- Are you striking a balance for the better good of all?
- Will you achieve the best outcome given the information and the time available?
- Are you being honest with yourself?

Again, this is not about becoming self-obsessed; class this more as a simple check-list of observations so that you can guide yourself through the situation. If you conduct these sorts of simple observations on yourself, they will eventually become second nature. Also, trying to trace these emotions back to their source will help you assess them with greater clarity and you will learn to appreciate why they have arisen. This won't always be practically possible, nonetheless do so when you can.

Self-management

Self-management is built upon self-awareness; therefore, you need to be aware of your actions before you can manage them effectively. Self-awareness is maintained in the present (rather than forgotten about until later) and it can be used to direct your behaviour. Without knowing what we are feeling we are at a loss to manage those feelings, therefore our emotions control us. That's usually fine when it comes to positive emotions like enthusiasm and the pleasure of meeting a challenge. But no leader can afford to be controlled by negative emotions, such as frustration, rage, anxiety and panic[28].

We can become a hostage to our feelings, and self-management is the component of emotional intelligence that helps to free us from this condition. You may have found that you have applied this control when undertaking what could be a nervous situation, as when turning up for a job interview. Or when maintaining your cool in a demanding meeting. It's what allows the mental clarity and concentrated energy that leadership demands, and what keeps disruptive emotions from throwing us off-track. Leaders with such self-mastery embody an upbeat, optimistic enthusiasm that tunes resonance to the positive range[29].

These more positive emotions and thoughts, enthused by self-management, will help to counteract those more negative ones, allowing the self-leader to stay productive when dealing with themselves and others.

Self-management in play will be: deciding what you will aim to accomplish rather than waiting to be told. Planning your day or week rather than waiting to see what others are doing or waiting to see what events arise. Being self-aware and observing that you are acting rashly, and altering your behaviour in order to suit the situation at hand. In relation to dealing with others, by taking responsibility for managing yourself you avoid forcing others to manage you, which may risk you to react and lose yourself awareness – in turn making self-management harder still. Which is usually due to the fact that we can lose focus on our emotions and how we are managing them in the moment.

An example of a more difficult situation could be when given an abstract, poorly defined assignment at work, or the need to organise a large family event without all the necessary details – with potential family complications involved. These are typical examples of where the situation can become overwhelming. In these circumstances, managing your behaviour to learn to emotionally adapt and accept the position will help you to make a constructive start and provide emotional stability. This will also help you take responsibility for your actions.

A practical step here will be to break this large assignment down by chunking it into manageable steps or tasks, then taking the time to identify which ones you are sure you can achieve, and resolving the rest, seeking help with understanding if you need to. You will end up in a much better place to succeed.

Also, visualising success of new emotional habits will help you to become more successful. The daily practice of visualising our objectives as if they already existed can rapidly accelerate our achievement of any (achievable) ambition. The process activates our creativity, imagination and then ideas. If we can see what an end result looks like, it makes it easier to achieve[30]. So, for example, repeated visualisation of how you want to respond and manage your behaviour to a typical pressured situation you commonly face, will be to your advantage. This could be a conversation with a difficult colleague or manager, or your attendance at more difficult meetings. How do you wish to conduct yourself? What new actions or mannerisms do you wish to strengthen? Visualisation of success is a great way to inspire you and builds confidence in these more difficult assignments that we need to undertake in life.

Most of the time when we are not even aware of it, we are talking negatively to ourselves, we are filling our minds full of doubts and worries that the majority, if not all, of the time never come to fruition. There is a clear difference between worrying about the possibilities of failure and taking the time to have a clearly defined period to reflect and plan for the worst, such that we can mitigate these risks.

This endless negative mind chatter can be our own worst enemy. Catching our negative self-talk and replacing this with far more positive statements is such a constructive way of boosting our own confidence in supporting ourselves to achieve things. Some of this comes back to being our own best friend.

Take a few years ago when I had to go for an MRI scan on my back to ascertain if I needed surgery, as I had injured my spine and had been in a lot of pain. Now I don't like confined spaces at all, from a frightening experience as I had as a child, and combined with not knowing what injury I had done to my back, it didn't help when I was pushed into that small tunnel with my arms above my head and then the noise from the scanner started – which to me sounded like an old tractor engine! In this moment, there's an element of positive self-talk involved to keep your cool and to stay relaxed. You are under the complete control of someone else, I mean, you can't climb out unless someone lets you out. And this to me was the worst part of all.

During my scan, I thought of the overall good that would come out of the activity; I could receive a diagnosis and move out of the pain I was in. Also, it was only going to last twenty to twenty-five minutes, and I wasn't in the far more claustrophobic situation of being stuck down a pothole or similar. I also praised myself for keeping relaxed and calm and when one test finished and the noise from the tractor-sounding scanner stopped for a few seconds, I thought, 'One test down – I'm closer to going home. Another test down…' and so on.

Negative thoughts could have found their way to the forefront of my mind to such an extent that I would have ended up panicking. But this is an example of where positive self-talk came in remarkably useful and allowed me to maintain a level head.

Social awareness

Self-awareness and emotional self-management are the building blocks to the third element of EI: social awareness. Once you are able to choose and manage your actions effectively through calm and thoughtful application you will be able to make practical use of the truth that everybody knows: your worst mistakes are avoided if you listen, observe and empathise more.

The moment when you are late for a meeting – you are walking rather quickly down the corridor, trying not to drop your laptop and notebook, and you enter the room ten minutes late, and as best you can quietly enter the room, but as you are edging your way around the table you notice there is a stony silence. This is not aimed at you, the looks on people's faces are telling you this as you observe them: there is an edginess to their body language, their facial expressions look cold and hard as if just the moment before you entered the room someone dropped a bombshell. One now unpopular person has just delivered some difficult news and you can taste the tension in the air.

The part of your awareness that picks up on that awkward 'cut the atmosphere with a knife' type of mood in the room is your social awareness. And to master this will help you to become a socially effective self-leader.

Social awareness is centred around the ability to recognise and understand the emotions of others. By observing their body language (which includes facial expression and gestures, etc.) and by listening to the moods of others, both when in meetings and in general conversation. So, observing and listening with an active interest, and observing and assessing as much about the mood and actions of others as you can. Tuning into others' emotions as you interact with them will help you get a more accurate view of your surroundings, which affects everything from relationships to the bottom line[31].

Becoming adept at growing your social awareness can really have a great benefit in understanding the culture and social rules of an organisation that are going on around you. These are mostly never spoken about, never written about, but are definitely there – deep and resonant within the organisation that you belong to.

One of the best ways to understand and be accepted (which will only aid progression) within the organisation is to observe and listen to others and to adapt your style to best suit the culture. Although everyone is different, as you study more of the people around you, you will notice commonality and trends in their actions and behaviours.

I already covered the topic of self-empathy back in chapter one, but one of the most important elements of social awareness is empathy; the ability to empathise with others emotions and what they are going through in their current situation. To endeavour to put yourself into their position in order to attempt to appreciate the issues that they are going through may be perceived as a weakness, however it's far from it! This is a major strength and 'feather in your cap' if you can act in such a manner.

Empathy is the mainstay of social awareness and a building block to self-leadership and leadership of others: to take the time and the responsibility to understand where others are at, and not to make excuses for yourself as to why you can't take the time to do so. This is both an expression of self-leadership and selflessness, which frankly set you above the virtues of others in a similar position. Modern bosses that see this type of behaviour as a weakness in their character are simply wrong; not displaying empathy is only a weakness in their qualities as a more conscious self-leader.

A few years back, I was running a small team on a project that involved some specific deadlines. We were a prime supplier supporting a new business change package for a major UK airport. So, you had tight deadlines, what's new there? you may add. Well frankly, there was one main difference: the manpower allocation in my team was tight, and I mean about 50 per cent under-resourced for months. Robin, a senior and valued team member of mine, was a new father whose wife had not long given birth to a baby boy. I think from memory his son was only eight weeks old at this point.

Robin was suffering with severe sleep deprivation, and the young boy's sleeping patterns had simply not settled into a good routine yet. Then, that Friday, he was looking to get away by about 5 p.m., but I regrettably had to stress that I needed him to stick around until 7 p.m. that evening to hit a deadline. Normally, there was no way I would have asked this of him, but we were so up against it – so I felt I had no other option.

Well, about 6 p.m. that evening we were in a meeting room looking at a screen at some figures for a report I had to send out. I was talking about the data, whilst facing the screen and asking his advice on something, when I realised he was quiet. Then, when I turned around to look at him wondering why he wasn't contributing, as he typically would, I found him asleep.

I put myself in his shoes and fully empathised with his situation. There was no way I could ask him to stay on any longer. How could I? So, even though we were going to miss our deadline for today and I would have to take the rap for this the following Monday morning, I then woke him up and sent him on his way. He protested, but my mind was made up. The guy needed to be back with this family, alive and well, and that was what mattered most.

Relationship management

Every interaction, good or bad, that you have with another person affects both of you in some way, and in order for us to deal with this effectively we require the skills of the last element of emotional intelligence: relationship management. It's fair to say that self-awareness, self-management and social awareness are about the present moment: being aware of your actions and responses to situations then making adjustments in your behaviour accordingly, as well as being aware of the moods and emotions of others – and this is where relationship management comes into play.

Relationship management is managed both in the moment and also formed over time. In the moment because relationship management is about the dynamic management of the emotional exchange with others as they play out, and over time as we need to manage our emotional relationship that we build up over the longer term, sometimes even decades.

If we take a step back and consider social interaction. This has been there since our ancestors developed their social exchanges back in their tribes, and this drives a lot of our behaviour today: our need to fit in and to interact with others. So, what has this got to do with relationship management? Well, a lot. If we don't fit in, then we feel left out, and we will do almost anything to change that and to maintain our social relationships with others – even lie if we have to. This is not a want, this is a need of ours, to fit in and have a bond and connection with others; it supports our emotional happiness.

Then, beyond that, we need others to support us through: love, care, parenting, advice, education, a helping hand, support in the workplace, etc. This basic need creates a dependency for us to interact with others, then interwoven with that there is an emotional exchange and the need to achieve things with and through others.

To an extent it's irrelevant how much we wish to achieve for our own lives and the need to get by on our own, as in order to self-lead we must be able to interact with others at some level. Whether we are conscious of it or not, our emotions play a large factor in this rela- tionship. An emotional exchange with others will affect both parties, therefore, we need to learn to take responsibility for the way we feel and also the way we conduct ourselves with others. Being difficult, awkward or even acting disingenuously with others will only lead to the other person mistrusting you, which is a terrible strategy to a build relationship upon.

Skilful relationship management can make the world of differ- ence both inside and outside the workplace and is a critical tool that all leaders will need to grow in order to successfully work with others or to achieve just about anything done in life.

When relationship management is played out effectively, we are in a greater position to build and manage our relations with others. We must look to do this all the time, as you never know when you will need your network for support. This does not mean you spend all day building your network, but where practical and feasible this is a good move. It also allows you to interact with people's different personality traits and quirks, thus building your confidence in your own social skills.

Make eye contact, read body language, engage thoughtfully in conversation and then respond accordingly in a relaxed and natural way. Even if this feels difficult and an awkward thing to do, it's a must to become a little uncomfortable in these social situations in order to improve your relationship management skills. I once know someone that joined a public speakers group purely to increase his social skills – as he was so nervous meeting new people. As the saying goes, 'You just need to do it and get through it'.

There is a whole myriad of issues we will hit when it comes to improving our relationships in order to complete tasks with others, and sometimes we need to adapt and change our behaviour in order to do this. Think of the colleague that you don't get along with, this could even be your own boss. Putting the other aspects of EI in place – self-awareness, self-management and social awareness – will help lift this relationship off the ground. Being aware of how you are around them, managing your behaviour, and picking up on their mood in the moment and also more generally.

What about the boss you don't like to work with, the one that is downright difficult to get along with, but you need to deal with? You need to establish some form of relationship in order to complete something. This can be a trying, exhausting and downright disappointing situation that you have to put up with, and you may feel like a victim. But if we are faced with these situations, we need to move through them.

First of all, establishing a level of connection with the other person is a good move; find out their interests, their likes, some form of connection between the both of you, and attempt to build on this. Take the responsibility for making the connection, albeit it may feel like gritting your teeth in the beginning.

Moving on from building a bond, you need to establish your interests and what you want or can do as part of the project at hand and to understand their perspectives and what they are trying to achieve. Almost to compartmentalise and create a dividing line between your tasks, thus creating some boundaries or interfaces between the two of you. If you can both be involved in a small number of tasks, then fantastic. Ultimately this is what you are looking for in order to build and manage the relationship, but this may not be advisable in the beginning. Ideally you will find a common purpose, one goal that you are both aiming for.

When appropriate, you will need to come on to the issue that is coming between the both of you. This may be a sensitive or delicate problem to try and approach, and rather than becoming anxious about it by endlessly trying to judge when the time is right, rather sense instinctively when to broach it.

The opportunity may be at the end of a constructive situation between the two of you, which will have at least built up some rapport, or it may be at the end of a successful day. This way of approaching things is much better than sweating over the attempt to make the timing right. But, take responsibility and have the discussion, and make it a positive outcome for the both of you, whilst trying not to make it such a big deal, i.e. don't take yourself too seriously – lighten up a little.

When I served in the Royal Navy, I had to work with all sorts of personality types with all sorts of backgrounds, and some of those people I honestly just couldn't stick being around. One particular character called Ted, who was in charge of the accommodation area, or mess-deck on board ship, I disliked with a vengeance, because of his narcissistic personality. He literally loved himself and threw his weight around – and I did not warm to this one little bit. And in the early days on board ship he took a particular distaste to me because he sensed my dislike for him, and he would pick on me. Which was not good.

But ultimately, we had to work and live together, so I took the responsibility of forging a path through my dislike for him, and therefore I was the one that had to mature in order to improve our relationship. If I waited for him, I'd still be there now, some thirty years later.

In these situations, you need to act responsibly and work to find a common purpose in tasks that you undertake, and this is what helps gets the personnel in the armed forces through the tough times; as well as watching each other's backs, of course!

In civilian life, things are altogether different, but common purposes are still there, alive and needing to be resolved. It's simply a case of making the effort to understand where the other party stands, and then working with them towards a successful resolution.

There has to be compromise somewhere along the line, otherwise nothing gets achieved.

You see, we are not simply just talking about friendship here: difficult relationships, especially at work, where we've little choice but to work with the other person, is something that we need to manage and think our way through, using the other aspects of EI as appropriate. Stand up for yourself and make yourself the responsible one in the relationship, even if this is your boss.

Take the higher moral ground and help set the scene for how you see the relationship working. Just make sure that you are using your self-awareness to assess how you feel and act, your self-management to alter and address your behaviour or your tone of voice and emotional exchange with them. Then, use your social awareness to assess the emotions of the other party such that you act appropriately, but all the time attempting to self-lead by knowing what you want and what is appropriate for the working relationship.

No one ever said that working, or personal relationships for that matter, were going to be easy. But, from bitter experience it gets much easier with practice, I can assure you!

NOW, OVER TO YOU

How will you aim to master your emotions? You will have been able to tell from this chapter that there is a lot more to the root of our feelings than you may have expected, and a whole variety of things affect them, from our diet, how we act, the decisions that we have to make, the impact of the media has on us, through to the amount of sleep and exercise we get. But now it's up to you to take some positive action in order to help ensure that you undertake management of your emotions. Because as you will have read, emotions can simply take over, to the point where if they get out of control and you are no longer in control – they are. And this is due to the fact that our emotions are a deep-seated component of our physiology.

One fundamental aspect of self-leadership on the other hand is about taking responsibility, and through the successful management of your emotions you both thrive and allow a more mature character to shine through.

Consider your emotional foundations. Assess them and review your average daily routines. How would you score yourself on these five far-reaching foundations – sleep, mental awareness, mental diet, physical exercise and physical diet – if you were to assess how well you were doing against them? Are you meeting them satisfactorily or not, meeting them to the best of your ability to give any opportunity of improving your emotional quotient (EQ)? Be honest with yourself, is there room for any improvement? Are you giving your physical and mental health, which directly influence your emotions, the best opportunity you can to grow?

The most straightforward model that I believe for emotional intelligence (EI) addresses the four principles as outlined above: self-awareness, self-management, social awareness and relationship management. These areas when focused on in our waking lives propel our EI forward and allow us to evolve as self-leaders and into becoming better people all round.

Primarily, society has thought in the past that it was our IQ that was the measure of success. On the contrary, if you now take the effort to focus your attention on these emotional intelligence elements, your IQ and EQ combined will provide you with a more rounded success, both in your working and personal life. Further reading on EI is: *Emotional Intelligence 2.0* by Travis Bradberry and Jean Greaves (Talent Smart, 2009).

PERSONAL CONTRIBUTION
JON CASSELL: CRANIOSACRAL THERAPIST

Hijacked By Fear

I work as a Craniosacral Therapist and have extensive experience working with people with physical and emotional trauma.

Emotions flow at different rates, but they should flow. Grief, for example, moves very slowly but it does move. It must move, or people can be stuck with it for life. Love flows – or it becomes bitter.

Anger, contrary to popular belief, can be positive emotion. Its purpose is to initiate change – just watch a bunch of puppies squabbling over their food bowls. Anger should flow rapidly upwards through the body and out through the eyes and the voice. That way it can do some good. The trouble comes when we choke our anger back, when we deny it its proper flow. Then it becomes stuck, quite literally locked into the tissues of the body.

The problem is that we humans are very bad at letting our emotions flow. They get stuck. We brood. We develop a short fuse. We get mysterious aches and pains...

Self-awareness is key! Being able to focus on our bodies enough to feel what's going on inside there. And that can be learned.

For more than twenty years now, I have been working to help people let go of their pain – and much of that pain has been emotional. Yet the strange thing is that all of this emotional pain has a physical dimension. In fact, I would say that it is virtually impossible to separate body, mind and emotions. They are each aspects of the others, and more. Healing the pain of our stuck emotions is almost impossible without accessing its physical aspect. (For further reading on the topic, see Peter Levine's book, *Waking the Tiger*, and *Focusing* by Eugene Gendlin, North Atlantic Books 1997.)

I remember being on a short course when I first started looking into this work. It took place in a marvellous, rambling old house in Cornwall, within walking distance of Lamorna Cove. It was a wonderful experience, fascinating to notice as we became able to access and free up these old, stuck patterns.

On the last evening, there was to be a party. Now, most of the participants were women and, when I walked in, they were all in there – dancing. A great cry went up – a man! Now, I can't dance. I have two left feet and no sense of rhythm. It's not my fault, that's just the way it is. So I fled!

A walk down to Lamorna Cove, I thought, that's the thing. So off I set. Now the road to Lamorna is steep (more of a path than a road, really, as I remember it). As you go down, there are thick trees to your right and a quite precipitous drop to your left. It was dusk and the light was beginning to fail – and then that feeling came over me... that feeling, deep down, that there's something in those woods – and it's looking at me – and it's got teeth. That ancient fear, the teeth in the dark forest, grew very rapidly and I found myself on the edge of panic. I stopped in the path. Two choices. Turn and run, or continue to walk, still feeling this horrible fear. I had already turned and run once that evening and I didn't intend to do it again.

And then the though hit me.... What had I been doing these past days? I had been on a course, learning how to process hidden emotions and old trauma.

Right!

I stood still in the path and led my awareness inwards, noticing all the sensations I could feel. Okay, now, what is the sensation of this fear? Very soon it showed itself. An intense fizzing, arising in my lower abdomen and flowing upwards, through my belly, through my chest and neck and through my face and head. Hot. And scary. As I stood there, just allowing these sensations to be, the fizzing started to lessen, to grow weaker. Essentially, I was gaining more emotional control.

It probably took no more than five minutes for the feelings to fade away altogether. And, as it went, I realised that the fear had gone, too. Thankfully, I had managed these strong emotions.

I continued my walk to the cove and then turned and strolled back, by moonlight now. It was lovely. I even put in an appearance at the party.

Emotion is of the body – and it can be released in the body. It's a skill, but it can be done.

Chapter 4

Embracing Failure

'Failure should be our teacher, not our undertaker. Failure is delay, not defeat. It is a temporary detour, not a dead end. Failure is something we can avoid only by saying nothing, doing nothing, and being nothing.'

Denis Waitley

Have you ever wondered why it is that some people will succeed through difficulty, setbacks or hardship while others will seemingly bounce back with ease? Those high achievers, who, regardless of the challenge put in front of them, seem to make good from things, while others crash in a heap, and wonder what on earth hit them. Is there some divine formula handed out at birth? A special blessing issued out in a queue that some just never knew about. You have to admit it, when you reflect, there does seem to be something going on behind the scenes – some people will achieve outstanding feats regardless of the difficulties and hardships they face.

For example, the corporate game changers who rise through the ranks regardless of their setbacks – where they give the appearance of bouncing back even stronger. Top businesspeople that have been bankrupt, only to turn a new business around and make it a real success. The standards set by powerful athletes that reach the dizzy heights of human endurance – even after meeting with injury or personal difficulty. Those that have suffered disabling war injuries but have returned with acute difficulties to then turn their lives around – some even competing in competitive sports like, for example, the Invictus Games.

There has got to be a connection somewhere. Well, there is.

What it all boils down to is how you perceive and how you respond to failure. You cannot have success without it! It's a bit like a lover's relationship, if you will, when you have met with success, you have undoubtedly crossed some degree of failure along your path. It's a given.

You see, with anyone who has achieved any form of success in life, stuck it out when the going got tough, had the guts to take the risks when others probably wouldn't, what it's all down to is their attitude – how they respond to the outcome, irrespective of what it is. Because people have come from all sorts of backgrounds and suffered all kinds of adversity only to succeed in a variety of different ways. Somehow, they bounce back – and make good.

But it all comes back to how you perceive failure, my friend. Then, if you find yourself there, having failed – however frustrating or bitterly annoying it may seem in the moment – leading yourself back out of that position, and back towards success. Therefore, by picking yourself up, dusting yourself off, and getting back on the horse, so to speak – you aim to hit your original target. Or maybe a new target, for that matter. But what you don't do is lie face deep in the mud full of self-pity. That attitude achieves nothing, and helps no one.

Likewise, when we do fail, we also need to appreciate that there is always a lesson to be learned as a result. Always. And then if you take the time for some self-reflection after a failure – there comes with it a direct and immediate positive that can be achieved as a result.

It's a given fact that failure plays a factor in how anyone achieves anything of substance in life, and sometimes these failures are considerable. However, if you consider your own life and reflect back on when you have achieved anything of any real significance, or even just got by and lived an ordinary life, I'm sure that you will agree that we all fail at times. It would appear then that failure, making a mistake, being at fault, however you wish to frame it, is part and parcel of getting by in the world.

It's also worthwhile to remember that it's always been with us. You only need to consider a small child learning to walk, and the number of times they fall, trip or stumble while trying. Even when babies and toddlers learn to talk, they fight to sound words, fail to communicate as their language range is limited, and I'm sure feel utterly frustrated at times. Still, they carry on regardless and always get there in the end, however difficult the fight may be, and this is because when those young children fail, they choose not to stop, and instead, attempt to capture a lesson to learn from every mistake they make.

However, much more importantly than that – they don't treat their failings as failures! They don't let those failings get the better of them, or blame themselves, or become shameful or feel guilty and beat themselves up. And if they do become despondent – which does happen – then they don't hold onto these negative emotions for long. They get back on with the job in hand.

My daughter could never naturally learn to cross the mid-line as a young child. This is a condition where we can't move our arm or leg across the middle of our body to perform a task. As an example, this meant that she could not put her left foot in front and across her right foot while she walked (thus crossing her mid-line) and vice versa. That condition, amongst other occupational problems she suffered, meant she had a real problem with her balance. During her younger years, she spent hundreds of hours in special occupational treatment for her condition. Still, she never complained – she just ploughed on through her adversity – and succeeded. Today she can ride a horse to canter, very successfully.

These simple examples demonstrate that to infants and young children failure is all part of our overall success; and there is so much that we can learn from our own refreshing attitudes to failure. Because we were all there once, we were those babies and small children determined to walk and talk. The ones falling over and over, and at one point making no sense at all in how we communicated – and we progressed, we succeeded. We just got on with it.

Failure, it doesn't feel good – but it can serve you

When we look at failure for what it means to us, when we fail, in that specific moment when things go wrong, it doesn't feel right, far from it. For example, if you fail an exam, or land the business deal you wanted, whatever it may be – in the moment when failure occurs – it all feels far from ideal. It can feel bad emotionally.

Also, when it happens, when we fail, there is a tendency to reflect inwardly and begin to feel wrong, foolish or worse; even society as a whole and the workplace are less tolerant of failure than they should be. Besides, when people hold a negative perception of themselves, it is not surprising that they feel quickly defeated when faced with challenges. Each obstacle, mistake or failure can seem like proof of what they already know – that they won't succeed and that they are not okay[32].

This negative reflection is a great shame and does not help the overall rewards failure can bring to us, rewards that have served many successful people across the globe and throughout our history. So much adversity, and learning from lessons in life, has led to success. It's one of the reasons why large business projects learn through smaller pilot ones. They want to see what has gone right – and just as importantly – what has gone wrong. So that they can learn the lessons of both success and of failure.

Failure, a stepping stone to success

If we can stand back and take a decidedly different view of failure, and begin to see it in a different light and acknowledge it, learn from it, understand it, and even to an extent befriend it, we will start to see its many benefits. Based on the fact that failure is a stepping stone to future success, it becomes apparent that your answer to the question why some excel in life and why others fall by the wayside is that they have failed – but not given up!

These people have led themselves through the experience of failure and have moved beyond it. They have somehow managed to make progress to succeed, however, painful and bitter the failure experience may have been. And more than this they have consciously decided to deal with the experience and move forward with their lives and not back away, as many would.

Failure will help us, not just when it happens, but also many years from now. It will also help those we encourage, mentor and coach in life: our children, our friends, our work colleagues and our teams. If we can seek out the juices from what failure is teaching us, it's not just what we learn from it – it will also potentially help generations to come. When viewed from that perspective, failure becomes a much bigger teacher than we can imagine; failure's lessons when used in the right way even grow and seep into the rich tapestry of life's future successes for years into the future, not necessarily ones in the present.

If we can view failure correctly and see it as a part of life that does and will happen, from time to time, we can welcome it. Not all the time, not every day, but we do have to accept that failure plays a role in life. Viewing it with the right lens we can come to accept and thrive off its back, and not just see it as the enemy to be avoided at all costs. Failure exists – fact. Failure happens – fact. Human beings fail – fact. And so, you can't avoid failure – fact!

I know failure can feel hard to take at times, and like everyone else I have failed. I've come up against a myriad of failures, some directly my fault, which can feel hard to swallow at the time. Still, I've learned to accept its bittersweet lessons in life, and even though it does not always feel good to fail, I stay determined to continue with this positive frame of mind: that I, and others, will learn due to my failures, setbacks or mistakes, whatever they may be.

THE ARENA

This quote below is from Theodore Roosevelt in his 1910 'Man in the Arena' speech:

> *'It is not the critic who counts; not the man who points out how the strong man stumbles, or where the doer of deeds could have done them better. The credit belongs to the man who is actually in the arena, whose face is marred by dust and sweat and blood; who strives valiantly; who errs, who comes short again and again, because there is no effort without error and shortcoming; but who does actually strive to do the deeds; who knows great enthusiasms, the great devotions; who spends himself in a worthy cause; who at the best knows in the end the triumph of high achievement, and who at the worst, if he fails, at least fails while daring greatly, so that his place shall never be with those cold and timid souls who neither know victory nor defeat.'* [33]

Down in the dirt is where real life happens, in the grind, feeling life's pressures; metaphorically wading waist-deep through the mud of life's experience and teaching process, is where we learn the most. The arena is an activity, participation, engagement; this is taking part, it is contributing, interacting with others, teaching, team-playing, leading, managing, loving, parenting, all of it and more. Being involved in something that you believe in and for a worthy cause, and not sitting back and remaining comfortable or languishing in life's pity party.

The arena is the battleground of life. The place where we fall, stumble, pick ourselves up and dust ourselves off, and head back into battle, whatever that may be. Besides, these activities are where life and living happens, where we learn, where we discover and explore.

Not from life's gallery, not being the onlooker who knocks our failures, points their finger at us and laughs at our expense when it all goes wrong – but down there in amongst it all – in the arena.

Life is teaching us all the time, in every moment and every day, but we forget it, we become lost in the moment. We end up lost in our thoughts, our emotions and our distractions. It's so easy to forget that life's encounters are informing us of where we need to improve and also preparing us for future battles, and that failure is just a building block in this process.

No one would be where they are today if we did not fail. If our ancestors and our families throughout history were not down in the arena of life, and doing things that they believed in, only to fail now and again, we wouldn't be where we are across the spectrum of life. Those involved in science, engineering, sport, the financial markets, medicine, drama, the arts, all of it and much more have learned through failure. Failure is a fundamental component of the process of learning and innovation. Some of us can and will detract, play safe or withdraw from what life has to offer, which is a great deal, so why on earth do that? What sort of life would that be? Life's adventures are too full of raw and unlimited opportunity to take these options. There are so many things that life offers, and failure is just one part of this experience.

In writing this chapter, I came across a commencement ceremony speech given at Harvard University in 2008 by the author of the Harry Potter book series J. K. Rowling. She gave a talk on 'The fringe benefits of failure, and the importance of imagination'. The following quotes are quotes from her talk:

'Ultimately, we all have to decide for ourselves what constitutes failure, but the world is quite eager to give you a set of criteria if you let it. So, I think it fair to say that by any conventional measure, a mere seven years after my graduation day, I had failed on an epic

scale. An exceptionally short-lived marriage had imploded, and I was jobless, a lone parent, and as poor as it is possible to be in modern Britain, without being homeless. The fears that my parents had had for me, and that I had had for myself, had both come to pass, and by every usual standard, I was the biggest failure I knew.'

She later went on to state:

'You might never fail on the scale I did, but some failure is inevitable. It is impossible to live without failing at something, unless you live so cautiously that you might as well not have lived at all – in which case, you fail by default.'[34]

Believe in what you want

Now, as we know, she went from the biggest failure she knew to be an absolute success due to doing the very thing she believed in, which was to write. What she didn't mention in her talk was that her mother died during the time she was writing Harry Potter, and at one point, clinically depressed, Joanna even contemplated suicide. However, I don't mention her to give you some rags to riches story; rather because she makes the point well that failure in life is inevitable when you are trying to succeed. You either fail because you try to achieve in life, or you fail by not living.

So, whilst we are not all J. K. Rowling, and neither we should be as we should not compare ourselves to her, she is a superb example of someone who survived significant failure and adversity, but also lives and thrives exceptionally well, with the Harry Potter franchise estimated at $25 billion in 2016, according to Wikipedia[35]. Nonetheless, Joanna herself falls out of the billionaire list due to the millions she donates to charity, which is fantastic to hear, and is the mark of a true entrepreneur.

Eventually, we all succeed if we try long and hard enough, but what constitutes success may be down to personal interpretation; it may not be the success we first imagined, but eventually, we do gain some form of success. I doubt Joanna, ever imagined the sort of success she would receive when she began to put pen to paper several years before her first book was published. I would imagine that her initial idea of success was a world away from what she has become today. Nevertheless, even after twelve rejection slips from various London publishing houses, Joanne still kept chipping away, only to hit it lucky on her thirteenth attempt.

She could have easily given up, and thrown in the towel, partway through that long, painful process of sending off a manuscript, have them review it (which takes some time), only for them to respond negatively. And then to have to start all over again, and again, and again, and again.

It's during these challenging times when you are failing, that the audience from the gallery, tells you to stop, to give in or give up. These are the times when failure makes you feel vulnerable, starves you of self-worth, and the times that try to sap you of every ounce of self-confidence you hold. These are times when we need to be brave and be bold. These factors ideally start and stay alive by you remaining personally committed to what you believe in, or else your intrinsic motivation will fall by the wayside. And so to stay in the game, you need to be internally engaged.

One direct way that will help you here is to create a list of promises or pledges that we make to ourselves *before things get tough – before we fail*. The reason for this being that if we don't create and believe in what we want to achieve, how can we ever stand the chance of seeing things through if things do become difficult? There is a likelihood that we will become downtrodden by mistakes, failures and the like. So, we need these commitments to steer and guide us in those more difficult moments, and they must be something we hold close to our hearts.

Some examples of personal commitments can be along the lines of:

- I will complete what I have started, even though it is tough some days

- I will still exercise, even though I have a busy and work schedule

- I will stick to my diet, while I love my food

- I will work at my relationship, even though I travel away frequently

- I will work towards promotion every day although there is competition

- I will increase my customer base regardless of rejection

- I will be authentic and honest even though I meet with dishonesty

This example list includes things that you will embody and want to live by whether you are failing or not. It also lists what you are up against, which makes it personal and specific to you, and it is a list that you may wish to live by coming through any adversity. It may be that you cannot live by what is on your list every single day of the week, that might not be practical, but these are the things you commit to yourself that you will continue to work towards them.

Importantly, what you list must mean something of value to you – real value – such that you can really believe in your commitments. Plus, they can also change, as you and your circumstances change. Therefore you need to review them regularly, and this will help provide you with focus and clarity. You need to be honest with yourself if you maintain that you are sticking by them – otherwise, they will not work for you.

Every time you review your commitments, you must believe in them. That detail is crucial. Become determined, stay focused, potentially even single-minded, not allowing the mental failure scripts of other people's experience and their emotional baggage to slow you down or stop you. This *will happen*, coming even from your friends, peers and family.

After a fall, ensure you maintain your self-worth

When you have fallen off your metaphorical pushbike again because you have failed and you are lying there face down in the mud, it can feel tough, terribly tough! And this is when the commitments that you make to yourself help to remind you why you need to keep going. Furthermore, when you do experience difficult times through failure and hardship, you need to ensure that you cut yourself some slack.

This can be as simple as taking a break, going for a walk, or treating yourself to a meal out. Allow yourself some time to think and self-reflect on where you are on your journey to success. A contrasting experience will provide a level of reflection and feedback and a feel-good factor for you to support yourself and help to maintain a healthy level of self-worth. At the very least, it will cause a mental distraction – which is what you will need if you are finding things difficult in some way.

In addition to rewarding yourself, while working towards your commitments, make sure that you practise self-love, by looking after your happiness and well-being. *Sometimes not to ask much of yourself will be the right thing to do.* For example, treating yourself kindly, not being hard on yourself, allowing yourself some flexibility in your routines, not comparing yourself to others, having a decent amount of rest and letting go of any perfectionist tendencies that you may have.

Remember, that those in the gallery, who may point their fingers and laugh when you fail, come and go in life. However – you are with you for ever – so you need to look after you and not worry about them. Not even for a moment!

FAILURE, CREATING EXCELLENCE

There is no doubt about it, from failure many good things come about. As well as the specialist areas that I mentioned on the previous pages – such as science, engineering and the arts – that have all benefited through failure followed by success, failure is a great teacher to each and every one of us – and that includes you.

You may have heard of the maxim *fail fast and fail often* which comes from the argument that if you fail often, you will learn quickly? Well, to be honest, when I first heard this expression, I thought it was ridiculous, a lot of old nonsense. I mean, why should we wish to fail most of the time, as the expression infers? Shouldn't we be looking to do the opposite – succeed?!

But maybe this expression does have something to teach us, after all. Whilst practically it makes no sense to fail all of the time, we should assume and adopt the mindset that we must readily accept small failures into our lives and embrace them. By this I mean, if you brush failure aside, and simply move forward without actually learning from the experience, then you have missed out on a very valuable opportunity.

You see every failure brings with it a most precious learning opportunity, and if we are learning, then we must improve.

Over the years, I've seen several people that I have come to work with embrace failure and build on the education that it gives them. One startling example was a gentleman called Peter who attended one of the public speaking clubs in my area. Peter joined the club hoping that the opportunity would help his stammer – which was an encouraging strategy. His stammer resulted in the poor man stammering with almost every sentence.

Peter bravely came to the club and attempted to speak every fortnight, where I would imagine most with his affliction would have stayed at home – but he refused to. A brave man indeed, and you could not help but admire him for it.

At every meeting, he would come and speak, and every meeting, he would stammer. However, over time you could tell that although he still stumbled over his words, he was managing his way around them more. He began to speak more fluently. It was beautiful to see. Eventually after more than a year in the club he presented a seven-minute speech – almost fluently – it was magical. And throughout that speech you could tell just how far he had come in his time with us.

At the end of his talk, the room of close to thirty stood and gave the man a well-deserved standing ovation. And Peter, well, he was close to tears with emotion. An event I'm sure everyone in the room will never forget. I certainly won't.

So, first things first, self-leadership and failure have a unique relationship. The relationship between leading yourself and achievement is about finding direction, an approach, a strategy in any given situation to hit your goal. If failure hits you consider three things:

1. Accept and acknowledge that the failure has happened and manage the emotional surge that is likely to strike you. The emotion will pass.

2. Then, if you then believe deep down you want to carry on, reflect on where you went wrong, and change tact, learn and adapt. Move forward with a new approach.

3. Repetition is the mother of skill. If you continuously repeat an exercise or task over and over again, then your ability to excel in mastering your skill or behaviour becomes self-regulating.

On reflection, I believe we can all forget the skills that we have mastered over the years and overlook the amateur-like position we all started from. And so, when we find failure hard it's a case of instilling those memories, those thoughts, into the forefront of our minds and hearts. However, if we adapt, persevere, and most importantly, believe we can succeed then in the end, we can all become excellent. We will become our version of excellent, which in the end, is all we can really wish for.

A striking personal failure

I had my own notable experiences of transferable learning from failure when I left the corporate ladder to become a partner in a small but successful training and consultancy organisation, as a freelance expert in my field – at the time technical management.

After joining the consultancy, I was initially successful, I worked around the UK and other European countries, and I was in high demand. I was hopping from one job to another, with little time to spare in between business trips. Admittedly, I joined the organisation after the 2008 market crash had set in, but again the work was there for a reasonable period after I started, and things were going well; indeed, I thought I'd cracked it.

Then of course, as the crash started to bite, companies were beginning to withdraw those two primary external support vehicles that provide essential support specific needs of their staff, but are still viewed by some as a luxury: training and consultancy. Things for us began to become tricky as we became affected because companies were reeling in their nets for a rainy day and keeping their cash firmly in their wallets. The vast majority of organisations fail to make the connection between the degree to which they meet their employees' needs and how effectively those employees perform[36].

Eventually, I went from feast to famine, and instead of the work coming to us regularly, with small amounts of time chasing work, everything flipped entirely on its head. We then began to spend vast amounts of time chasing jobs while getting the odd piece of work; which to me became simply exhausting.

This outcome continued for a while, and things were deeply strained for me as I began to live off mainly savings. By this point, I was seriously contemplating leaping back into my old industry sector. Then out of the blue, I was approached by a previous client of our company, who'd been there before my time, about a potentially lengthy consultancy contract. They wanted us to meet shortly afterwards, and I began to do some research and put together a pitch for the work. In the background, we were progressing efforts to partner with a larger company from northern Europe, with whom we were more likely to clinch such a contract due its size and our combined experience.

However, there was only one annoying catch: the client wanted a pitch from us ten days hence. Now, our European counterparts couldn't make their proposed date, and our potential client would not move the appointment – so we had no option but to go it alone.

If we clinched this contract, and with an immediate and substantial client, this would be ideal. Not perfect, as you should never rely on just one customer alone. However, I would have cracked my more immediate problem with my financial difficulties, and things could have regrown from that point.

My business partner and I arrived tired on the client's site on the day of the pitch having both travelled several hours to reach our destination, and due to heavy snowfall the evening before, we had to walk miles from the train station as public transport and taxis were few and far between.

Overall, the session appeared to go well initially, but you could tell as time went on that the potential client was not convinced that we could handle the job. Admittedly it was huge in size, and would require a considerable footprint of consultants on-site to deal with it. Even when we tried to convincingly portray how it would involve our partnership with our European colleagues, who were highly specialised in this particular area, it was still not enough. The customer would not even hold out for a second meeting to include our future business partners.

At that moment, that point was raised, I second-guessed that they had already seen their ideal company, and were playing a numbers game with us, i.e. they had to meet a set number of potential consultancies to meet an internally agreed target, although I will never know.

These moments are not great at the best of times, and in times like this you have to maintain a perspective of *you win some, you lose some*. Which, I'm sure, we can all relate to. But then again looking back, this situation was too much of a game-changer for me, and the world felt like it was about to end a short time later.

At the end of our meeting, we left on good terms, as always in these types of business meetings, but from their body language and the mood of the room we knew that although we'd done well, we were not convincing enough. I boarded the train home a short time later, I was drowning in self-pity and anger, as I knew that my time with my current business partner was up, and I would have to move on. I felt I had personally failed – cataclysmically.

I felt the forces were against me at the time, and I was blaming everything: the market, bad business advice, myself, my business partner, the whole damn situation. However, the current situation was unsustainable, my savings were drying up, there were bills to be paid and mouths to feed and my taxes were due. So, with these real demands I had no option left, but to jump back to the world I knew. And let's just say that I made the bridge to earning for my family and survived that transition – I'll leave it there, for the moment. But, it is moments like this when you feel kicked in the gut that the emotions strike your very core.

I find it alarming, to the point where I want to laugh hysterically, that when you research this topic of failure, there are so many glory stories that address adversity from significant failure – they gloss right over the specific painful and hurtful periods. The times when you are down and can't think straight, when you can't easily lift your head high to gain some perspective on the situation.

When your emotions are dragging you down badly, these are also the times when the vulnerability sets in hard, and you see and feel things from a hugely different perspective than usual. You see the worst in situations, as your thoughts distort your view. But you must understand that this is your perspective while you are in this state; it is not real and is short-lived. I know I and many others have been there. You may think in this state that you will stay there, but you won't – don't worry. You will make it through, and life will improve.

In the end, you always make it through.

'No man is defeated until is he defeated within.'

Eleanor Roosevelt

SOME LESSONS TO LEARN

Emotions like the ones I've just described, after a significant failure, are natural. Nevertheless, while you are in this state, you need to aim to see past, the present and into the future, as to retain these problematic emotions and live with them will only stifle your progress in moving on. And move on, you must. You must see the actual reality of your situation to heal. You have been kicked in the gut hard, yes, but you cannot stay there for ever. You have to move forward anyhow, but you also need to move on emotionally;

by making managed, positive advances that will help with the emotional healing process.

Don't rely on others to make these steps forward for you, but take responsibility. Otherwise, you will not grow from the experience and therefore never fully heal inside.

Now, these painful and uncomfortable feelings will come from several sources: your standards like perfectionism or high ideals, the rules of others set for you, and even the norms of society that you accept into your mindset; perceived failures are usually down to you comparing yourself against others. Make it your goal to ascertain and self-reflect the cause of these feelings, and once you work out the answer, this will help you to learn for the future.

Now, going back to my story, shortly afterwards, I moved on by making some concrete steps to recover from my predicament. I gained some focus and took direct action to help make sure that we could pay our bills, but I knew that I needed to take some constructive steps in relation to my emotional state.

Even months later, I was still carrying the emotional baggage and needed some solid direction as the experience had been so demanding. I therefore hired a professional coach and we worked over several sessions to understand what the failure had taught me; what lessons I could take from it and how best to make progress. During the course of these sessions, and since, I have learned several lessons from my failure, which I now teach. They are:

1. To quickly accept failure. It's happened, get over it and move on, self-direct and take steps to improve your situation. Progressively and consciously take positive actions to push through and past the failure hour by hour, day by day.

2. Avoid all or nothing thinking. That is don't fall into the trap and begin to feel you are either a success or a failure in life and business. This position is not valid for anyone. We all have

aspects in life that we are good at, and others where we are not so good.

3. Practise self-compassion. Be kind to yourself, let yourself off the hook and do not under any circumstances beat yourself up after a failure. Remember, we all fail at something.

4. Don't enter the blame game for the failure. It's a circular argument, and you only waste energy. (More on the topic later.)

5. Carry out some due diligence or common-sense checks, whatever is appropriate, to ascertain once fully satisfied whether there is any point continuing after a failure. But be careful here not to give yourself a get-out clause.

6. Remain self-aware and sincere to yourself and change your mind if necessary. To change your mind is typical after a failure, where you are experimenting and realise your endeavour was not for you in the first place.

7. Assess the cause, to ascertain how you can learn from it in any way or whether it was a no-win situation. But even then, you can learn from the endeavour.

8. Assess each aspect that did not go well and why you did not perform at your best. And if you were going into a similar situation again, what would you do differently? What would your new approach be to improve things, and why?

9. Don't directly compare yourself with peers, competitors, colleagues and clients when you fail. Comparison is futile, as each person in each situation is entirely different from the rest. That is, each of us and our experiences are unique.

10. Take concrete action steps forward and make new progress based upon the whole experience up until now, and be comfortable with your new direction. Ensure that you maintain your new momentum with energy, remembering to adjust this new direction, if necessary.

11. Go through a period of feeling gratitude for the learning experience. It would be best if you did this when you have fully understood what did not go well and what lessons you have learned, as well as reflecting on what did go well. So be grateful for both and maintain your sense of self-worth.

I have already taken these lessons to resolve issues in other areas of my life, and I've also used them to see off other potential failings before they have transpired: both in business and personally.

We are a product of our failures in life; that is, after a failure, we are never the same person we were before. And to remain beaten up and twisted due to failure means that you have lost. Use the above steps, regroup, develop, learn and evolve your emotions and mindset from a major life failure, for ahead is a positive growth experience, and you will be led through failure and back to recovery and progress. J. K. Rowling showed that with tenacity, strength and focus on the thing that she loved she could turn her world around when it appeared so desperate. And that story, at least, is a light for the soul when failure hits hard.

I have taken the above lessons, which can be grouped as summarised sequences, to form the following diagram.

'Most people have attained their greatest success just one step beyond their greatest failure.'

Napoleon Hill

EMBRACING FAILURE

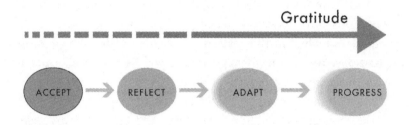

PERSONAL GROWTH BEYOND FAILURE

To lead yourself successfully beyond failure, you must heal, grow, learn and act in a different way than you did before. You may, however, not wish to repeat whatever course of action led to the failure; this is of course really natural if you firmly believe that you will fall into the same trap as before due to circumstances beyond your control.

Put your hand into the lion's mouth, and you may end up with a nasty bite.

You may not wish to learn, of course. If the failure is related to a topic or activity that you genuinely don't care about or have no interest in, then why would you? In this instance, it will be evident to you that you don't care. But, if you do care, even to the extent of just trying to avoid getting your fingers burned next time around, following the eleven steps on pages 158–60 will help. As you take action, consolidate and reflect, make adjustments to your approach; you will learn and be more successful.

But what about the inner personal growth that occurs as a result of a failure, the growth that takes place in your psyche? This aspect of growth is what I am going to cover next.

Failure builds in resilience

Beyond failure, we can hurt, especially if it means something to us; and if we hurt, we feel pain, distress or grow anxious. These sensations can distort our feelings and change our outlook on things, and when in this state, you will tend to see the worst in situations. You will not feel good, and you will not feel at peace with those around you. Furthermore, if failure hurts emotionally, it will naturally invoke our fight and flight response, addressed in the chapter on Emotional Mastery. And once the amygdala, which lies deep in the brain, detects danger, our mind will move into survival mode. As a result, we will unsurprisingly want to walk away from the failure; or quickly run in the opposite direction – hoping not to be seen again.

But in these moments, we ought to catch ourselves and recognise what is occurring inside of us. This is because if we observe our body's reaction when going into survival mode, and make an attempt to stay as fully conscious of our natural response, with the aim of preventing this from worsening, we can gain a much more significant and far more self-revealing learning experience.

In survival mode, you tend to react and can even panic, as opposed to considering things more slowly and rationally. But, if you recognise after a failure or mistake that you are emotionally attached to the outcome, keep your conscious mind engaged and in the present moment. These thoughts and sensations will primarily come through your self-awareness. Then through self-control you slow down your thoughts and reactions, and then move on to acknowledging the situation, and finally taking the step to forgive yourself. To summarise, you are progressively working through the experience of failure by taking steps forward; then you can look to learn and move on from the situation. Making less of a disaster of things and making it more about the learning experience.

You need to remember something utterly incredible, in that after a personal failure, where you feel emotionally hurt or worse as a result, we are not the same person as we were before we failed; we change, we grow in character – we move on inside. So, if we are going to change, then make a conscious change for the better. If you can evolve emotionally from experience, and there is no reason why you can't, then this can only be immensely beneficial for you.

This is one of the best places from which to see personally related failures and how individuals respond to them. Now, typically the ego will edge you out of the way, and most of us will not wish to discuss or even admit to their failings openly, and even when they do, agree that they are personally at fault (and this is primarily due to the fact that they feel more vulnerable having failed). It takes a courageous person to discuss their failings wholeheartedly.

However, over the years I've personally seen individuals within organisations grow from failure, even some that give the appearance that they shirk off failure, only to get back on with the job in hand as if the failure was nothing, as if it had just been made minutes before and was part of some dim and distant past event. A shrewd frame of mind if you can adopt it.

My conclusion is that these people know they will eventually claim their prize, that through the practice of failure, they instinctively know they will ultimately triumph. Just consider one of Richard Branson's business failures, when Virgin Atlantic Airlines almost crashed before it started.

It was in 1984 when Branson launched the airline, with the aim to give passengers a better flying experience. While he had little experience, he saw a bit of opportunity. Still, his new venture nearly failed before it got off the ground. Virgin's initial test flight was a rented Boeing 747, but a flock of birds flew into the engine causing a considerable amount of damage.

Without a working plane, Virgin couldn't get certified and therefore could not start to carry passengers. It couldn't get money for the much-needed repairs without certification. Branson stayed optimistic and did not panic. He got the repairs done quickly through a restructure of his companies and pulled money from other ventures. The airline achieved the much-needed certification, and Virgin's inaugural flight from Gatwick to Newark was a success.

In my experience, these types of individuals typically rise in business and within organisations, or even if they don't, are at least renowned for great achievements. Once you can see this in a person, to see them literally rise past failure and move forward and grow in resilience, then you know success lies in wait for them.

Resilience built in layers

Resilience is a prized quality, both in organisations and individuals. It was originally a scientific term, taken from the Latin verb *salire*, 'to jump'. The 'resilience' of a material is its ability to return to its original shape after being compressed or stretched. In the twentieth century, developmental psychologists began applying the term to children's ability to deal with trauma. Now it is a useful management concept, describing an organisation's ability to deal with change without getting bent out of shape – and staying that way[37].

An organisation in the context above can be a company, a school, a charity, and of course, you can also take this concept of an organisation to the family unit. But any organisation or group is made up of individuals, and it will be those individuals acting like a team that brings about any organisational resilience. But then deeper down it will be the individual's resilience with their own dilemmas, issues and chaos and seeing these through that brings about a broader resilience.

To build some resilience, on an individual basis, you must first take specific steps towards this. As we saw in the chapter on Emotional Mastery, physical exercise is one of the primary drivers that help to strengthen resilience since it helps emotional management, promotes recovery and cognition, thus directly assisting an individual's ability to adapt and bounce back from stressful situations and failure alike. Then you have other practices such as meditation or yoga, or additional stress-releasing activities that help release strain within the body. These activities will help install a layer of emotional resilience in the first instance.

Then the act of failure can cultivate resilience, through the control of our emotions and the way we act through and beyond failure; always maintaining momentum to see past the failure itself and see it as a growth experience, looking forward to solutions. Humour is also an essential strategy in order to remain resilient, as humour promotes mental and physical health.

Also, never forget the importance of mentors that have had similar experiences and can share their lessons learned. When being guided by a mentor you can lean into their support, and just this on its own, with a guiding hand giving you direction, can create a layer of resilience and increased confidence in your actions. In all, the way that we act to maintain our self-control by injecting action and certainty into each moment helps to build in resilience. It has to. Action creates momentum, which creates more certainty.

We must sometimes be subjected to stressful experiences, to feel the hurt, pain and severe emotional response coursing through us so that we can heal, recover and bounce back, and bring about an additional individual resilience within us – like a layer of insulation that thinly surrounds us. It's as if the actual act of failing big and going through a challenging experience brings about a coating of mental toughness, against potential future failures. All of which will lead to eventual success, if we strive forward for long enough.

Failure, resilience and self-confidence

The relationship between resilience and self-confidence is closely linked, as one will feed the other. Our ability to be resilient will support our self-confidence in times of failure or adversity. And if we maintain a rich self-confidence, this in turn will feed our psychological resilience when we encounter failure, enabling us to keep going by trying again, adapting our approach or changing our direction. Whereas resilience is the capacity to cope and bounce back if we encounter failure and adversity, self-confidence gives us the ability to tackle our challenges, to seek out our dreams with much greater certainty. It is our ability to remain confident, within the context that we are happy with, and provides us with our power.

However, while failure can grow resilience – when looked at in the right light – it can hack away at our self-confidence if we allow it to. And this can be a devastating blow for us, as self-confidence is the foundation stone of self-leadership.

Developing a good sense of self-confidence, through activities such as good communication, positive self-talk, achievement – especially making those more bold achievements – keeping your mental saboteurs at bay, are all activities that will contribute towards growing both self-confidence and also developing a self-belief. This self-belief is essential as it is this inner grit combined with an inner determination that will help you see yourself through life's difficult times, which includes our own failures.

Without any self-confidence, we are practically finished. Our emotions will be low and running on empty, and we will not have the inner drive to wish to clamber forward with those challenges that we will hit, even in everyday life, let alone those greater demands in life and the workplace. Low or no self-confidence is like pushing an enormous rock uphill; this is how it feels.

After my career failure, that I described earlier in this chapter, my confidence was running on empty. It is tough even to climb out of bed in the morning when there is no fuel inside of you, no get up and go, never mind taking on anything in any way challenging during the day. With your self-confidence and self-esteem running low, or even on empty, you suffer from the feelings of listlessness, pointlessness, isolation, as your certainty has died, and this is simply no laughing matter. You feel like you can't achieve, don't want to achieve; you feel that you don't want even to try. Plus, this is the last place we need to go inside.

Self-confidence helps provide a feeling of self-worth, a belief in our abilities, and is needed to live a happier and fulfilling life. One of the great shames of our modern working world, with many households having both parents out in work, the challenges of our digital age that is transforming the labour market, and an ever-growing comparative streak in our world cultures, is that it challenges our self-confidence.

Therefore, as we need our self-confidence to grow, we should develop our resilience to help maintain it such that we can continue to make brave moves in life, to take risks, to take the steep path and to lead ourselves. And when failure does strike, which it will, after the initial sting, we remain bold and full of confidence in the abilities that we enjoyed before we encountered the failure. This way, we help to maintain our overall happiness and feelings of self-worth, to stare back into the face of more potential failure and adversities, and smile with a broad Cheshire cat-style grin; knowing that we will learn, succeed and triumph in the long run. Hence failure will never be the dictator of our overall success.

'Man often becomes what he believes himself to be. If I keep on saying to myself that I cannot do a certain thing, it is possible that I may end by really becoming incapable of doing it. On the contrary, if I shall have the belief that I can do it, I shall surely acquire the capacity to do it, even if I may not have it at the beginning.'

Mahatma Gandhi

LESSONS AND YOUR RESPONSE

Your response to failure will dictate how quickly you recover and also the effects on your mental and emotional state, not forgetting those around you, as the more prominent the failure, the higher the likelihood it will affect others too. But you could also consider if you don't like the word failure, in your mind replacing this with the word '*lesson*' as your emotional state after failure is everything. So, if you believe that you are learning something, then you will cultivate a different relationship on how you view the '*failure experience*'. It's only a word change, I know, but it's a really important word. So, if you wish to replace '*failure*' with '*lesson*' then do so. Still, I will continue to use the word failure here, as this is the topic of this chapter.

Disconnect expectations from the result

Failure is a disconnect or detachment from the desired result or expectation versus the outcome. In effect, it's not what you or others around you expected to happen. However, let's not worry about others for the time being, as concerning your self-leadership and your overall response to failure it's you that you need to think about and where to concentrate your efforts. Then in turn, if you respond more positively to failure this will have a more positive impact for you, your future actions and your mental and emotional state; therefore, also for those around you – thus your response is critical.

Any failure, unless it was expected, or even wanted, or small, will typically sting or hurt a lot initially. Significant failure can also feel devastating, but you can't remain in your ever-circling thoughts; you have to think more constructively than that. If overall success in anything brings about failure, which it does from time to time, then success is where the focus needs to lie. The focus needs to rest in taking action and making constructive steps towards success.

Consequently, when you think failure has hit, have you genuinely failed? What was the cause of the 'disconnect'? Is the difference between your expectation and the actual result your perception, or reality? And by this I mean your expectation that you had at the outset may be incorrect or misguided? Plus, the actual result – your perceived failure – may be for the better in the longer run. It may even suggest that the ideals that you were placing upon yourself were too high in the first place, especially if you are a high achiever.

There are times in life, we can push ourselves too hard only to realise that through adversity or failure, it was our high expectations that set us up to fail in the first place.

Whilst working late earlier in my career I spoke to a colleague, who seemed to be boasting that his working hours had jumped from sixty per week, to over one hundred, for his second week in a row – in keeping with his high standards. But it was no surprise to me that this extreme and absurd strategy had him out for the next three weeks with mental exhaustion.

So, this simple example can be expanded to greater and demanding tasks that we set for ourselves at times. I'm sure we all have someone that we know that has placed too many demands on themselves, only to find that they incur a severe health condition like a stroke or a heart attack. Then it is only after the incident when lying in a hospital or convalescing at home that they reflect on their actions and discover that their health condition was a direct result of the 'high expectations' that they set for themselves.

Hence, when we fail, it's a healthy exercise to reflect and appreciate what was the cause of the disconnect and try and understand the reasons why. Here, you need to do two things: look internally at yourself and then look externally, outside of yourself. Look for the causes that gave rise to your predicament. Even though we may blame others for excessive pressures, we are usually also to blame for setting our expectations too high.

When you look at yourself, assess whether you are trying to please others, whether your original set of beliefs were wrong in the first place? Maybe as stated on the previous page you have set your standards too high. Or have you misunderstood the task what was needed in the first place? Perhaps you have met an excellent standard when 'good enough' would have been most acceptable. On a similar vein, maybe you tend to suffer from *perfectionist paradox*, meaning, that when striving to make your work perfect, it makes you so restricted with apprehension that it becomes an all or nothing procrastination. You end up not doing anything at all. Hence, you fail from the outset.

Your self-awareness and appreciation of any restrictions that you are placing on the task in hand that may lead to failure is a must. Here the typical causes are high personal standards, a false belief, your understanding, or even due to your concerns.

Identifying the cause will help you to understand why you failed and, importantly, for you not to be hard on yourself. If you believe that what you are thinking and feeling is somehow preventing you from making progress, and therefore causing you to fail from the outset, then you need to honest with yourself and admit this. Being brave with yourself costs nothing and is likely to pay dividends in the future. If you feel stuck in this position, now is the time to reach out and seek the support of a mentor or coach. There's more information on mentoring or coaching in the next chapter on decision-making (see page 213).

External factors as a cause of failure

When you look outside of yourself, do you have any unrealistic expectations set on you by your family, partner, or when in the workplace from your boss? These can be a common source of idealistic standards. If any of these factors are the cause of your failure, then realising this is a must. Then the second step is to take action to prevent a repeat of this in the future.

Even tight resources or time constraints are genuine external factors, which can make you feel absolutely frustrated when you find yourself squeezed by them. However, quick acceptance of the fact that they are out of your control is needed to help you regain a degree of composure and help you move forward again. Taking the attitude of, 'I can only do what I can do with what I have,' is a prudent and practical approach to self-preservation and sanity.

All of these potential reasons can have a real bearing on why you or your project failed, and why a failure occurred in the first instance. The trick here is to remain objective and keep asking yourself what the cause of the disconnect is. And when you establish what the reasonable cause or causes were, put a plan into action on how you are not going to fall into the same trap as before. Therefore, making progress to help ensure that next time – you succeed.

'You aren't failing until you start to blame.'

John Wooden

BLAME

Some amongst us will blame ourselves for failure, even if the failure is no fault of our own. But there is no logic to self-blame as it gets no one closer to achieving their eventual goal.

Self-blame is a form of self-criticism, a kind of negative self-talk that we can bombard ourselves with as a result of failure. Worse than this, we may express feelings of shame or guilt. However, there is no need to consider both shame and guilt, as there is a closer relationship between them than we may first assume.

Although there is a long-standing assumption that shame and guilt are highly distinct emotions that represent opposite ways of experiencing failure, there is, in fact, little theoretical or empirical reason to assume this. Shame and guilt are more alike than different; the small differences between them are a matter of degree. So here I will refer to these feelings as simply shame. And state that when we do feel shameful due to our failures, they are a common expression of self-blame.

People who feel shame lose perspective and tend to internalise and overpersonalise everything that happens. They say to themselves, 'I'm to blame for what happened', in the process demeaning themselves. But they also feel helpless, and don't believe there's anything they can do to change the situation. The internal critic in their heads continually judges and criticises them, telling them that they are inadequate, inferior, worthless.

These forms of self-castigation, as direct result of self-blame, cause an unnecessary waste of energy, time and valuable resource, and can damage your self-image and reduce, if not kill off, your self-esteem. And although these are psychological pits that we can fall into and not choose for ourselves, if you see yourself heading down the road of self-blame aim to correct things as soon as you possibly can.

You first need to forgive yourself. Even if you are the direct cause of failure, there is simply no point beating yourself up and making yourself feel much worse than you already do. It will also help to correct your self-talk, as you are most likely to be living in your head with the inner critic telling you how guilty you are. Driving in as many positive messages as often as you can into your thoughts, discussing and sharing your issues with a trusted colleague or friend can often help. If things are altogether challenging for you, then consider seeking out professional advice through counselling, and practice self-compassion (see page 47).

Anyone that places blame on themselves for failure, mistake or blunder, even if it was not their fault, is not doing themselves or anyone around them any favours. But, understandably, these emotions are impossible to merely shake off; therefore, the approaches left are great healers and need to play a part. And for this reason, allow yourself time to heal and take action to remedy the cause of your feelings.

Placing the blame externally

The other response that we can take as a result of our failure is to place the responsibility on something externally or, worse still, hold resentment. Now, while there could be a legitimate reason why you have failed, external to you, and as such you have been prevented in achieving your goal, through no fault of your own, you feel the strong urge to blame something or someone. This urge may even be seething through your veins, but this wish to condemn will turn into energy that I'm afraid you will only expend unnecessarily.

Newton's third law is: 'For every action, there is an equal and opposite reaction'. And used in this context it means that the thoughts that you create in the direction of blame or even as something as substantial as resentment, due to a failure, generate energy that is most likely to end up making you emotional, overheated or even irate over an outside influence; also something that you may have no control over.

As they radiate, your thoughts affect everything in nature. Physics already recognises this fact as applying to sources of physical energy: any light, whether a star or a candle, sends its waves throughout the quantum field of electromagnetism, going as far as infinity in all directions[38]. Hence, this blame on others is wasted energy, and will only in turn affect you physiologically, and potentially those around you, too. And this effect will be in direct proportion with the negative energy that you create. Put simply, you will directly impact your health and are likely to affect those close to you, in response to believing that you are taking the correct course of action by venting blame at something or somebody.

Acceptance of the situation is the quickest remedy to the result of external forces causing you to fail, painful though it may feel initially. Thus, this will bring you back to a starting point, where you can rebuild your energy and recoup your thoughts ready for action once more in the direction of success. We've all been there, feeling anger and annoyance at outside influences affecting our achievement. But accept it quickly, learn from it, and move on and protect your energy for what you need it for – your success, and your happiness as a result.

'Learn to let go, this is the secret of happiness.'

The 14ᵗʰ Dalai Lama

NOW, OVER TO YOU

Do you believe that you can embrace failure in your life? That may seem a leading question, but given the nature of this chapter, you need to ascertain if you can see failure as a growth exercise. One that regardless of how it may seem when failure happens, you can self-direct yourself through the outcome you didn't plan for and towards a brighter future.

I'd like you to conduct an exercise. Here you will take some past failures that you believe you have worked through and see how they have benefited you. If you can, reflect and take three poignant failures, so ones that stick out in your memory, but all from different life experiences. Aim to disconnect yourself from any pain or blame you felt as you went through the failure experience itself and instead focus on the results, the person you became as a consequence.

As described in this chapter, failure is a disconnect or detachment from the desired result or expectation versus the outcome. But please review your experiences and focus solely on the positive benefits. Maybe this is a change of mindset, a shift in a relationship for the better or you grew more self-confident as a result? Perhaps you have become emotionally stable from the experience, and therefore you find similar situations more comfortable to handle. Even if the lesson learned is as simple as you now know what to do differently, such that you can enjoy a better experience in future.

It can be a number of these. Possibly there is another outcome not mentioned? But identify your lessons learned and what now happens for the better as a result. This exercise should show you that if you look at the outcome differently, you can now see how you have benefited from the experience.

Make it your goal to remember that when we experience the arena of life and become actively involved, we are going to hit obstacles; but this is where real life happens. It's the active participation that keeps us on our toes and gives us the edge in our life experiences. Even so, you should be able to tell from the exercise above that failure does create greater excellence, and those more significant failures will also make you more resilient as a person. But in all, you must learn from your experiences and look to embody failing, in that you look past the initial sting and see only growth in your future.

Failing teaches us so much, and if we incorporate its lessons into our thinking, then we can learn a great deal. Therefore, use future failures as a learning opportunity. And then, there is only one thing that can happen as a result – you grow as a person. While you come out with a different outcome, you end up with a better future.

PERSONAL CONTRIBUTION
CLIVE SMITH: PROFESSIONAL AUTHOR

Failure Is Not A Problem

I am professional author and have written a factual history book about a family relative who took part in World War II. I sometime give talks about it, which can lead to strong promotion opportunities, and I was invited to an interview/audition for one such talk. It was something that I had done on a number of occasions, so I didn't feel the need to prepare greatly for it. I have a standard presentation that I tailor a bit and cut down to fit in with the time frame requested.

I was the first one up and was feeling a little nervous beforehand, as is usual. I felt that I made an okay pitch. I answered a few questions and felt that everything had gone well. I certainly didn't sense at that time that anything was wrong.

A week or so later I received a reply telling me that I had failed the audition, listing a series of points that included such things as 'my presentation was poor'. Although the reason for failure was all my own doing, I was overly surprised and shocked by the outcome as I really wasn't expecting it. I hadn't even considered it as a possibility and so felt angry – how could they have got it so wrong? But now I found myself in an unfortunate position. Being an author, my art and my income suffer if I can't promote my material, and now I'd lost a wonderful opportunity to do just that. I was stunned.

Initially I began to blame the interview panel and took no responsibility for the outcome; after all, it's the easy way out to feel like a victim when something goes wrong in life. I felt that the criticism was harsh, but then when I later cooled down, I reflected on the experience in more detail.

I think I had misjudged the audience, so there was a useful lesson to be learned here, that even if you think you know what someone is expecting it is a good idea to ask for clarification if it's not obvious. Don't become too careless either, just because something is second nature. I think I hadn't researched properly what previous topics speakers had covered, so I hadn't gauged how my presentation would fit and whether it would be of interest. Really, I should have researched areas that I thought I was strong in to avoid getting caught out. I also made the mistake of thinking that I was demonstrating a presenting style rather than content, and that the material I was actually presenting didn't matter so much.

In trying to rationalise the situation now, could going first on the day have helped with audience attentiveness? I realise though that by the time they had heard six or seven more presentations they would have forgotten all about mine, and so would have remembered the later speakers and therefore more likely to be favourable to them. I should have presented some key, memorable points to make mine stand out more. Also, it's human nature not to give top marks without having something else to compare to, so I realise that I had become the entry level for the audience to compare others to and lost out to perhaps better speakers as well as to the order in which we'd presented. This is something I didn't necessarily have control over and had felt somewhat frustrated about at the time.

On reflection, the feedback was very useful to me. I didn't like what I heard, but it was free advice, and if you can personally mature and grow from such a setback you can use it to your advantage. This example of a failure has made me change my mindset to see it as a positive experience rather than negative one. Also, to use my failure as a learning exercise even though it really didn't feel like a positive experience at the time – quite the opposite! The lesson I had to learn was to ensure that I simply couldn't afford to be so complacent. And that going forward I would treat the situation and the other parties with the respect that they deserve. Because I'm a skilled author in this area, it's important to me to get it right. If you go the extra mile at the preparation stage, you will reap the benefits further down the road.

What overall lesson did I learn? Well, learn from your mistakes in life, because they will happen. The trick is not to be defeated by them!

Chapter 5

Decision-making

*'It's not about making the right choice.
It's about making a choice and making it right.'*

Jim Rohn

I believe we would all love to make great decisions. Make a sound one, and it serves us well. Personally, I thought I was a good decision-maker, several years back; however, I was not. Not at the time anyway. I've improved somewhat since, but little did I realise that there is more to this subject than most of us know – or are even consciously aware. But like any muscle in the body, we need to work at it, to improve our ability to make a good decision on a more consistent basis. This decision-making muscle, which we all have, needs to be developed and tested out there in the real world. It's not something we can try out in the classroom, well not without *real-world* results. And results are exactly what you want from making decisions.

With decision-making you can theorise and evaluate until the cows come home, and they probably will, unless you can commit and make your decision in a reasonable period. Still, smart decisions made well make the difference.

On the other side of the coin, you can be armed with half the facts, not think things through nearly enough and go out into the world making decisions, but mainly shooting from the hip, and create a whole load of issues for yourself and those around you. For example, if you made a major job move and were not armed with enough details of the new role, it will only work out if you are fortunate to have landed a good position. Whereas gathering sufficient evidence about the move beforehand will fill you with confidence and provide more clarity about whether the move is to be a good one. Whilst you can never be one hundred per cent sure, you will at least move into the new role armed with more facts and greater clarity at that point in time. And with big decisions such as these – it can make a real difference!

A good decision, made with accuracy and consistency can bring so much transparency to a muddled situation, and can set you in the right direction, quickly. Which is why we need to achieve a better grip on decision-making so that we can lead ourselves through the maze of choice in life.

It's useful to point out, however, that different people will make decisions in different ways. And there are those that will try to steer clear of any significant form of decision-making whatsoever. People who want to avoid more meaningful decisions will hate to commit to anything, to nail their idea, best guess or conclusion to the mast. But this is not trying to mock this mode of thinking, as I'm sure that at one time we have all been there – I know I have. But I believe it's useful to point out that it exists – and if we fall into this mode of thought we should recognise it and resolve the drawback somehow before it causes an issue further down the line.

This manner of thought only means that there is an underlying shortcoming in our thought process, for a whole variety of reasons, which I will expand upon later. But on reflection you must admit, as I'm sure you would if you were honest with yourself, that we are usually the last ones to admit our own failings. So, if you feel you are falling into this trap, aim to remain self-aware that it is taking place, and seek support in order to move forward with your situation.

On this theme, there are times when we can't even see our short-comings, not until we experience them, that is, until there is some form of comparison between our expectations and our results. And sometimes this can be a result of a decision gone wrong. But what can feel equally as bad to some (but not all) is the expectations of another that we trust and respect when it becomes clear to us that we have let them down in some way. And this is another example of what we want to avoid when we make our choices in life.

Ideally, we want and need the best outcome for everyone concerned with the decision, with the information and the time we had available. Sometimes this is simply not possible! But if we at least endeavour to achieve the right result, then at least we can sleep peacefully at night.

STRONG EMOTIONS CAN CLOUD CHOICE

Let me let you in on a time when I was making a decision, an experience that stopped me in my tracks. The kinds of thoughts that were running through my mind when I was faced with a difficult choice.

The experience drove me to continually improve my decision-making skills and attempt to master the subject, as it froze me as no decision has before or since. At the time, I was completely perplexed about what to do, but fortunately, I managed to create some momentum again.

It was partway through my corporate career, and I became tired of my job and had a desire to move on. I had been leading a large team in an organisation in the digital communication industry and had just about had enough of the slightly frenzied nature of the organisation. Overall, I did enjoy working for the company – it installed a work hard play hard culture, which I fed off for a while – but I felt that I needed to experience a new company culture, and broaden my leadership experience.

I therefore went out and searched for a new position, and after a time, found a new post working for a much bigger company. The position was a more demanding managerial role and would take me out into a different industry sector, which held a massive appeal to me. This was working for a giant in the IT sector but working directly alongside front-line healthcare staff of the National Health Service, which pushed massive business and technical change directly into large UK general hospitals. The responsibility of this role was a sizeable step-up from my previous position, and I knew it was a big personal stretch, but I was keen to go for it.

Then came crunch time, I decided to resign and take the new job. I believed I had a good insight into the position through an ex-colleague that worked for the new organisation, so I felt I had a good view on the situation.

Deep down – I knew what I wanted – and therefore, I resigned from my current post, and that's when the sparks flew. My current company did not want to lose me and frustratingly presented me with two counter-offers. Now, this would have flattered me in normal circumstances, but now it frustrated me – a lot! It created unnecessary complexity in what, to me, was a simple choice. One of these offers involved more money but I would retain my current role. The other was a different position with lots of variety and working for a great boss, but on the same pay.

Well, this sent me into an absolute tailspin, and the more I thought about it, the more I could not make a final choice. It felt too huge an emotional problem for me to resolve. Although I had already officially resigned my current post and verbally accepted the new offer, my current company gave me one week to decide which option was right for me, but only after I pushed back for more time. I then made matters somewhat worse by foolishly using this extension to consider it, probably out of courtesy. After all, I now had three options on the table, and these situations don't come around every week. Consequently, I was far too close to see the wood for the trees, and I was now unable to stand back and view the situation from a higher perspective. And, within a matter of only two or three days, it began to become too much to deal with.

Maybe you have been in the situation yourself, where the amount of choice begins to cloud your ability to decide, and you begin to feel overwhelmed? It's far from fun, but is this exactly what can happen when strong emotions become entangled with choice. They distort our ability to see clearly, and the faster we can work our way out of this predicament the better.

In my situation the agony got so bad it was overpowering my judgement. I felt paralysed by indecision, but why? It was just a choice after all, and it had seemed entirely clear what to do up until this point. No matter how objective I 'tried' to make myself feel, or how I 'tried' to lift my standpoint on things, I simply could not gain a broader perspective on the situation. However, in those moments where I could reflect on my circumstance, I wondered why on earth I had bothered considering the two counter-offers? Why did I not merely laugh at the prospect of staying? Why hadn't I walked out of the door by now?

In these more lucid moments, I was incredibly angry with myself. And I felt that I'd shot myself in the foot. It was the first thing I thought about in the morning, and the last night at night, and then again sometimes even in the night. I felt utterly stuck! Although I wanted to leave the company, the organisation put a strong case together to keep me that in itself injected fear into the equation, which in reflection made me reassess what I was doing. In essence, it had diminished my power somewhat. It grew a fear of the unknown in me, a fear of leaving a post that was comfortable but one where, admittedly, I knew was no longer growing me.

Until this point, I believed in the new role. It was a brand-new challenge and in a completely different business sector and felt like a golden opportunity. However, all those rational thoughts were slowly being swept away with a tide of new and unwelcome emotions. Then as a consequence, all of those thoughts that I was having of my new offer now felt like someone else's memories.

All kinds of excuses and muddy thoughts were running through my mind and I realised I would never be able to make this decision by myself. I needed a mentor – someone with some serious clout and experience who would be able to help me stifle my emotional response and gain a degree of objectivity on this matter.

Reaching out for a mentor, someone you can really trust to guide your thinking, might seem an obvious thing to do when you are *not* in a crisis, but when your thinking is all distorted, it's easy to forget that others can help.

When you are in the painful position of being embroiled in indecision with a heavy choice to make, you need to strive to gain perspective on your situation. It needs to be achieved through some self-reflection and honesty. Once done, then I suggest you self-direct your way through your murky logic to a good advisor of choice.

In my case, I sought out a senior figure from my current organisation that I felt could help. On the face of things, it seemed like reverse logic to seek support from within the organisation, but gut instinct took over, and I reached out to him. I believed that he had enough emotional intelligence and responsibility for me to trust him, which in my case was essential.

With my heart in my mouth I called him one evening after work and remained honest and ran through the entire situation, and what was going on in my head. I discussed my options and how I was feeling. We had some open and honest discussion with neither of us jumping to conclusions or clouding the issue with company bias. During that call, he didn't express an opinion, and also did not look for me to make a decision there and then. Thankfully, he was considerate and empathised with my situation, and we agreed to meet the next day in the office to discuss the situation further.

After I ended the call, I felt such relief as I'd managed to get the whole situation off my chest, which was precisely the support I needed. I realised later that evening that I knew my choice, my mind was now entirely made up. The call had been the right choice.

We met as agreed the next day, but within a short time, he perceptively detected that my head had already left the firm, and I was moving on. We then went on and had a friendly conversation about my present organisation for a while more, where he flattered me and sought my advice on a few company matters. Later, I left his office in a bit of a daze, humbled but elated.

I sat in my office chair for some fifteen minutes before I got on with any work and as I stared out of the window, I realised that I'd just painfully learned two primary lessons in difficult decision-making:

One: never make important life choices based on intense emotional bias as they only blur your judgement.

Two: choose your advisors well as their influence can completely illuminate a clouded mind.

A few weeks later, I started my new role, which tested me to the limit at times. However, I later went on to have one of my biggest career highlights as a result of my move. This was when I worked directly alongside the UK's NHS on such a wide sweeping national business change programme. And after two and a half years of hard slog we went operational at 11 p.m. on a Saturday evening, which happened to be my birthday. I will be forever grateful to have worked at the side of such a great team.

'We all make choices, but in the end our choices make us.'

Ken Levine

DECISION-MAKING AND SELF-LEADERSHIP

Decision-making has a process behind it, a series of thoughts we have in order to arrive at some form of conclusion, for us to take action in some way. Sometimes decisions are needed as we will run out of time while we ponder or delay, sometimes the choice will feel too demanding, and we will become stuck. At times we will not want to decide as it may feel like too much pressure. However, typically, our thought processes will be subjective, internal, wrapped up in memories and feelings from our unconscious mind. We will then make decisions based upon something profound inside of us; at times, we never really know why we made a particular decision. It is not surprising to discover then that the unconscious mind has a significant influence over our decision-making, with the decision being made deep in the brain seconds before our conscious mind is even aware of it.

Daniel Kahneman covers this well in his book, *Thinking Fast and Slow* (Kahneman, 2011), which addresses the differences between the way we think, and refers to it as two systems. The first system, SYSTEM ONE, is fast thinking, and is thinking done almost instinctively or automatically with practically no effort from the thinker; no conscious control.

This system, when trained and skilled, can get things right, and decisions can be made accurately and incredibly quickly. For example, a trained firefighter or an experienced financial analyst make instinctive conclusions when faced with on-the-job decisions. Even a skilled and capable parent, when confronted with a badly behaved toddler, will act on their innate parental talents.

All of them will use their intuitive responses and split-second decision-making in challenging or more everyday situations that arise, and will typically respond in a precise, mature and proficient manner. Usually, their actions will bring about precisely what is needed in times of crisis or out-of-the-blue occurrences.

However, Daniel describes that SYSTEM ONE can also get it wrong! SYSTEM ONE is gullible and is heavily influenced, as it uses 'cognitive ease' of illusions of truth and enjoyable feelings. For example, a cognitive bias is sometimes followed in recruitment decisions, which can be based upon personal experiences, societal stereotypes, your emotions, thoughts, and a conversation you may have had earlier in the day where you feel you had to justify why you needed to hire – which is preoccupying your mind. Which could lead to an expensive mistake.

We can be lazy decision-makers

Our rational minds can apply the law of least effort on occasion, relying on intuition and making a quick but inaccurate decision, where at times we need to apply more thought and consideration to come up with the correct answer. These are times when we can slip-up. I've seen this happen in my own experience in business – four-, five- and even six-figure decisions being made where emotions played a significant role in the decision-making process. Essentially, the decision is made limited facts to back up the choice – which can be reckless.

It is in the moments where more attention ought to be applied that Daniel says is when SYSTEM TWO should step in. This is where conscious thought is applied to a decision.

Now, SYSTEM TWO involves thought processing but is more complex and mentally draining. We can naturally recognise this system, as it's when we apply more concentration and consideration to the thought process, as we are using it. So, typically this is where we apply more rational decision-making to a particular choice or situation. Normally it takes time and is harder to use this mode of thought. Where we have to soak in more information to provide an informed decision, but more important decisions do need to be made with a deeper level of thought.

Your manager at work or partner at home may be waiting impatiently, and not have the time for your SYSTEM TWO thinking when being decisive is required, but sometimes this laboured thinking is precisely what is required to make a good choice. Here, when SYSTEM TWO thinking is needed you may need to take responsibility and stand your ground on those bigger, more critical decisions that we all face from time to time.

So, this is a process that comes into its own where more difficult decisions need to be made. And conscious self-leadership springs forth when it comes to more conscious decision-making.

Self-leadership is a conscious choice, a conscious relationship with you and the world around you; to lead yourself you have to embody more conscious choices over your work and home life. Therefore, it is perfectly reasonable to expect that you should aim to apply more thought to the decisions that require more intentional thought. Of course, this can only happen where it is practical to do so, and where the decision warrants it. Some examples will be: a crucial business decision, a career change, a house move, a relationship choice. Decisions where the outcome is of some value to you, of some real emotional or financial importance.

When dealing with items of importance, especially with regards to you and those close to you, ensure that you give your choices of significance the energy they demand so you end up with a positive outcome.

A DECISION-MAKING PROCESS

There are a small number of steps to help you make more mindful choices, but first and foremost we ought to recognise that we need to consider the decision consciously, meaning we must make it less subjective, less internal. Not just mull things over in our heads and try and decide, with thoughts churning around in ever-spinning circles, or for that matter be unnecessarily influenced by someone or something else. Then, even if we are influenced, we should take the time to reflect and be in honest agreement with the idea. And so, we decide more consciously.

The steps below are set out to help you gain more clarity with your own business, personal situations or challenges with others. They are designed where the decision requires a good deal of thought, and not choices where you know what your answer needs to be, or even identify you will naturally work it out. Also, they are not for those everyday situations when we know quick, instinctive responses to on-the-spot decisions will suffice – which of course, do have their rightful place, but we should remember can be prone to error.

These steps are for self-led decision-makers where the final choice is a life changer, a business changer, a relationship changer, a game changer. They do also count for the smaller decisions where you are paralysed by indecision or analysis paralysis and cannot move forward for one reason or another.

These steps are for when we know that we need to be decisive, and we owe it to ourselves to resolve things more systematically, more methodically, with more conscious and careful thought. It's with these more significant decisions that we know – deep down – the outcome counts. Sometimes, really counts! And so, if you are a seasoned professional, faced with a choice on which microphone to purchase for audio conferencing calls, these steps are not for this type of situation. On the other hand, if you have to make a recruitment decision for a post in the organisation or a five-figure business decision, then these steps are intended to support you.

The first and last points on the following pages are not steps in themselves. The first is general guidance to support the decision-making process. The latter point, after step 4, is an outcome from the decision-making process itself. Please note that after steps 3 and 4 below, I have inserted additional information that adds value to the step, in order to provide more context and to look at practical problems that can be faced.

Guidance for steps – appreciate that you need to decide

The title above may sound like the most obvious thing in the world to state, and like it's not something that we need to consider in our decision-making, but it is.

Some may not be open to decision-making, even subconsciously. Examples being that they may not put themselves in a position such that they are informed enough to make decisions, or arguably a more common problem is that they may not even want to be decisive.

Looking at the first example, I used to work for a boss that never put himself in the position where he was fully aware of what was going on around him – and so he couldn't see the need to decide. I imagine he may have felt more comfortable simply sitting back. He never set up those regular meetings with his staff; they were more ad hoc, and took place very occasionally. And he also never fully listened to what others were saying to him, or he didn't step up and ask the more difficult questions on things he never fully understood. It was only on rare occasions that he put himself in the right position where he was informed enough with adequate information to decide – and therefore this caused problems.

In this situation, when we are leading others, we would need to ensure that we adopt an observant mindset and gather the information we need to realise that a decision is required – it's fundamental. Then to apply enough focus on the right things, especially if you occupy a crucial role in work or life, is the next stage.

The point being made here is more about being in the correct position, taking the responsibility to organise the correct lines of communication on a regular basis, genuinely listening to others, being self-aware of what you want out of any given situation, whilst not remaining so steadfast that you can't alter your view on something.

Also, it is about adopting a mode of thought which is open to exploring new situations, and the opportunities that arise in any given moment; not being closed-off to the world or the environment around you. And asking the more difficult questions. It's highly advantageous to have members in your team that you can trust with information, and this is gained through building relationships with them.

The second example would be where you have to admit you need to decide; and maybe you have recognised the situation in yourself in the past? I think at one time or another we have all been guilty of this. So here you may begin to kick the can down the road, so to speak – you consciously delay the decision. And therefore you kick the can for another day, but when you come across it again, you do exactly the same. You kick it again.

Here, I knew of a businessman that was approaching retirement age and did not want to make the difficult decisions with his businesspeople about the world post his retirement. Who would take on his tasks, how would he manage the knowledge transfer? How would the whole succession plan happen? What would life be like post retirement? And therefore, he kept putting the act of making the decision off for another day. But in doing this, another year or even five years can pass without any practical steps being put in place for his successor.

With the bigger decisions, the questions can feel hard or even a little scary, and you may not to want to commit to being decisive at all. And in these instances, you must admit to yourself that at some point you need to meet the fork in the road. With more critical decisions there comes responsibility – and no one will give you the solutions on a plate. Admit to yourself that there are tough choices to be made.

And I know, in these situations, it can feel hard. However, there comes a point when the can can't be kicked down the road any further. You have to do something with it.

In these situations, we need to be honest with ourselves – maybe even brave. Contemplate and come to the conclusion that sooner or later the decision needs to be made and simply commit to a date when you will decide. And be optimistic, see into the satisfaction beyond the decision and see into the more enjoyable things that you could be involved in post the choice you need to make. This is where you should focus, beyond the decision and on the enjoyable and more interesting aspects of life that lie thereafter. There will be good times beyond the tough decisions, so we need to lean into them.

Step 1 – Know What You Want

Once you realise that a decision has to be made, you need to know what you want out of your situation. And this can sometimes be the hardest thing to achieve, as there are so many influencing factors that can make us change our minds. It would be best if you believed in what you want inside, deep down. Not just glimpsing a surface thought influenced by an outside force or factor. Deep down, you must feel and trust in the result you envisage.

Overall, the best decision-makers will aim to see into their outcomes – even envision them. In my own earlier example, when I was looking to move jobs, I already knew what I wanted: I knew that I needed to swap my position for my career progression. However, the choice was made all the harder when not one but two counter-offers were thrown my way.

Therefore, I had to fight my way through the maze of choice being put in my direction towards my goal. And this is what can make things all the more robust for you, as if you decide what you want – and fix on your goal – you can then keep this focus in mind. Then dodge the obstacles if they come.

A checkpoint on this, however, is to keep an open mind about the specific outcome. Essentially, remain flexible, to a degree. You don't need me to tell you that in life it is somewhat impossible to control external events, so don't try to. While directing your focus on what you want, do see the envisaged result as more of an 'acceptable outcome'. Therefore, if curveballs or other surprises do get thrown in your direction, then you may need to factor these in positively. You never know, you may get a better result than what you anticipated.

Going back to my earlier examples, if your decision is a five- or six-figure business decision on the timing to launch a new product, a last-minute market downturn may need be to factored in for a later launch. Which, in turn, may give you more time to prepare. When making a new recruitment decision, you will need to rethink things if your preferred candidate of choice changes their mind about your job offer, for one purely on the basis it offered higher pay. And chances are, in this situation, that they were never indeed the right candidate in the first place.

And so, while you should be focused on what you believe you want, this step is also about self-reflection and asking yourself questions. Given the information at hand, or with a turn in events, – what outcome would you like to have happen? The outcome may be a single event, a list of results; it may be a cumulative outcome that will grow over time. It may be a state of mind, an approach to life, an intention to do something more, to have made a choice on a job and be content and more comfortable.

Your desired result or outcome doesn't necessarily have to be something material or concrete. It could be that you have concluded that you are not happy with your overall behaviour towards someone in your life, and you have a strong desire to improve it. However, importantly, make sure you are in control of the outcome. If you are not in control of this, you may waste all of your efforts.

Think ahead and aim to forecast say six months to a year onward, or whatever timeframe is appropriate. And in a single statement, consider what you want, but remain flexible on the specific result. Moreover, by reflecting, try to find the steps that must be taken to achieve this result.

Here, you are setting your intention to establish your identity in a forecasted setting in the future, and this is a catalyst to creating change and resolving some of the major issues that come with choosing an option.

Now, at this point, don't try to make the decision; you are merely trying to gain perspective on what may influence your choice. It could be as simple as committing to decide, which, when we are paralysed by fear is a bold and courageous step.

'The first principle is that you must not fool yourself and you are the easiest person to fool.'

Richard Feynman

Step 2 – Gather the Facts

It is by understanding the facts, where you refer back to what has given rise to the reason for a decision having to be made, that you can hope to gain some clarity and make progress. If you familiarise yourself with the facts and conduct some due diligence, you may be able to make the decision instantly as you become more familiar with the question.

The reason for the decision could be a demand, a complication, a predicament, a business challenge, or a personal challenge. Also, if you gather the facts, it could become crystal clear that you don't need to decide at all. It can also help to ensure that you are trying to solve the right problem; therefore, you will indirectly check whether a decision is necessary.

When we fact gather, we are also testing out assumptions. And we will typically accumulate assumptions through previous experience or limited understanding. Therefore, part of fact-finding will be testing our assumptions by asking questions, gathering data or analysis to support our limited knowledge or understanding.

One side effect of fact gathering is that time passes, and on occasions a situation in which you feel you may need to get involved addresses itself. This point is especially true when the decision is directly about people. I experienced the situation myself when I had a team member who was beginning to underperform noticeably. His performance became more and more of an issue, and I knew because of his temperament that he would have become vocal had I broached the subject. Admittedly I was not interested in an emotional outburst. I was likely to become cross due to previous experience.

I was assuming all sorts of potential issues: internal politics, team dynamics and so on. And so I held short and private one-to-ones with a small number of trusted colleagues who worked with him more closely, and neither was proving decisive to finding a potential cause. And this therefore led me to believe it was a personal issue.

In the end, I purposely delayed the task of approaching him. Still, I did keep a keen eye on his behaviour, to see if things would work out naturally. Now, this is not the action I would advise or usually take, but I had an intuition – that in this situation it was the best approach. I believed that if he wanted to open up, he would do so in his own time. And low and behold, his performance improved. I had no idea if the cause were genuinely a personal issue that was distracting him. Still, things did resolve themselves in the end. Thankfully, for everyone involved, he settled in again.

On the other hand, if there is a genuine need for a decision to be made which concerns you, then it is your prerogative to do as you wish. You can sit on the fence with your arms folded at this point if you want to, you are in charge of this one. Effectively, you ignore the decision.

This approach is useful if for some reason you haven't got all of the facts or you are not content, for whatever reason, to move forward with being decisive at this point. If you choose not to decide, this is a decision in itself and gives you back control over your circumstances and your involvement. This approach, in the right situation, is the perfect strategy.

I have seen this tactic used by many as a delay tactic as they don't wish to get involved with an event. One such example is a fellow business friend who will purposely delay answering to some solicited email requests, as he believes he can't or does not want to commit or get involved unless absolutely necessary. Now, sometimes this will be new work enquiries, and so he is essentially turning these potential clients away. But also, what he is doing is protecting his time and energy to focus on what he believes to be higher priority.

Effectively, he is factoring a level of time and emotional management into his routine, which I think is a prudent move as long as it's not to his overall detriment.

If you wish to press ahead with a decision, see what you can do to gain as full an appreciation of the situation as you can. This response may mean you need to gather details, figures, data, which can include searching for your emotional reasoning. And potentially seek out the opinion of others. It is the act of taking in enough information to help you decide the right thing at that particular point in time.

Just note, that you will never get the moons to align, meaning there will always be more to learn and more facts to understand regarding a choice. Still, you can't soak in information for ever. No one has all the time in the world. Even though, sometimes one feels it would be a wonderful thing to have control over.

Step 3 – Consider your Choices

The options are important. Possible options can make or break the decision in hand. Used well, they can transform how you see the outcome, as the possibilities can easily influence the result. That is why, after you explore some of the options, you need to take a look back at what you wanted and see if these match, or change in any way. For example, after you explore the options, a new one may come to mind that you never envisaged before, and then you need to consider if this matches your original goal or not.

One thing you want to avoid is *narrow-framing* in decision-making. This is where you define your choices too narrowly, therefore seeing them in binary terms. We ask, 'Should I move jobs or not?' instead of, 'How can I make this current post work?' 'Should we get rid of a more difficult team member?' instead of, 'How can we put steps in place to turn their current behaviours around?'

Here, you may be surprised to find the new option influences what you wanted in the right way. It may offer you an alternative you never thought of before.

I began to use this approach several years ago when on complex work tasks, and it makes an amazing difference to how you perceive things. Thing become more concrete – more obvious, and I have even been known to doodle on a whiteboard to aim to explore all the choices available, using a mind map of my own.

I once spent time with a client who simply could not see his way through a complex project issue with so many variables involved in terms of options available, which meant he did not know quite where to start. But just by spending one hour going through his choices on a whiteboard – everything began to become understandable to him. Even though he was the expert he had become almost paralysed with indecision as he was trying to solve quite a complex problem completely in his head. And he felt his options were limited. He may have been narrow-framing himself? But seeing it drawn-up on the board, with the options and the relationships, things became clear to him.

This step is the point where you mentally walk through the options, then either sketch these out or communicate them to others, whatever is appropriate for the situation. Even use a simple piece of paper to draw them up. Either way, you are getting the options out of your head, and purely the act of writing them down will sometimes provide more awareness of the possibilities that you have never considered before.

This approach will be especially true if there is an emotional attachment to the options available. After you do this, assess them, and rule out the less practical options immediately.

Concerning your possible options, ask yourself:

- **Feasibility:** what am I capable of doing?
- **Impact:** what will the effect of this be?
- **Desire:** what do I want to do?
- **Outcome:** what feels the right thing to do?

These questions can be used for more general decision-making also.

Consider alternative choices

As an extension to step 3, you might also employ a lateral or creative thinking process.

So to take one step back from the situation and reflect on your position. This can be done by discussing your situation with a trusted source, or even sketching out your situation using a mind map or similar, as discussed on the previous page, whilst you consider what other choices may be available to you.

Most of us think laterally if, for example, we are planning a holiday. Our minds become creative, whilst we consider hotels, activities, attractions and the like. We compare one list of where we want to go against another. With our wishes and our budget, we try to make things work because we want the holiday to be right for us. Therefore, our minds naturally become fact-gathering machines, as we have a different thought pattern running. Another idea is to use humour in order for us to think more creatively. When we feel light-hearted and witty this usually injects new thinking into our thoughts and the choices we may consider.

And so here you are trying to assess any alternatives that may be available to you that you have never evaluated before, but without initial commitment. No commitment at this stage allows you to be creative with ideas.

There may be dependencies here or additional things that need to be put in place to allow these less apparent options to become more viable, hence the reason that they were not in the first list, you should have created, against step 3. There is the possibility that this step is not necessary, as you may have concluded all the options, but if not, continue with this additional sequence.

Have a look at this list below of possible things to consider that can help to bring about additional choices. While assessing these, consider again the 'know what you want' material in step 1.

Keep in mind what you believe you want from your situation. Do any of these factors expand your list of options? Again, assess your options and exclude those that aren't relevant.

- **The physical aspects:** finances, furniture, location, equipment

- **The relationship aspects:** business, personal

- **The risk elements:** business, safety, emotional

- **The time-related elements:** can you create more time, reassess your calendar, prioritise events?

- **The emotional aspects:** can you reduce conflict, take on more responsibility, make a positive step, stand and be counted, go with your heart?

When you have studied the alternatives, in itself a hugely effective exercise of exploration and consideration, assess them then exclude the choices that you believe are not relevant. This way, you make decision-making more manageable for yourself. This stage will give you much more control over the situation.

Facing difficult choices

Much can be written on the ways of making difficult choices as part of the decision-making process. Typically, not all choices are difficult and most decisions can be made effortlessly, without much conscious decision-making at all, if any.

But we need to be careful, especially when it comes to more predictable situations, that we are not just 'switching-off' when we believe we are making more routine type choices. Familiarity can breed contempt, especially when attempting to make decisions in more time-pressured situations, or even simply when you pay less attention to them.

It is fair to say that we typically don't know if we have made a wrong decision until we see the consequences, but we can inject errors into our decisions if we don't give the outcome the seriousness it deserves. Essentially, the errors in decision-making often come when we overlook vital information, or we choose to focus on incorrect or irrelevant information, or we make more assumptions about the situation than are warranted[39].

I have seen the above situation many times in the workplace, when people look for an easy answer. People will tend to rely upon their intuition in order to assess a decision, when actually more time is really needed to assess a problem. In a lot of instances in time-pressured situations (that can be superficially imposed) we ought to protect our time to consider decisions, especially where there is more at stake – even if the boss doesn't like this answer!

On occasions, to make a choice can feel bitterly hard because all the options appear to be on an even par, and this can make decisions feel simply impossible. The more personal the choice you have then the harder it can be. Some large supermarkets have even lowered the amount of choice that they have on offer, as they see too much variety in a product range as pushing customers away from being able to choose. So, to use the same approach when you are faced with a difficult choice is the first good strategy you can take. Reduce what you can choose between and make things more manageable by assessing what you believe is important to you.

When faced with a reasonable number of somewhat more difficult choices, for example two job offers, some people will start to make a list of pros and cons, using this as a way to resolve a decision over a somewhat difficult choice. This on the face of things can seem like the most practical place to start, and yes it will be. At least it gets things out of your head, which is the last place you want to be when faced with a difficult choice!

But pros and cons will be rather dimensionless without *reasons*, as Ruth Chang expertly put across in her TED talk: 'How to make hard choices'[40], meaning, 'What are the *reasons* that you have for seeking out why you should make a decision on a particular choice?' Our reasons should be our prime motivators. You should need a damn good reason to make any important choice.

So, we start with the choice, and if one choice outweighs the other in terms of having a positive merit and we feel drawn instinctively towards what we know is right for us, then the answer easy. Then, simply make the decision to make the right choice. But what about choices that are not so easy to make, when everything is more or less equal.

Here, as with my earlier personal example over my counter-job offers, you will naturally feel that you are between a rock and a hard place, as the comparison is more or less impossible. Then, to take the action to list the pros and cons will make you start to explore what is out there. You can then add to this by also scoring these pros and cons out of say 1 to 5 in terms of what they mean to you; their importance factor. A pros and cons list is a simple decision-making tool in that it requires no real skills or application to use it.

Here you can write the pros, or the positive aspects and outcomes of a decision or course of action. As an example, for a job opportunity, they might be:

- Increase my skills – 5
- New location – 3
- Increase my network – 4
- More pay – 4
  Total score = 16

Then with the same job move the cons, or negative aspects and outcomes of a decision or course of action, might be:

- Increased travelling time – 4
- Risk in moving job – 3
- Increase in working hours – 4
- New people – 3
  Total score = 14

The scores can then simply be added up, and the higher the importance to you, the higher the score. And in theory, the higher the score, that choice is then up for more serious consideration. However, the drawback with this approach is that the choice may become hard because everything is more or less averaging out, so there is no obvious merit of one job over the other. Then you need to consider *why* you should make one particular choice.

Ruth then describes that this can be done through exploring the *reasons* to take one option over another. This will then create a much more powerful rationale in terms of *which* you should choose. Here, time should be taken to self-reflect and ask yourself the following questions:

- What would each choice open up for you that you may like/dislike?

- Who will you become if you take one choice?

- Where do you think or even wish each choice will take you in say five years' time?

- Which choice or which aspects of each choice do you stand for?

- Do you want to be the person or carry out the activities that each choice will bring you?

In my earlier example I had no reason to stay with my company – I knew this hence why I didn't stay – but admittedly needed to involve someone else in my thoughts. And this is also a good idea for you, to involve an advisor to discuss the reasons why you should make a certain choice.

From what you know about the choice and your list of pros and cons, what actually matters to you most? It's a good idea to write this up in a short document that you can reflect upon. Really, you are writing your future, leading yourself to create more certainty in your future in a world full of uncertainty. Which in itself will create more conviction and can shape your character in a powerful way.

Step 4 – Make the Decision

If you feel you have addressed all the options available to you and have explored the possibility of alternatives, now is the time to make the decision. Fundamentally this comes down to the simple step of choosing from the options available. If you are blocked, then identify what is preventing you from making a decision.

Assess what these blocking issues mean to you, understand them, appreciate them and then ask the question, are they genuine issues? Then, if they still prevent you from choosing make it your aim to remove these aspects that are blocking you and then make a choice. But see the opportunity first, create the rationale, the reason, the justification, the motive, the emotional drive behind the decision if need be. You will need to believe in a decision to generate the momentum to move forward with it.

When we take a step back and look at the practical aspects of making decisions in the everyday world, we need to appreciate that several elements will influence us and prevent our progress in reaching a definitive conclusion. Take, for instance, the fact that some people have real issues in making decisions – they flounder when faced with personal ones, and when in groups would rather hide within committees or agree with someone else. So, if you are on the fence with regards to a particular issue, with no real vested interest either way, then sitting on the fence is likely to be your best option.

However, to make decisions is a fundamental aspect of self-leadership, and if the decision concerns you, now or in the future, or with a colleague or someone you hold dear, then you need to muscle in and become involved. I agree that this does not always feel easy for several reasons, which will be covered later in this chapter. However, unless we can decide, we can't move forward, and nothing gets done. Do remember that if you can't conclude a decision, which does need to be made, you will not choose a way ahead, your goals cannot be met, and your progress can quickly grind to a sudden halt.

One consideration when decision-making is that if you believe it is the right thing to do, then simply make the decision, and allow things to unfold after the event. Thoughtful and astute decision-makers, like serious business owners, will not always have all the resources lined up before making a decision, they believe and trust in. They make the decision first, and then allow things to unfold and then find the resources after the decision has been made. Yes, this introduces risk. But then again, if we didn't introduce risk into our choices at times – we would get simply nowhere in life.

'In any moment of decision, the best thing you can do is the right thing, the next best thing is the wrong thing, and the worst thing you can do is nothing.'

Theodore Roosevelt

Help, I'm stumped

I have seen, and I'm sure that you have too, people stumped, stopped in their tracks and racked with indecision because they simply can't decide; they wish to look for more information or off-load the problem. Worse than this, they can't even conclude that a decision needs to be made, as they can't see the problem or dilemma for what it is. I've seen both colleagues and clients in this position, where they can't see the issue that stares them straight in the face. This is usually down to poor judgement, lack of experience or even contention with an emotional issue that prevents them from making progress.

After I ran a consultancy session on a client site trouble-shooting specific management issues, I once stayed back with one of the managers as she asked me to discuss a problem she had. She almost made it look to the others in the room that she had forgotten something, but this was a ruse to stay behind and confide in me.

Now, she had come across reasonably confident during the day but ended up in tears around a set of business decisions she felt she could not make. It didn't take me too long to fathom that it was not the decisions themselves, but the added pressure she was under to make them. Admittedly, it sounded like she was under a lot of pressure, but also felt she could not reach out to someone for help. It took less than an hour for us to help solve her issues, which were not complicated, and she could have resolved them herself but felt too distraught.

Eventually, she left with a smile and more confidence. But before she left, she came to the conclusion that she needed to be strong and address the cause of these pressures to provide her with relief from her suffering. In her case, her boss. Here, she needed an up-front conversation with him to reflect how he came across to her. In addition to this, she needed to find a confidant, as a relief valve, just in case.

This can be an issue for all of us at times, where we are blind to the predicament that gives rise to the decision-making difficulties in the first place. The only real solution is to continue to work on your awareness of the situations you find yourself in, where decisions need to be made, and build a mental landscape of the environment around you. As I touched upon back in step 1, you may still need the reliance on the awareness of others that you can trust. So, if you can't see the predicament in the first place and it's your responsibility to do so, then ensure that if others do they inform you. Then you listen, understand and take the responsibility to act on the information provided.

Large and small decisions

Small decisions will be easier to make than large ones, of course, which is a little obvious, but it's worth stating because if things don't go to plan the outcome may come back to bite. The likelihood is though, it's no big deal; and in the world at large, it is – no big deal.

Some outcomes to decisions will go wrong – fact! That's life. But, if you have put your best effort into achieving the right result in the first place, without overdoing it, then you have done all you can. You can always choose to *course correct* or select another option at a later point if things don't go to plan. The world won't end. In the process of trying to make a decision, with so much else going on around you, it can be difficult to remember this when you are in the thick of things. But remember, it is useful to not be afraid of making decisions by being fearful of the outcome. Even if the result has not gone your way, then you can always make another decision, and continue until you achieve what you want.

I find in life that some of us can zone in on things in too great a detail, but by making the wrong choice this is where we learn. Nothing comes to us by accident, and we still learn and grow through when things go wrong if we look deep and hard enough into the experience. So, aim to remember this when making your decision. You'll still be loved if it doesn't turn out exactly to plan.

More significant decisions may feel all the more monumental, and this is all down to past experiences, your frame of mind and perspective. For example, a five- or six-figure decision, or who to release from the organisation when going through a financial crisis. All easy to say, but harder to do I know. However, the higher you climb the ladder within an organisation, the more you will see that wide-sweeping decisions are considered every day, but the more abstract the position your mind needs to be in making those decisions. So, the CEO of an organisation will be involved in many choices but will not be involved in the minutiae of details, due to their position in the company. This low level of detail cannot be considered unless there is a considerable risk associated with it.

Those in these types of posts cannot move organisations forward unless advice is sought, considered and decisions are made with as little fuss as possible. However, it is worthwhile pointing out that even CEOs are not consistent in their decision-making abilities, and nothing tests the courage of a CEO more than making big business decisions. Therefore, none of us is alone in finding our choices a real challenge to make, at times.

The mindset of making more courageous decisions is down to regular practice, being bold and making the commitment to make them, nothing else. These are in themselves strong abilities, but perspective and dedication to be decisive are the simple qualities required to be applied, and emotion is typically removed as a factor.

The only time that emotion should play a role is if the decision is made in the moment, rather than at a future event, and something resonates with you that it is the right way forward. Ultimately, if an emotion overshadows your judgement to the effect that your focus is clouded – then take it right out of the equation, stay factual and do not let it steer you.

No one was born a decision-maker

Sometimes we need to remind ourselves that no one was ever born an ambitious decision-maker; in fact, no one was born a decision-maker at all. Consider the most astute decision-maker you know – at one time, they simply didn't know how to. They always learned through experience with possibly some context-specific tuition, or even researched the decision-making topic through case studies and the like, to support their skills. However, every situation will feel unique in the moment to those great decision-makers – because it will be. In addition to this we are all conditioned by our experiences and knowledge.

You also simply can't always take a practical problem into a classroom before you need to decide on your choice. And there is always some minor nuance that makes things in every situation that bit different. One small variable like timing, cost, people, the financial climate or even the weather can make a difference to the result.

But, even the smartest of decision-makers amongst us learn as they start to make them. And they too must have certainly failed a little in the process, things must have backfired, they had to. By a process of deduction, if the outcome to every decision that someone made always succeeded, then they would be classed as faultless decision-makers. And I'd love to meet anyone who claimed that lofty status. Therefore please, don't believe you can't learn the art of being a good decision-maker. As by having a clear understanding of what you want, fact gathering, considering your choices and measured application – whilst your emotions are kept under check – you can.

Either way, our great decision-makers throughout time selected their choices. But they learned from their mistakes, and over time, they got better at the process. They reflected on their results and made adjustments due to lessons learned. Therefore, a simple way to improve decision-making skills is... simply to make them. Start by making small ones, make them consciously and regularly.

Neither nervousness or lack of self-confidence should be mistaken for thinking that you are about to make the wrong choice. Nerves are, in fact, a good indicator that you are about to stretch yourself in some way or take yourself out of your comfort zone. These feelings are remarkably close to sensations of excitement, as the symptoms that indicate nervousness and excitement in the body are so close. So, if you attune to these sensations and tell yourself that this is excitement and feel the exhilaration in the moment, then this will act as a level that should help change your mindset from a less confident perspective to a positive and more determined one.

Outcome from steps – take action

Once the decision is made with a choice selected, something must then happen; do not procrastinate or wait for the situation to be perfect, it never will be. Try to define the ideal situation for a parent of a newborn child. There isn't one. I should know, being a parent of two. Any decision never feels good enough, but the child is loved regardless. If the preferred choice selected is still relevant, then it's time to take some action.

By taking action you will also demonstrate to yourself and others that you are serious as you will naturally create momentum, which will, in turn, reduce your fear; and some action, any action, is better than no action at all. With this, focus on the solution by being solution-oriented and avoid unnecessary distractions, the ones that appear to try and set you off course.

I always find that the energy created by taking action outweighs the fear and any trepidation that was there in the first place. Action is motion and this creates more momentum. I mentioned during the introduction that I have parachuted. Well, I can admit that when you are sat on the edge of an open plane door for the first time in your life with a 15,000 foot drop beneath you all other decisions in life pale into complete insignificance. I knew what I wanted, or I knew my 'acceptable outcome' (which was to land safely, I may add), and there were only two choices available at the time. Jump, or claim there was a problem and climb into the back of the aircraft for safety. I chose the former.

With the wind whistling beneath my feet, and where everything felt completely unnatural, and with all my natural instincts saying to me, 'Don't under any circumstance even think of jumping!' – I did. I took action and lived to tell the tale. And do you know what? The excitement and inner momentum grew in me the very second I did jump – and the experience felt incredible.

Now I get not everything can be likened to a parachute jump, but it certainly focuses the mind! And when your decision has been made you ought to focus your intentions on your successful outcome, as this will help direct your thoughts and your actions on bringing about the right result. This result will come about due to the energy that you create and attract while you are active. It's incredible what happens when you act on a task and expect success, what astonishing results come about. When you create a drive and an energy in a specific direction, you will create a momentum that will take you in the direction of purpose.

Unless the action is in the moment and you are responding instinctively to something, then to plan is the first and most crucial stage you must undertake for a future event. You don't wish your plan to fail, so set about considering your next steps towards your 'acceptable outcome' you ought to have thought through (back in step 1). Again, however, if through observation in this phase, you realise that you made the wrong decision, rework the problem and make a new decision, then self-direct yourself on to a new or altered path.

Nonetheless, there is no shame in changing your mind based on an assessment of your approach; in fact, this is an excellent and mature method of taking action. When taking action, be fully conscious of what is unfolding, listen to others, observe and reflect on what your intuition is telling you. Be guided by the situation and don't remain resolute with your original decision. Decision-making can be difficult at the best of times; therefore, be open to change, adapt or improve things when there is a need – or when things don't go to plan. Overall, allow yourself to make productive progress on your choice in hand and adapt or rethink where necessary.

'No plan survives first contact with the enemy.
What matters is how quickly the leader is able to adapt.'

Tim Halford

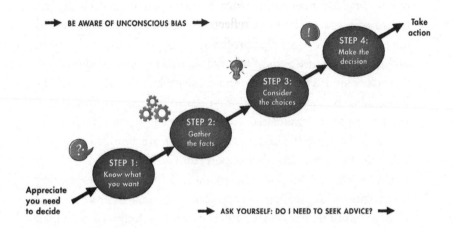

SEEKING GUIDANCE WITH DECISIONS

While we are making decisions, there will be occasions when we may need to involve another for support, even for a simple sanity check. This support can come from a variety of sources: a friend or associate, a partner, a work colleague. However, when making a more informed or fundamental choice, and to support or help refine your thinking, you may need to seek additional support, even professional assistance.

It is a self-led, and responsible, act to personally find the right support when making significant business or life-changing decisions. There are times when we are too close to the woods to see the trees. We can't gain the perspective and need the support of a good advisor, as I spoke about in my anecdote at the start of this chapter.

The appropriate support can move you forward drastically in your thinking and thought processes, and dependable assistance or advice cannot be underestimated. Highly skilled business leaders seek professional help (sometimes external to their organisation) for their thought processes when it comes to decisions, as they realise the value of its importance. Simply put, they appreciate that the value of their thinking reflects the outcome of their success. These more formal types of professional support typically come in two types: a mentor or a coach. But you don't have to be a highly skilled business leader to reach for this support, you simply have to be self-aware and honest enough to know you need the support.

Mentoring and decisions

A good mentor, which could be a friend, work colleague or professional mentor, will usually have the direct experience that they can share to see the mentee through their hardship concerning their choice. The mentor's experience should provide direct exposure to assist the decision. If they don't have the expertise, a well-chosen mentor will still have enough related experience to assist you, their mentee. The mentor ought to be able to provide enough trusted support to lead to improved decision-making, or at least help to guide you through the choice that you face. One crucial factor is that if you seek the advice of a mentor, they must be able to empathise with your situation. They have to, in order for you to trust their advice, as typically they influence your decisions through their experience and related expertise.

Coaching and decisions

The performance or executive coach helps clients gain clarity about their values and how this will impact a decision. It will also help clear the real from the imagined, which helps the client to solve real problems. Typically, these forms of coaching will help the client organise their thoughts and priorities around the decision and will help them to assess risk and the options with a level of clarity to avoid common decision traps. A good coach will not direct your decision but will allow you to gain a level of mental clarity so that you can reach a more educated and thoughtful conclusion; or at least, will provide you with enough mental tools to enable you to take the responsibility to make a decision or similar ones independently.

Clean coaching and decisions

Clean coaching is a way to help someone to uncover the structure, or 'invisible architecture', of their thinking, by tapping into the metaphors they use to describe their experience. It is based on a simple set of clean questions developed by counselling psychologist David Grove. Metaphors generally operate at an unconscious level, and by paying attention to them, it's possible to gain access to a more in-depth and embodied level of experience – the patterns that run our lives, our truth. Modelling the structure of experience via metaphors allows access to internal processes that are generally unconscious, and when you can 'see' how you are thinking, this can guide your decision-making. Clean coaching also often results in an exciting new insight or the recognition of some new possibility[41].

SOME PRACTICAL PROBLEMS FACED WHEN DECISION-MAKING

Emotional involvement with groups

Shrewd decisions made in the moment using emotional intelligence are valid in the right circumstances. If you use emotional intelligence, such as self-management and self-awareness (covered in chapter three, Emotional Mastery) well, it will help you decide in less time. Also, these qualities can be employed as an essential guide to help determine a more successful outcome.

At best, this is mostly based upon your field of expertise, and at least, life-related experience of one form or another; but it is filtered by emotional reasoning. It is totally feasible to accumulate a lot of knowledge and experience with limited facts, but then to employ good emotional intelligence to a decision and typically come out on top. This is true of professionals, or well-seasoned experts in their field. They will typically get the outcome of their choices right – even if the results are not that accurate or exact.

Besides, across the world, decisions are made like this every day that do have *good enough* outcomes. Good enough meaning that there is less need for absolute accuracy of the outcome of a decision, as long as the overall result is achieved.

Many modern software products are pushed to market this way, with a fix-it-later approach – as long as the deadline is accomplished. Take, for example, software applications, such as those used in the smartphone. Many thousands of decisions are made along the development journey, to get the product *'good enough'* to ship to market in time, with the software updates to fix known problems being applied after customers have purchased the product. And this approach will be agreed by the project team. In the grand scheme of things – it will and does work. And this approach will for many similar scenarios.

But what when good enough just won't work? When the outcome to a decision really does matter, say for example in organisations where the repercussion of getting it wrong are huge. Where the outcomes to decisions need to be more definite, even clear-cut. For example, the recruitment of an ideal candidate for a senior position in a firm or selecting the most suitable company to lead a major marketing campaign.

At times you really do need to get the outcome to a decision right. However, it's fascinating to note that there is expertise coming across from various chambers of science and industry that have provided helpful hints to support decision-making, which can be used in organisations. But a comprehensive framework for achieving quality decision-making throughout an organisation is still rare – almost three-quarters of companies have no formal corporate-wide approach to making major, complex decisions[42].

Besides this worrying factor, group decision-making can be critical here in ensuring the correct outcome is achieved. But be careful. In previous decades there has been a great deal of research that has demonstrated the superiority of group-making decisions over that of even the smartest individual in the group. There is one exception to this rule. If the group lacks harmony or the ability to cooperate, decision-making quality and speed suffer. Research at Cambridge University found that groups compromising brilliant individuals will make bad decisions if the group disintegrates into bickering, interpersonal rivalry, or power play[43].

This means that groups can turn out to be smarter than individuals in making decisions, especially in organisations. This is due to the fact that they will be using a common language and operate in the same culture – but only if they exhibit qualities of emotional intelligence. If they don't, then the likelihood is no decision of any use, or even one at all, will be made.

Therefore, if there needs to be a group decision, it is wise to ensure that those present are emotionally qualified to support the discussion. The self-leadership aspect involved here will be to use your own emotional intelligence to ensure that you focus on the end result, and therefore avoid being caught up in any emotional breakdown or wrangling within the group. Both of these elements will all work towards helping you and the group involved to ensure that you get the productivity you initially hoped for.

I've seen this for myself once too often. In my first position on leaving the forces, I was involved in a meeting on whether the company should make a counter-offer to one of our senior technicians. Julian had been with us for four years, but he now wanted to resign and move on. It was a relatively simple decision in my eyes – we needed to keep him. If at heart, he still wanted to stay.

The real sticking point was that he had upset one senior figure in the past, who just happened to be in the room. And with hindsight, this should have been a warning to us all – but we didn't take heed. And so, rather than see the bigger picture, this senior player was more than happy to see him go! He was very vocal about this point, and was quite outraged when it looked like a counter-offer would be made to keep him.

Now, there were six people in the room due to the gravitas of the situation. We were a company of only fifty or so and losing anyone vital was a real blow to us. Julian had been with us for four years and had built a superb reputation, overall. And I felt he had fully redeemed himself from the upset he had caused anyone in the past. This event in question was over three years earlier, and since then, Julian had greatly matured his approach to his work. Now he had become a dependable advisor to our sales team on some of the technical aspects of our product line. He was also handsomely rewarded with two good salary increases during his time with us as a result. But on the other hand, this senior figure held a petty grudge.

As I remember, even though two of those present were company directors, the meeting quickly broke down into an argument, in which I refused to get involved. It was a petty and embarrassing situation and was only stopped abruptly in the end by our CEO. The look on his face was a picture. He was disgusted by the behaviour.

In the end, we did make a counter-offer to Julian – but disappointingly, he turned us down. I was the one that had to approach him, but his mind was made up. It was a sad loss to us, but thankfully for his sake, he was set on his course and already looking forward to his new career move.

Our own emotional involvement

Now, we don't always have the opportunity of involving a group in our decisions. And when we don't, we should be a little careful of applying gut instincts where strong emotions are involved in situations that do need rational conscious thought. For example, if you make investment decisions, you will need to rely heavily on removing emotions which are nothing to do with the investment choice. You could be having a superb day, and feeling on top of the world, but the emotional influence should be prevented from swaying an investment which is abundant in risk, in any way. Instead, the investment facts are the only things that should be considered to help bring about the correct stock speculation.

Here, it is useful to note that you are all the more likely to take risks when you feel happier or excited, compared to when you are feeling sad or depressed.

A good exercise here will be, to be honest with yourself and recall a time when you know you were influenced by emotions when a cool-headed decision should have been made instead. Then reflect on how you could have handled the situation with more conscious rational thought. Good emotional intelligence, covered in chapter three, Emotional Mastery, should be understood and applied to help avoid your emotions unnecessarily shaping your most essential choices in work and in life.

Emotionally biased decisions can be disastrous, and I have seen the best of people encounter the worst of experiences, as their emotions run away with themselves, as in the example on previous page. Rarely are emotions like anger, frustration, resentment or jealousy necessary in the professional workplace, or even in the home environment, but they do occur. Like me, I'm sure that some of you have seen these kinds of emotions used in the workplace.

Still, most of the time, the offenders are let off the hook and the situation usually blows over with no long-term effects. But to use those extreme negative emotions in what should be rational decision-making in the working environment or similar can be tantamount to professional suicide. And the reason for this? Well, these are the moments that count. They are metaphorical forks in the road, where things such as money, jobs, quality, design, strategy and assets are directly affected. And negative emotions entangled in such important topics should never be welcomed.

This then brings us to one of the problems with decision-making when you are too emotionally involved to make a decision. Equally as bad is when your emotions are influencing you to *such a degree* that you make the wrong choice, but are entirely oblivious that you have done so. Now, this will typically be a decision where the subject is too close to you and you are not introducing some good emotional management, thus are not creating an emotional distance between you and the choices you face.

You may even feel in the moment when faced with a difficult decision that is affecting you emotionally that you wouldn't know where to start with the idea of managing your emotions, because they are overwhelming to such a degree that you can't think straight. Also, the longer you have to make the decision, the worse things can appear.

I think though, to be fair, we've all been there at times; tied up in an emotional knot over making a choice which can feel like a monumental hurdle! The solution for this is all about gaining perspective on the situation, which, as highlighted above, can feel tough in the moment. However, one of the quickest ways to do this is to change your physiological state, and to do this, you need to take some physical action. Recent research in clinical psychology has shown that the fastest way to change an emotion is to change the behaviour attached to it[44]. Thus, changing your physical actions and behaviours will have a direct impact on your emotion; you don't have to wait for your emotions to affect your actions.

To stay embroiled in an emotion-saturated decision-making process is pointless. Do something else! Listen to music, watch a movie, go for a walk or conduct a pastime or activity you enjoy. If none of these activities work, then use physical exercise, within your limits, to provide enough physiological stimulus to help you to gain perspective.

'Logic will not change an emotion, but action will.'

Unknown

Some people will probably resort to things like yoga or meditation, or some form of relaxation, maybe a massage. Sometimes stilling the mind can help, but it will not help in every situation, especially when you have been overwhelmed and this problem is sucking away at your soul, a decision that is so overwhelming you think about it first thing in the morning and last thing at night. But hey, when the problem is that bad, and you are struggling to work out what to do, you need to take some serious responsibility and apply some essential fundamental leadership qualities by giving yourself a break. It's not fun when things reach a bad point, and it would be inappropriate to come up with some cheap recommendation, or some pseudo sophisticated – sounding advice.

No, when struggling, give yourself some time out and take a step back, maybe try to find some ridiculous or amusing aspect of the situation to provide yourself with a helpful perspective on things. Find humour in the situation, remind yourself not to take yourself so damn seriously and choose for the time being – *downtime!* In this instance, this is the responsible thing to do, this is your personal power action, and it is all part of the art of self-leadership.

Too much information required to make a decision

Another problem in terms of decision-making is the amount of information that is presented to you or that you discover at any one time, thus making the decision seem impossible to make. Barry Schwartz, in his book *The Paradox of Choice* (Harper Perennial, 2004) found that a relative's accounting firm was offering 156 different retirement pension plans. No one in their right mind would want to deal with this amount of choice and would want to walk away with no decision made whatsoever.

Furthermore, in practical circumstances when faced with too much information you are being overwhelmed, and the natural tendency would be to switch off as you are now inundated with facts. You encounter a state of 'analysis paralysis', whereby you have so much rich detail that you're perplexed and cannot move forward. Some of the details you have uncovered will be useful, but likely some of them worthless, or at the very least misleading.

Now, without stating the obvious, you are not a computer, and you have to remember this. You are a human being with a human brain, and to actually find yourself in the mode of thought where you believe that you can process your thoughts while being inundated with information, data and choice is unrealistic. If you are open and honest with yourself – it is actually unfair on you! Essentially, this is a form of 'information overload', which essentially is a cognitive flood of facts and figures, be they in writing, verbal or both, that will overload you and prevent you from being able to form any conclusion whatsoever.

Therefore, you need to be able to be self-aware of what your limits are, and when there is too much input that demands you to process too many choices all at once – take personal responsibility and put a stop to it.

Practical ways to deal with too much information when making a decision, over and above what has been outlined above, is to be down-to-earth about it. Ideally, retrieve the detail from your head and write it down, which allows you to focus more clearly, as your head is the last place you want to have to wade through to find the factors involved. Writing it out will help relax your mind and also help you to become more objective with the data.

In addition, time-box how long you will act on the decision, or even split this into sessions. If this is a particularly tricky issue, then some degree of management on the problem will help your confidence levels as you strike a degree of control over the situation, which is what we need when it comes to significant issues.

Some years ago, I had an experience with a demanding series of work-related challenges which were going to affect all of my team. It was clear that a series of difficult, on-the-job decisions had to be made.

The first session ran for a whole working day, and the team was tired and jaded, and they contributed a lot less after the initial few hours – mostly due to the amount of data. I realised that I needed to time-box these sessions. The only way we could apply any useful thought to the process was to continue with two- to three-hour sessions, held over several days, and more importantly, at a time of day when we all felt we would be at our most productive, which was typically late morning.

We completed the sessions and successfully cracked every issue we faced. We took decisive actions – and we managed to stay awake the whole time. (I'm not being flippant when I say this – I have attended meetings where people have actually fallen asleep. I'm just highlighting that being alert is crucial when important decisions have to be made.) By scheduling our meetings at this time we were able to stay focused, sane and engaged – and so get the job done.

Large amounts of information that have to be dealt with by you will need 'to be chunked down', and by this I mean being able to take charge and break down the amount of information we need to address. Still, consider the fact that there is a priority choice underneath all of this; a real aspect that needs to be genuinely considered is lurking somewhere in this quagmire of detail. So, you need to be able to chunk this information up into smaller, more managable, pieces. Consider sets of data such as priorities, customers, subject area, impact and risk. Then filter on what is not useful or required to remain influential and strike a conclusion.

The aim here will be to have the data broken down and selected, as best you can, to come to the right decision, and it is in these sessions that you look to see what the real decision or decisions and options are.

Don't be reduced by decisions

One source of a decision that needs to be made will come from a pressured situation. A common place for this to happen is in the workplace, but not always. Here, I'm regarding the situation where you have the decision thrust upon you, where you are already struggling to cope with what you have already. This can typically happen in the workplace, where you attended a meeting and left with an action with a difficult problem to be solved. Or a team member or colleague comes to you with a dilemma that requires a complex choice to be made. In the moment this can feel hard, as even though you are burdened you may feel a new sense of heaviness come over you. One where you may feel you wish to escape your new predicament.

In this position there is a chance that this new weight can feel too much, and it might be. In that case, you need to assess if there is now simply too much complexity that you are already dealing with to address this curveball. Therefore, you simply choose not to accept this additional responsibility at the present time, and then a decision has been made to delay choice-making. You consciously move it to the back of the queue of work you face. In this case you've already self-led your way out of the circumstance for the time being.

But you must acknowledge and plan to come back to the issue, when appropriate. Even if you do not agree with the new problem to be solved, you must acknowledge to yourself that you will need to revisit it. Be accountable to yourself.

The other way to deal with this is to flip the situation on its head and consciously see this as a new opportunity or opening for a better outcome. The reason for taking this approach is that choices do not appear for no reason. Simply put, your thoughts need to focus on whether these choices are relevant to you in the moment. If so, then adjusting to a more assertive and challenge-oriented mindset will open up a new and possibly greater outcome.

Move past the discomfort of what can easily be perceived as inconvenience and start to perceive a new and somewhat different outcome. Fully accept what you believe is the right decision as being the priority. This outcome may be simply the way you need to spend your time, or when time is invested this may be exactly the opportunity you were looking for. Even if not, it is bound to affect the outcome, so take responsibility and embrace the situation.

'You may not control all the events that happen to you, but you can decide not to be reduced by them.'

Maya Angelou

The incomplete picture

The definition of the incomplete picture in this context is when you are in a position where you need to make a decision, and either you have a lack of facts to make an informed choice, or the data you have is worthless. This circumstance puts you in an awkward position where you cannot appreciate the size of the problem or enough details of the choice you are up against. This brings with it a host of issues, and in some circumstances can feel somewhat worse than if we have too much information, as treated in the wrong manner it can give rise to a host of difficulties.

Decision-making, where the decision counts, but where there is a lack of detail, is a non-starter. It gives you no confidence, and the likelihood is you that will have a poor outcome and will suffer the consequences as a result. The exception to this is where you are going with your gut instinct, where your knowledge and expertise in the area of the decision is sound. In this instance, unless you can obtain additional data or you can seek counsel, then the only option open to you is to use your gut instinct. Reliance on this means you will rely on the feeling in your gut, your inner compass, to help guide you, and this is a must in the instances of a no-other-option approach, or if you firmly believe that this will give you the best answer in the moment.

However, gut instincts can only take you so far in life, and anyone who operates outside of a sound decision-making framework will eventually fall prey to an act of oversight, misinformation, misunderstanding, manipulation, impulsivity or some other negative influencing factor[45]. Therefore, decision-making using gut instinct should be kept to an absolute minimum unless these moments can't be avoided for any reason, or you are skilled in the area of your decision.

The other side of the coin is where you have the information to make a decision. But still you understand the detail is inadequate or even worthless. Examples being the wrong figures for a critical financial decision, or the incorrect customer survey results for an up and coming marketing campaign. Whatever it may be, if you are the sole or a key decision-maker, bad information can be tempting to use; but this is a risk. Worthless information should not be treated differently from a complete lack of information, but as we base our assumptions on limited evidence, it will be very difficult for you to ignore this worthless data without a significant effort in self-monitoring and self-control[46].

The conclusion leads us to the understanding that we must remain conscious and in the moment when presented with suspected worthless detail, and not fall into the trap of trying to make it work. We can always reflect on past experiences and use this internal reference point as a guide as to the best way to proceed. Experience in doing this when making key decisions pays off in dividends, as long as we are suffering a strong emotional bias.

There is a chance, if we don't manage our position we may fall foul of situations where a decision comes our way, and we deduce that we don't have the facts to make a choice – but plough on regardless. It's true that there are situations where we perceive that we have no choice; for example, in the circumstance where a challenge has been handed to us by our line management or similar that requires one or more decisions.

Nevertheless, if this happens, line management will typically remain accountable for the outcome, which means they will have to give an account for their actions with regards to the result. For them to make us responsible for being decisive, with a lack of information, is hugely unconstructive and potentially detrimental to the task at hand; and more importantly will reflect on them if things don't go to plan, and they are still in a position where they remain accountable.

Now, there may be a legitimate rationale why there is a lack of or no information to hand; for example, it could be unreliable, too expensive to retrieve, there may a time delay involved and so on. However, the circumstances where you are being pushed by others for answers to big decisions, in the certain knowledge that there is not enough understanding to make a sound one, is at best deeply irresponsible, but it does still happen.

This has happened to me on several occasions. In one particular scenario, I was asked to help make a decision for a new client. They wanted to invest in a new and expensive business management application to improve their working practice. This job was not standard practice for me, meaning a client had never asked me to do this up until this point. So, I was in a brand-new and strange situation.

There was a sticking point, however, in that there was a lack of concrete data to defend whether a roll-out of their selected application would be successful. Therefore, this could all go badly wrong. In all, this could have been overwhelming for me – so I needed to keep things objective and maintain focus. And by objective, I mean the criteria by which the decision is based upon. I had to collate facts, and not merely gather someone's subjective judgement or feelings about a new product. That would have spelled disaster. The roll-out of this application was predicted to be huge, and the impact of business change very expensive. And so it needed to run smoothly as possible.

In the end, I managed to refine things through interviews with personnel, on their working habits and current working practices. I also sat for hours with a trial copy of the product and created dummy projects for demonstration and consideration. On several evenings I sat until almost midnight until I was happy with my efforts. In all, this gained a degree of confidence in me as to whether this new application stood any chance at all in being rolled out successfully – thus preventing it backfiring. In all, my efforts were taking the focus away from me and on to a fact-finding mission, which at times was a test of my resilience.

Furthermore, I then applied percentages to my confidence factors, risks and assumptions. Therefore, because I did my work, I again kept things as objective as I could, so the conclusion could be more independently reached based upon my findings.

Nevertheless, in similar circumstances, there is not a whole lot more that could have been done. The right decision was fortunately made, and the investment worked out. But these can end up as difficult conditions, so the bottom line is to collate objective criteria and keep things practical. Where there is a lack of clarity, self-direct yourself and create it – whatever decision you face. Create some objective evidence and data, which can be discussed and considered.

The aim then is that the information you gain can be used to move the focus away from you and on to the decision in hand. This should then help promote a healthy and impartial assessment, and hopefully armed with this data – the right choice can then be made.

Delegation or joint execution

The other circumstance that you should be conscious of is where you may not be the right person to decide. As self-leaders, we must be fully conscious of the fact that to make a decision, we have to have enough facts and figures, and do not have the expertise to make the decision, especially when dealing with a large and complex choice. Although when it comes to the subject of delegation some leaders will battle with perfectionism, as they can't see some decisions as unimportant. And here we need to either come to a decision quickly or delegate it.

However, those that have perfectionist tendencies find it difficult to assign their decisions as insignificant. As part of their nature, they want to feel in control. But why? Because imperfections bother them more than they do other people. If something goes wrong, perfectionists might feel explosive frustration or a niggling sense of irritation that's hard to ignore, and they don't want to take that risk[47].

At times those leaders with perfectionist tendencies are more accustomed to being in charge and cannot see that some decisions matter less. Here there is a real need for leaders to be more conscious of their matters in hand and how they are arriving at their choices, and to recognise their perfectionist tendencies through a level of self-awareness and manage them through a degree of self-control.

And there is another aspect to this: we practically can't know everything about each subject in hand that we encounter, and cannot be everywhere at the same time. It's not possible! And if we ever find ourselves in this position, then we have to be responsible people and give the responsibility for decision-making to someone else. It simply has to be delegated.

Now, this is not a 'get-out' here, although it can be viewed that way. What I am talking about is the off-loading or delegation of the problems to someone, who is better placed than you to make the choice.

Admittedly this can be awkward in a business or even the family environment, as the problem can become entangled in position. For example, within an organisation, who '*should*' make the decision due to their position, versus who is the '*right*' person to make the decision due to knowledge and understanding of the problem? If it's not you – then lose the ego – and hand it over.

Even joint decision-making can add a refreshing feel to a somewhat difficult choice! In all, we must recognise that good self-leadership is to accept our faults and limitations and who is best placed to be involved and take the responsibility to engage those that can help. Giving up any sense of pride or ego in favour of attempting to reach the right outcome is sometimes an absolute must, especially when there is a lot at stake. To make a decision is good; to have help to make the right one at times – is a must.

NOW, OVER TO YOU

Decisions could be viewed as a stumbling block or a bothersome step to the future. Still, if you consider with the right mindset, then they can represent a new future, a departure from our current circumstance. An original path to travel down or a unique opportunity to realise when a new prospect opens in front of you.

Reflect for a time on your approach to making decisions. Consider some meaningful choices that you have made in the past. Ask yourself how they have sculpted your current character or have given you the life that you have today. Are you happy with the choices you made? Do you have a pattern to the choices you make, or how you make them? How self-aware do you honestly feel you are when you make your choices in life? Think about some significant decisions you have made in work or life and reflect on these questions. Please don't simply skip them, they are too important.

While you can't change the preferences you have made up until today, using your previous experience, you can change the way on how you decide from this point forward. Think into your future decisions – how will you make them, and what ones will you make? All of the choices you make today will make a difference to who you become tomorrow and who you are years from now, and so make them as consciously as you can.

Be mindful of cognitive biases, or illusions of truth where you may be making a choice based on how you feel in the moment, as opposed to a more logical decision. Sometimes these choices based upon feeling are correct and intuitive, but on occasion they are clouded with emotions, and this can be a risk when there is a lot at stake. Take a more mindful and self-aware frame of mind into your day such that you can aim to make the right choices when they arise. Seek advice when needed if you are too close to the decision being presented but make the responsibility of your decision your own. Own it!

When faced with those more challenging decisions, use the steps outlined in this chapter to help guide you to a more definite outcome such that you process your moves with clarity. Not all choices need systematic steps behind them; the gut makes some decisions through experience and circumstance. However, do learn from mistakes made from the past or even if they do occur in the future. Aim to do this to the extent you can more consciously refine your leadership and trust yourself – with a higher level of expertise – and a better understanding in your hidden talents.

PERSONAL CONTRIBUTION
A FORMER RIFLEMAN OF THE GREEN JACKETS

Wouldn't it be great if regrettable decisions were limited to ones born out of stupidity or foolishness?

Decision-making is without doubt a core skill that every management leader or employee will need to use at some point in their career. Indeed, many employees because of their role in the organisation are sometimes routinely forced to make complex decisions under intense pressure. It is essential therefore that the decision-maker makes the best possible choice in the shortest time possible as well as being able to show the reasons for the decision. Generally, the more senior the role, the more difficult these decisions become.

Good decision-making usually goes hand in hand with good and effective leadership. It should be based on sound knowledge of the subject matter, a clear aim to achieve a successful outcome, plus a full and comprehensive understanding of the various options available, and finally the confidence to carry the decision through to a successful conclusion.

My own experiences in decision-making were initially forged in the slightly darker world of various military conflicts before I went into business, although in essence the guiding principles surprisingly remained the same. In truth, over time as I became more experienced in the 'dark arts' many of my decisions fell into the category of 'intuition' despite having a 'decision template' that covered every eventuality imaginable – even death. Fast-moving decision-making became the norm and therefore, equally unsurprisingly, I remember very few of my better decisions – despite one or two sailing pretty close to the wind. They must have been okay though because I am still here, as are most of my then companions.

Sadly, however, good decision-making is rarely honoured or acknowledged outside of the environment in which it was made, whilst bad decision-making hogs the comedic limelight on YouTube. However, one decision I remember well (not made by me, thank goodness) was in 1966 during the Malayan/Borneo Emergency, when British Forces were deployed to counter the ever-growing communist insurgency into South East Asia. Even the decision made by the individual concerned resulted in his death – read on and try and identify the few simple faults in his decision-making...

After two weeks patrolling east of the Cameron Highlands in central Malaysia, our Iban scouts detected the signs of a large (thirty-strong) armed force of communist insurgents. After a further week they were eventually tracked to a heavily wooded hide set in a natural bowl in the landscape. It was decided that an attack would go in at first light (fire fights in the jungle at night are rarely carried out due to the impenetrable darkness). Moving into various attack and ambush positions around the hide just as first light was beginning to filter through the tree tops, the occupants of the camp began to rouse and start their morning routine before moving off to intimidate, kill or destroy whatever kampong (jungle village) they were going to target that day. Clearly believing they were perfectly safe and far enough away from any roving security forces, a number even began to light open cooking fires, which only helped to illuminate the scene throughout the clearing. One fella even sat crossed-legged beside one such fire and began to strip and clean his weapon.

On a pre-arranged signal all hell was unleashed and pandemonium reigned throughout the hide as automatic and explosive fire began to tear into the hide and its occupants. However, despite the rate and volume of fire being brought to bear on everything in the clearing, the seated and crossed-legged insurgent calmly began to reassemble his weapon before the inevitable happened and he was swept away in a burst of automatic fire.

So, what was wrong with his decision?

Despite undoubtedly being an able, capable and experienced jungle fighter and operator, he failed to instantly analyse and in seconds make the right decision when it really counted.

1. His 'intuition' and 'logic' should have made him instantly dump everything and get into the relative safety of the dark edges of the clearing.

2. He and the other insurgents were completely overconfident in their tactical nous, and as a consequence had no prepared plan of action (options) in the eventuality of such an incident, or intelligence on the opposing forces attacking them.

3. Cognitive bias instantly came into play as indicated by thinking he had the ability under fire to enable him to reassemble his weapon in time and fire back.

Would a better decision have saved his life? Given his circumstances and the opposing forces he faced – probably not, although it might have prolonged it a little longer.

The parallel that can be drawn into business or personal life from this story is that we should be able to draw on our instinct when trained to do so. We can rely upon this when faced with an immediate snap decision. Overconfidence does not replace excellent planning, and therefore you should not leave yourself with the option of no choice whatsoever. Also, never become too arrogant and believe that you can choose to resort to a rule of thumb. Choosing to adapt and make an intelligent decision based on the circumstances is the right thing to do. Maybe you won't be in such a drastic situation as the enemy above. Still, even out of the armed services, some decisions can make the biggest of differences to the outcome.

Chapter 6

Leadership of Others

*'The quality of a leader is reflected by the
standards they set for themselves'*

Ray Kroc

We now come on to the incredibly exciting subject of leadership, not only the leadership of others, but also the relationship between leading others and your own self-leadership – as you cannot have one without the other! The two work in harmony and you must realise this important relationship between both. In essence – you must lead yourself, before you embark on leading others. It's that simple.

Take for example, the very idea of the head coach of a topflight football club looking to inspire, train, discipline and also gain the respect of his team members. If he is undisciplined, a terrible decision-maker and cannot not build relationships, then it is an altogether preposterous situation. It simply would not work! He would not be setting any standards, and more than that he would not know what was needed from within to lead; he wouldn't understand some of the basic principles of leadership. Therefore, if you lead others, leadership must always flow two ways – both inwardly and outwardly.

Throughout this chapter I make use of the word 'team' or 'team member'. This is essentially anyone that you directly manage, lead, coach, motivate or inspire in order to get tasks done together, to co-create, if you will. This could be your direct reports at work, committee associates, troop members, players of a sports team that you coach or even members of your own family. Frankly, anyone that you are in a position to lead either formally or more casually like family members – which for some, can be much harder to lead than direct reports in the workplace! But please don't tell my kids that.

The expression 'to co-create' may sound a little odd to some, but essentially that is what happens when you work with others to achieve a mutually benefit outcome; even if your team member will do the majority of the 'hands-on work', so to speak.

Leaders are those that will change the belief systems of others and help them to see beyond the present situation in order to co-create. Leadership of others can feel tough to those that are new to it, and even to some that have had that responsibility for some years, but it's a fundamental component to getting things done. Leadership is everywhere, it's in our companies, schools, charities, hospitals, even at home leadership is prevalent. And when we reflect back on history at what has been achieved through team leadership – innovative product launches, team sporting achievements, scientific and medical breakthroughs and even human survival – it goes to show how important and necessary leadership is in our lives. Leadership is a key principle of our human race.

I'm sure that we can all relate to a story of leadership, whether it be in a business, a political environment or even a sports team that you support. One such prime example is Martin Luther King Jr., who became the dominant figure in the American civil rights movement. King, who was a well-educated Georgia-born minister, at the age of thirty-five was the youngest man to have received the Nobel Peace Prize. He received this for his non-violent resistance to racial prejudice in America.

Ultimately, he had a goal. A goal that would change people's minds so that they would come to the same opinion. As such, he staged non-violent strikes, protests and speeches. He fiercely ingrained the notion of non-violent protests into his followers' hearts and minds. After his home was bombed, what did he do? He and his members fervently prayed for their oppressors in church pews[48].

Regardless of being arrested and assaulted several times while he carried on his pursuit of a vision that all men and women were created equal, and that they should enjoy the same rights and privileges – he carried on. He presented what was arguably his most famous speech – 'I have a dream' – in 1963 to a live audience of close to 250,000 in Washington DC, as part of a civil march. After being prompted by a member of the audience, King, spoke from the heart. Here, he injected a most moving line and vision which was that 'he hoped that his children would not be judged by the colour of their skin but by the content of their character.'

The result of this extremely moving and influential speech was to put massive pressure on the American administration at the time to push the civil rights bill through Congress. Both King's speech and the march on Washington were accredited with helping to secure the civil rights act in 1964. The act, which ended segregation in public places and banned employment discrimination on the basis of race, colour, religion, sex or national origin, is considered one of the crowning legislative achievements of the civil rights movement[49].

So, if you are new to the task of leadership or simply need a reminder, you ought to realise that you are also making history in some way as you are touching other people's lives and will therefore make a difference. Even if your influence is relatively small compared with the example above, it's still every bit as real – and even more real to you. And when you get it right, when you inspire others and see the change in their eyes and in their hearts through your leadership, it really can be a magical thing!

LEADERSHIP AND MANAGEMENT

On the subject of leadership, just to clear up one point before we continue – please don't mistake management for leadership. Some managers will think that to check tasks done by individuals against a schedule or to deliver status against effort achieved and to plot this on a weekly report is leadership. Nothing, however, could be further from the truth! To assess task priorities and provide work estimates is not leadership. This will not move mountains, and it will certainly not change people's belief systems.

Nonetheless, some managers will believe that to micromanage their team will somehow drive them forward to meet their mission and achieve that glorious feeling of inner success. Or they believe that the best way to deal with an individual's inner conflict, perhaps due to being caught in a downward spiral of scepticism at the organisation's poor goals, is to roar at them to get on with their job; and then to go on to black-mark their progress. While in fact, the truth is that those who perform such or similar acts should not be in their positions in the first place and should take a damn good look in the mirror to find their inner conscience!

Don't get me wrong, good management is an important asset to any organisation, make no mistake. But management without leadership is rather two-dimensional – and does not make the leader.

What we need is that extra dimension to bring the work alive and to move people on and inspire them. What will ignite the flame and draw out the best in people is done through leadership. And when things are tough, when the product launch looms large, or when an army needs the motivation to go into battle, or even the sports team who are sat in the dressing room about to go out for the final play-off and stuck somewhere between childish excitement but riveted to the spot with fear – people need someone to climb down inside their souls.

In these circumstances your team will need their spirits lifted and be given that final push to leap back out there and do it one last time. They don't need management, just pure gold-coloured leadership. To light the touchpaper inside them and to lift their hearts so high they will jump up and out there and get the job done. This is pure dynamite. This, my friend, is the task of ultimate leadership.

'Leadership is lifting a person's vision to high sights, the raising of a person's performance to a higher standard, the building of a personality beyond its normal limitations.'

Peter Drucker

EQUIP YOURSELF FOR LEADERSHIP THROUGH SELF-LEADERSHIP

The more exposure you have to life's experiences, both good and bad, the more you have to offer others. The rich lessons that you have learned in life including self-belief, adaptability and resilience, and even the failures you've encountered, are all great lessons that will enrich how you lead. However, this does not mean that you have to amass decades of life experience beyond school age before you can do so. Start now and get perfect later – you must act from the position that you are in. Especially if you, like most of us, have been given little choice when you need to lead.

Still, virtually all of your life experiences will enrich your leadership skills in one way or another, so do not hide from life. In addition to this, as you mature and self-develop those skills and traits that lend themselves more directly to your self-leadership skillset, you will also grow to a degree the tools that will come in useful in order for you to lead others. These skills will include self-confidence, self-efficacy, the ability to influence others, emotional intelligence traits, acceptance of feedback, good conversational and listening skills. Also, most importantly – the need to stay humble. Never ever forget that one.

To take the time to self-develop these skills will pay dividends if you are ever in a position of leading others. And it is not just one of these skills that you will need to develop, for example self-confidence, but a whole variety of different abilities, as you will encounter a multitude of different experiences and circumstances. Some will be straightforward, and others will be more trying. Even so, let's make no mistake: when you achieve the results that you look for as a leader – it will be hugely satisfying indeed. Your team will appreciate it, too!

In conjunction with these skills, you will require your development of the more general life skills that allow you to underpin your self-leadership, i.e. the ability to take care of yourself, cook, wash, shop, communicate with a level of clarity, self-organise your daily routine, look after your health and be organised. These life skills will provide a decent foundation in order for you to both lead yourself and to lead others too. Never forget the basics, they may just save you when the going gets tough.

Let's make no joke out of this last group of skillsets, they are vastly important in life! It's absurd the number of people that have made their way through education and into employment with a healthy intelligence and a good 'common range' of abilities and level of awareness but cannot even organise themselves properly – never mind anyone else. How bad is that!

What is more concerning would be the situation where these people are put in positions where they need to lead and direct others. A reckless move in my book.

No, a certain amount of foundation skills are involved in self-leadership and self-organisation that we must each have achieved prior to leading others. This is not to say that we must be a master of the black arts of self-leadership and fully groomed in order to be in a position where we set the direction for other people – as when put in these positions we ought to be allowed to grow. Then fail at times.

But, positions of leadership require responsibility. And before we carry this out, we ought to have achieved – at least – a bronze award in the basic self-organisation and self-leadership skillsets. After all, it's only to fair to everyone concerned.

YOUR CHARACTER AND POSITIONING

In addition to these points above your depth of character will be of prime importance to you when you lead others. To a certain extent, you need to be thick-skinned, as they say, or in other words you will need to be able to take a certain amount of constructive criticism and failure and still remain positive. Always make the attempt to look at the bigger picture. This will prevent you from spiralling downwards and feeling dejected when things get tough; a form of self-preservation, if you like.

The last thing we need when leading others is to become miserable and down about anything at all. This does no one any good least of all you and may mean that you are taking yourself and the situation at hand far too seriously. And so, having the ability to laugh and find humour in what can appear difficult circumstances can, at times, be the best medicine you will ever need to restore your resolve and remain grounded. This helps you to relax with the team, as opposed to *always* leading from the front, by creating a false leader's character that may not fit with you.

One related and important point that I learned during a leadership programme in the Royal Navy was that you shouldn't always lead from the front anyway, to ensure a team gets over the line. This learning point happened to me through sheer instinct. I was grouped up with a team of six on one particular leadership exercise, where I was placed in charge. This test was a log run. And that meant that I had to get a team and a log around an assault course so I could be assessed on my leadership skills.

For most of the demanding course, which was wet and muddy, I led from the front. One where I shouted and motivated the team to push on over a tough terrain. It was only when we had to get the team and this cumbersome and heavy log successfully over a nine-foot wall, did I realise that the right thing for me to do was to stay in the middle of the group. So, as I maintained a position on the wall, effectively I was the last one down. Yet by doing this it gave me a clear view of the team on both sides of the wall so I could see the whole team. Here I could use people more effectively and could also help those that were struggling.

This approach was notably praised afterwards as a good method of seeing the entire team, and it taught me that leading from the middle or even behind – can be key to the team's success. At times, dropping back to ensure the slowest member keeps up will be an essential step to a team's achievement. Which may mean taking the time to understand and appreciate their struggles. Always being at the front will not give you a whole team view.

LEADERSHIP AND CRITICISM

Positive or constructive criticism can be a good thing, if you are prepared to accept this as a form of feedback and allow it to grow your depth of character, and understand where you are going wrong as a result, then you can correct things in the future. In my first few weeks of basic naval training I learned incredibly quickly that constructive criticism is not really directed at you at a personal level, rather at what you have done or are doing. Which is an important aspect to remember, when handing out constructive criticism yourself: focus your attention on the action and not the person. This is especially true when dealing with children; direct any criticism at what they are doing and not at them personally.

Although when I joined the armed forces, me and my troop were screamed at on a daily basis for doing this or that wrong, and it became par for the course! Techniques such as these are all part of the plan to both improve your character and attempt to break your spirit and resolve. In order to survive, you had to learn not to take the comments personally. Rather, we had to appreciate how to learn from the message being conveyed and adapt our approach to make sure that we did not make the same mistake the following day. I mean who needs their ears ringing for making the same mistake two days in a row? Surely one is bad enough.

If we go back to the topic of criticism that is perhaps directed at you from what others have said, it may be perfectly correct, i.e. they may have picked up on a genuine point. A character flaw, big deal – we all have them. But the likelihood is they are exaggerating it to make a greater point of it, or even to make themselves feel better. Except, if you don't allow it to permeate your inner self and get the better of your resolve, it helps to create a greater resistance to positive criticism. And this allows you to adapt your approach as a result. A beneficial outcome, when you can look at it in cool, calm reflection.

My own personal experiences have taught me that the only way to learn to deal with criticism is through exposure. You need to be exposed through action in order to learn this one. But we can plan ahead for it, as through action as a leader we will automatically hit criticism at some point. Therefore, as we know this in advance, we can plan to respond to it and not react when it comes. We can do this if we self-regulate our response; i.e., we don't react by biting back or similar. Rather, we listen and digest the criticism, and ensure that we don't take it personally, even by asking the other person delivering it what they meant. Maybe by asking them to provide other examples?

Even make slight fun of your shortfalls, if appropriate.

This dialogue can be a good thing as it will then allow you develop a clearer understanding if this criticism is fair – and if it is, accept it. Also, if you genuinely don't believe it is – then don't! Politely reject it. But whatever you do, never take criticism personally, under any circumstances, as it can start to erode your self-worth. And life if just too short for that one.

A leader in the making

To accept positive or constructive criticism and general feedback and then adapt your approach as a result, will have such a beneficial effect in the long run. An example I saw of this was several years ago when I used to work for a manager, let's call her Beth. Now, I'm afraid to say that initially I didn't have much respect for Beth; which I later recognised as a character flaw in me. She came into manage an existing quality assurance team for our technical communications company.

Most of her new team were stuck in their ways. On the other hand, I was also relatively new, with a different role in looking at change and process improvement and worked mostly on my own in the early days. But when I did work with her, I drew some rash conclusions about the way she behaved. For example, she appeared to give less thought to things, a trait that I did not admire in others at the time.

I observed that even in meetings, where she was trying to assert some influence, she got talked over on several occasions by some assertive characters; it was a hugely commercial sector we were in, and this shaped the culture of the company. I didn't partake in this behaviour, as it was not in my nature to act in this way, but the way others conducted themselves didn't help to build my confidence in her. And in the early months, I'm sure that others must have had their doubts about her also.

Well, over several months things began to change, and I actually began to admire her. I even found that I started to model some of her leadership traits in order to improve my own, as I began to realise that Beth was a fighter and would never take anything personally. Almost to the extent where she used any questions or criticism of her approach or ability as fuel to drive her onwards and challenge herself.

Following criticism, she appeared to always try harder, by making small adjustments to her style and being careful never to make the same mistake twice; sometimes she made even bolder moves than before. But one thing was certain – she stood out!

Even the time when it was announced publicly in front of a one-hundred-strong department that her role was to be changed, due to a divisional shake-up – unbeknownst to her – she afterwards acted with absolute charm. The way it was announced was frankly a managerial blunder, and she did look shocked when she heard the news. But over the coming weeks she simply got on with the job and was magnanimous about it.

She used to roll with the punches, as they say, and come in the next day with the attitude of… 'this is a new day, so let's get on with it'. It was incredible to witness, and you just knew that this attitude was something special and something to be admired. These were the very reasons why I modelled some of the behaviours I admired in her.

Well, approximately eight years after she entered the company doors and about three years after I had left to seek pastures new, Beth had moved from manager of a team of around twenty or so to the position of company vice president.

Criticism is par for the course whenever we attempt to represent something the crowd doesn't. Beth did this instinctively; she stood out like a sore thumb, compared to how other managers of a similar position conducted themselves. If you take criticism personally it can drag you down – if you let it! But you ought to let it fuel you like Beth did.

See the challenges as an opportunity to look to improve or adapt your approach. Over time you will become used to it and you will come to realise that the criticism is nothing about you anyway. It's actually the shortcomings of the critic. The onlookers who think they know better but are actually too frightened to stand out themselves. Too scared in their boots to make the wrong moves, to have the willingness to take the fall-out if they screw up and then learn from their mistakes as a result.

Know that the problem never lies with you if you are true to the well-being of yourself and your team. Remember, leaders never follow the crowd and this can make you a target. Believe in yourself and understand that 'being is more than doing'. This means that (and don't overanalyse as this can take away your momentum) if you focus on yourself and become more self-aware of your very being, how you tick, how you act, how you think, and are more mindful of your actions, this will give you enormous freedom and self-confidence in your actions when you do lead.

And don't just sit there and 'try' to be the best leader that you can be, as 'try' never works... never. Commit to it, commit with your every will, and then through intention and through action it will come about naturally.

'In dreams begin responsibilities.'

William Butler Yeats

TO LEAD OTHERS – IT ALL STARTS WITH YOU!

In leading a team, we also need to inspire, to uplift, to mother and father (within reason), to console, to mentor, to coach, to direct and to energise. But first of all, it all comes back to ourselves. Little old me.

For us to influence and set the direction for others in our team, we must first of all do these things for us as individuals; and a lot of that can come down to the need for us to remain our own best friend. You simply can't afford to lead others if you are experiencing inner conflict. So, first things first, we must manoeuvre ourselves on track.

Can you imagine working for a boss that was contrary or kept changing their minds every five minutes over something. How would that make you feel? What impressions would you be left with? No, that approach simply won't do. Therefore, we need the stability in ourselves in the first place. And a lot of this comes down to doing the work to appreciate and fully understand the end goal that you are want to achieve, and at some level, having the self-belief that you (with the support of the team) can handle it. Since if we don't believe that the end goal can be met, then how can we lift others to believe, and more important than that – trust in us.

Trust is the glue that has the capability to unite a team and to hold a team together. Needless to say, if you lose the trust of the team then you will lose your ability to lead the team – fact!

There again, sometimes the end goal isn't crystal clear. We may know what we are trying to achieve at some high level, we understand the mission in hand, but all that we have been provided with is some sketchy high-level plan or instruction that everyone knows will change and become more detailed along the way. And in these circumstances, we need to be honest with our people. After all we have to respect our team for the human beings they are, with all their different capabilities, I agree, but all are responsible people who want to do their upmost to support you. And unless you know to the contrary, as a leader, give your team members the credit they deserve. This will build in trust in everyone involved.

In these situations when the end goal isn't clear, you have the responsibility to ensure that as a team you look for the missing details together – share the responsibility – and always look to discover the answers in a positive light, and as a unit. Yes, occasionally with humour – in order to retain some of your own sanity – but always with a view of striving to achieve and make headway in what sometimes can be a difficult position.

Needless to say, the more risk that we have to undertake in our projects, the more important the mission we aim to achieve, then the more science we need to put behind it. When there is more risk at play, you must ensure that you analyse, deliberate, discuss, bounce ideas off others in order to collect all the facts that you can. But in either situation when you have made it your responsibility to fully appreciate the mission in hand, the risks involved, and committed yourself – and have the team do the same – then at least have them take a degree of team-ownership of the mission, and you can begin to start the journey together. And this joint team effort is paramount.

In order to inspire the team, we need to use a visionary style of leadership (more on this later). We need to share the dream and create the inspiration in order to influence the team to achieve. And to do this you have to appeal to their hearts and minds. You need to get underneath their skin and one way to do this is to set the vision.

One fulfilling aspect of leadership is to inspire and to move people enough to believe what's behind the goal to be achieved. An inspirational leader will move their team emotionally to become excited about what needs to be accomplished over and above the seemingly senseless drudgery of everyday work.

So, although it does start with you, you now have yourself and the team engaged and can create a belief in yourselves. Take ownership and together start to act as a unit attempting to solve your problems, as they spring in your direction, collectively. But with you at the helm. When a team harnesses the intrinsic motivation behind the mission then they will run under their own influence for some time. And this is also true for the leader that sets the vision – create your own intrinsic motivation behind the goal, that self-desire, that self-interest and when you talk, inspire and involve your team, and together you will create something magical.

'Coming together is a beginning.
Keeping together is progress.
Working together is success.'

Henry Ford

AS A LEADER CONNECT WITH YOUR TEAM

A story that I touched upon in the chapter on Decision-making, was back in 2006 when I had the absolute privilege to head up a team on a major National IT and business change programme. The team size grew over time, but initially we were a relatively small team of four. The project was set up to replace a brand-new health-care system in several large hospital sites, and like virtually every project it had its fair share of complications and difficulties. My team's role was to support the confirmation that the new system was 'fit for purpose' in situ, as this new technology was to replace live working business practices. And like our customer, we faced a whole host of challenges along the way.

Although I was assigned the title of manager – and yes, the responsibility of that position was hugely apparent throughout my time on the project – at this point in the story I was mainly applying leadership principles. We were still in the early days of 'bedding in' as a team. In the stage of 'norming' in terms of team development: appreciating how to use tools and working practices. We were still getting to know each other's strengths and weaknesses and impor-tantly bonding as a unit.

I had managed to introduce some good leadership practices but nothing was to prepare me for a conversation that I had one evening with Robert, one of my stronger team members. We both walked out of the office to go home but instead began to reflect back on what the team had achieved, and I was also trying to set the vision for the next few months ahead. I think at the time this was as much for my benefit as his. Since we were only a few short months into a long project, I needed to hear and remind myself of the plan that we were forming.

Then Robert turned and said something I had never heard before: 'You do realise that this team will do anything for you, you know!' 'What do you mean by that?' I asked. 'The team, they will do anything for you, as they really believe in you,' he responded. Well, I was gobsmacked by the comment, to say the least. I'd never heard anyone say anything like that to me before. I'd been leading teams in one guise or another for around ten years by this point and had been a member of several teams in the past, but I'd never heard this said about anyone.

Was he crazy, mad?

Nonetheless, he was one of my stronger team members and he didn't appear to be running a fever at the time, so I suppose I had to respect his thoughts. I did feel humbled by the comment, but also hugely grateful and I thought of nothing else on my journey home.

If you have ever had such a kind comment, it can take you off-guard to such an extent that you may start to become more self-conscious, but this will pass. Allow the gratitude to sink in, but most of all – try to prevent it from feeding your ego.

Now, I must admit, from that point forward it did made me a far more self-aware leader, as to be completely honest I didn't know how I managed to arrive at this point. And for the next few days while at work I probably felt a little too self-aware, too conscious of my techniques, to relax. But after I managed to work back into my natural rhythm, I made it a commitment to learn how a leader could move a team to a position to think such a thing.

Over the years I have had the great fortune to work under or associate with a small handful of brilliant leaders. Who I would have followed to the end of the earth. But why? And it's not just me, this is what team members will do, if you gift them with great leadership. Well, after doing some research, self-reflection and watching other good leaders, the following are aspects that need to be addressed in order to help a team to gel with you as their leader. I could call them steps, but in reality, it never works that way because life and the way a team forms – while working the mission in hand – is so dynamic that steps in a particular order simply don't do it justice. So, I will call these elements. However, to contradict myself a little, number one is definitely the first aspect to work on.

1. Build the Relationship

Whether you are leading a new team or your existing team has been joined by a new member, the first thing you need to concentrate on is building the relationship – but keep it healthy, i.e. don't get too close. You will want to create a rapport with the team in order to build in trust. Essentially, for a team to want to listen and really pay attention to what you need to say, and importantly act upon it with sincerity, trust must underline everything. It is fair to say that in the early days there will be no real depth of relationship formed, and the only thing you can do about this is to start to work on it.

Surprising to some that lead, your team will follow not because they have to – but because they want to. *Create the want in them* and you will begin to see good behavioural changes. And rightly so, relationships with some team members will take a little longer to bond than others, but keep the faith in the process and these slower burners are sure to come around.

On this project, I built the relationship in a variety of ways. One was through social meetings; we ensured that we had the occasional self-funded meal out together, with good open and fun conversation. Another way was to pay an interest in the team members' personal circumstances. For example, one team member rented a local property and spent time away from his family whilst on the project during weekdays. Here I paid a genuine interest in his situation, and also would make sure that on a Friday, he got away as early as he could so he could get back home to his family over the weekend.

I typically kick-started off the working relationship through one-to-one sessions with new team members, through discussion on a variety of different subjects – and not just work related. Also, if you take a genuine interest in them, this will help pay dividends for the future, as the working relationship goes both ways.

As leaders we need to take the opportunity to get to know our team and treat our team members as genuine people, not just a resource headcount, to achieve what we want and when we want it done. After all there will be times when you will completely depend upon these people, where their input will be vital to your success. We also need to ensure that we self-manage our behaviours and frequently reflect on how we come across.

I'm sure you do treat your teams like genuine people already, but we all need to remember that 'what goes around comes around', as they say, and even working life can be full of twists and turns. Meaning, there is always the possibility that one day one of your team members could potentially become your boss and will be passing out the work in your direction. It happens, believe me. Maybe not for the organisation you are in today, but some other association in the future. Even if they don't become your boss, they may become your friend, your long-term career companion or whatever, and needless to say – they have families also! It's not just you.

During the time you start to build the relationship with the team (and needless to say it's a relationship that must be maintained over the course of the project) there will be tasks to perform, and essentially you need to have the team on board in order for things to work. This will be a cyclical process: building then maintaining the relationship, performing team assignments on a continuous process. Being hard on yourself and the team in order to attempt to make things as slick as possible in the first few weeks (even months) after a team has formed, or after newer members have recently joined, simply will not help.

Relationships take a while to form. And I understand that in being a self-leader and trying to make things work, you will have ideals and either mental or written goals to work towards. But when teams are still 'forming', as leaders we need to be easier on ourselves and the team, as there are a whole host of team and individual dynamics at play. Therefore, things are not likely to be slick at first, so manage the situation and self-manage your behaviour by remaining flexible and tolerant with regards to team contribution in the early days. Simply put, a new team that is taking shape, or a new team member that has joined an existing team, will take a while to settle. Give out the right messages, relax a little, and allow the team to form.

2. Ensure a Positive Transference of Leadership

To build on the relationship aspect, but a topic that anyway deserves to be discussed, is the subject of transference of leadership. For leaders to lead others they need to have the ability to attract followers. This may sound obvious, but it's actually not that simple. Regrettably, as times are changing, it is getting harder to get people to follow. The changing structures of families are no longer working in the leaders' favour; more single-parent homes and dual-working-parent families have begun to create work environments in which people value traditional leaders less.

How so? Well, Sigmund Freud, the founder of psychoanalysis, found that his patients kept falling in love with him, regardless of their sex. He concluded they were projecting (or transferring) experiences and emotions from past relationships on to present ones. And that transference can occur immaterial of the sex of your team member or of you as their leader.

So how would transference work in our environment and how can it go wrong? Well, an example could be a team member, who as a young boy always sought praise and comforting appreciation from his father, which as a result made him feel good and secure. There is nothing wrong with that. But he may look for the same kind of praise and appreciation from his leader by transferring the emotions he felt from his past relationship with his father on to his leader. If they have that praise and appreciation, then the team member will feel good and the relationship will blossom. However, if he doesn't, then things can go horribly wrong and the team member may suffer from an emotional outburst, creating a rift or worse still a complete breakdown in the relationship.

Behind every leader-follower relationship there are rational and irrational motivations. The rational motivations we see day-to-day in our teams will be the standard ones, including money, power, status or job promotion. The irrational motivations arise from images and emotions from our unconscious – that we project on to our current relationships. For example, the relationship that a team member has with their boss. The experiences that we encounter with our past relationships can influence our present ones.

In summary, because our families shape our behaviours and influence our motivations, they play a considerable role in shaping our current relationships and what we look for in them. So, although I'm not necessarily promoting transference, as this will happen naturally, I need to highlight that you ought to be aware of its existence and to work to ensure that it remains healthy and kept to a minimum.

However, let's not misunderstand something here – followers look for leadership! Followers are as powerfully driven to follow as leaders are to lead. And when they don't find it, this can be incredibly upsetting and frustrating for them. I've personally seen outbursts, on the brink of fights in the workplace, that are purely down to the lack of leadership, i.e. team members yearning to be strongly led but instead left with no clear direction, which they both want and believe is needed!

These instances are likely to be a breakdown of transference, as the team member can't find what they are looking for in their leader. Hence you need to be critically aware and mindful of this component of our psychology and be prepared to create a healthy transference between you and your team.

At its best transference can serve as/be harnessed as the emotional glue that binds team members to their leader. People in the grip of a positive transference will see their leader as better, smarter and more charismatic than they really are. They are also likely to take greater risks on the basis that the leader is happy they take them. So, unless the leader has a strong grounding in reality, and creates absolute transparency between both parties, the leader can easily become undone by their team members' positive transferential projections.

As a self-leader both self-awareness and self-management are key here: in other words, being deeply aware of your position as leader, and of your own faults and limitations, and being mindful of these when dealing with your team members. Don't let the relationship between you and your team member make you or them believe you are something you are not, or can achieve something that you can't; that is, keep to the facts!

And be aware of countertransference, which is your own transference projecting on to your team member. That is, you are transferring your own relationship issues on to your team member. Rather – be relatable – and keep to the facts of your specific relationship with your team member. This way, you can keep it real.

The more people know one another and the rules of the game, the harder it is to project, and the more unreal the projections will be. Therefore, work to keep the relationship grounded. One way to do this and to prevent the relationship getting in the way is to reward team members based on performance and not the relationship, and make sure they all know this. This way you can build a healthy working relationship and keep transference to a minimum, but any transferential projections that may remain should only be positive[50].

3. Hold Their Attention and Create Desire

No team will be more on board with a mission if you climb inside their hearts and minds. Once you have achieved this, to a degree the task of completion becomes a foregone conclusion. Even if the target changes, even when the curveballs come in – and they will – if you can manage to lift their hearts and inspire their minds you will feel as if you can class the job as done. You can't of course – but that's how it will feel – as you will adopt the impression that the energy will carry them to the finish line, whenever that may be. And to an extent that will be true, as when the hardship kicks in and motivation is impacted, if you can create the initial energy and momentum, it will be such an important step in the team's future to successful achievement.

I managed to achieve this by involving the team in key decisions, and providing them with suitable responsibility for tasks. As well as standard weekly meetings I always loved to hold ad hoc meetings to discuss topical subjects, or when there was an important or sudden need for a decision – or even a policy – that needed to be made where I felt their input would be valuable.

Here, I would get the team to put their ideas and views into the mix, and used what valuable input I could. I would often get them to take the lead on topics, where I believed they were capable. These meetings ensured that their views were employed, and it also boosted their morale and their inner drive to make things work. After all, if we were using their input they would see their contributions being employed.

In the achievement of any goal as a team, we must act as a team, and this means to share the idea of how we will achieve the task together. This will not be possible when using the wrong style of leadership, like the commanding style (more on this later), as we need to explore the goal on the basis that as a team we need to work on the task together. Even if this is just at the planning stage of the process.

Therefore, in order to inspire them, we must have the team involved in shaping the idea. Through conversation, through dialogue, and physical drawings in whiteboarding sessions, which are great for grey-area problems. Get individuals engaged and have them see the end result, how will it look, what will it feel like? The more they can talk about and embody the end result, the greater your chance of team success. If you don't involve the team you *will lose their interest* – it's a fact. And it is your responsibility as the leader to have the team work at this aspect of task-shaping.

You can appreciate that there will be some members who don't contribute a vast amount at group sessions such as these, but encouragement will help. Taking the lead at these sessions will allow you to act as coordinator, which helps in your position as leader, but importantly also allows you to stand back and help people come forward with ideas and contributions. This will help them feel involved and valued, which is an important need of theirs, and as the leader you need to welcome this. People will act upon what they think and feel at any time, therefore be aware of this fact for the duration of the team's life together.

Be mindful in these situations not to dominate these types of discussions. The primary objective is to achieve the best outcome for the team and not for you, so tricks such as handing the pen to another and taking a seat or when they are speaking and making their attempt to contribute, actively listen and act upon what they say – as opposed to controlling the conversation with what you think will help.

Actively encourage the whole team to contribute from their position and their perspective. There may be some who are not as experienced as you or other team members, but this is all part of their learning experience, and as a leader you need to appreciate this and incite personal growth in them. So, allow them to make mistakes in the planning stages, but at the same time you may be surprised at what great insights you hear. Nonetheless, you must take responsibility for drawing a conclusion on what you have discussed or heard and go with this as the way forward to the next step.

Your intention is to progress the project, and encourage creativity and your team's active involvement in order for them to be right behind the mission in hand. Your overall goal here is to encourage your members on board, to make their time productive, to unite them with the assignment in hand, thus helping to take care of the overall mission.

4. Give Them Responsibility

For some leaders, the hardest act of all can be to give away responsibility: to delegate. However, this is a must in order to flow work through others. It can be hard for several reasons, but more than likely it will all boil down to only two:

- You may feel that the job will be better achieved if you do it.
- Or, your team member may do the job better than you.

Both may be correct, of course, and each assignment given to a team member is given on its own merit. The trick is to give responsibility away responsibly. And this means making reasonable and responsible steps to ensure that you have assigned the task correctly and made every attempt to ensure that each of them has understood the task and its objective.

On one piece of work, initially we had a relatively small team, and I had to judge where I believed a team member would contribute or thrive on a specific task. This was based on how I saw them contribute or how they'd performed on particular tasks previously.

But on other occasions – I had no darn choice – and due to the limited team size, someone simply had to pick up the work. Sometimes it would either take them right out of their comfort zone, and potentially it would be all too much. But if this happened, by keeping a close eye on their progress I would step in and support. And where necessary, I would roll my sleeves up and get involved. Here, I'd hold short one-to-ones, and used open and transparent techniques ('transformational conversation', which is covered a little later) to establish how things were coming along. This way, I could keep a close eye on progress, and also – equally as important – let them know that I cared.

To agonise over giving away responsibility can feel like a tough one, more especially to someone that is being overcautious and is more averse to risk. Here, it's wise to break the task down into manageable chunks and to make the effort to hand out the assignment with reasonable care. This will help those that feel the wish to maintain control and do the assignment themselves, or fret over the possibility that it won't be carried out properly unless they take over. Just doing this can be a sticking point for some leaders, and if you are one of those that find it hard to assign tasks, it is something that needs to work to get over. I'm afraid there is no other option here.

So, going back to the idea of giving responsibility away responsibly, this should help solve this challenge of delegating tasks, if you find it difficult. You need to also accept that for practical reasons, if you take too much on because you feel you need to maintain a degree of control, it can damage your health.

It's natural to share tasks and others must make mistakes. I realise that sometimes this can be a little annoying when you have put so much into making something work, but even after you chunk the task down and reduce the risk in something going wrong, there is still the chance that your team member will still screw up.

And so, there is only one way to solve this issue – do what you reasonably can but allow the team member to take the responsibility and allow yourself the freedom to give the task away. And then move back to your own work and try not to screw that up.

You can always check in to see how things are going and provide mentoring if you don't feel the task is being completed to your reasonable satisfaction. Good self-management to control that influencing nature comes in here, and there is a need for you to note that nothing is worse than being on the receiving end of a leader who comes across as picky and interfering.

To be on the receiving end of micromanagement typically demoralises a worker – and reduces the opportunity for creativity. Only employ it if you really have to, and then only in short bursts, otherwise you are likely to lose them. Whilst they may not physically walk out the door – they will end up demoralised!

If, on the other hand, support and genuine help is needed – then step in. Otherwise allow the team member the independence to get on with the task and grow in confidence and ability as a result. And that as a leader is part of your job anyway – to grow them.

You may find that your team member does a great job, even better than you would, in which case, regardless of how you may feel about it, this is a great result. You are there to lead and that is an immensely responsible task in itself; the fact that someone may outshine you with a particular task that you have assigned them will only reflect well on you both. On them more than you, but that's life as a leader, get used to it. In this instance you ought to feel both proud and satisfied. To have a team member that is creative and diligent is a successful result and is to be congratulated.

Leadership is not about you!

One hugely important rule about leadership is to realise that 'it's not all about you', it's about your team. And from a practical perspective this is a much better place to be in as opposed to having to find someone else to take the task over from the team member concerned. So, praise their successful achievement of any assignments. And although not everything can be celebrated, nonetheless it is your responsibility to acknowledge success in some way. Even a simple 'well done' can make all the difference!

One thing we must bear in mind is that although you can have several people in the same room with similar experiences in life, they will all interpret information differently. This will be based upon a whole variety of factors that will influence their assessment – education, expertise, past experience, their personal situation and even their state of mind are just some examples. Therefore, as leaders of others we need to be mindful of this fact, and although we can take no responsibility over our team members' individual situations, we can take responsibility for how to communicate a task in a way that others understand and can work with.

I once heard a project manager attempting to explain his points and deliver a task to Andrew, a colleague, who had taken a few weeks out due to an illness. As the discussion ensued you could tell from the language that was being used that Andrew, who was on the receiving end of the conversation, was not happy with the task, probably due to the time out of the office. However, the project manager continued to talk to him in what I can only describe as 'standard project management task delivery': sounding short of time and to the point.

Anyway, I went off for a short meeting and came back some thirty minutes later only to find the project manager still talking to Andrew. But by this time, you could tell from his body language that Andrew was so laid back that something fundamentally must have changed within him. But, on listening to the sound of the project manager' voice I realised the reason why. He had completely changed his tone and body language and was taking a far more understating position, but more importantly he had also sold him on the task. Andrew by this point was completely up for the job, and as far as I'm aware did a fantastic number, which that project manager praised immensely.

This is a prime example of someone giving away responsibility in a responsible fashion, covered earlier. He gauged the mood, then that of his team member, then adapted his approach accordingly and created a win-win situation.

5. Maintain Good Communication

Good communication can make or break relationships, literally! We all have off days or off moments, and the wrong words come out due to an emotional surge, or more simply, you 'put your foot in your mouth', so to speak, and say something a little embarrassing. These mistakes, however, do not let us off the hook with the fact that we need to ensure that communication is one of our top priorities when leading others; and to continue to work on this.

Through good communication we build trust and rapport with others and this understating is paramount, not just for good leadership, but for great leadership. In Dale Carnegie's book, *How to Win Friends and Influence People*, (Vermillion, 2006) he points out that people are far more interested in talking about themselves than listening to you. And this is a fundamental mistake that some make, i.e. they think that if they talk about themselves all day long they are building a relationship with the other person. Wrong, I'm afraid. And if this is the way you played out your last conversation – then you need to stop and change your approach.

While this message holds true in helping you to achieve a bond with someone else – asking them good questions about themselves, their family or their circumstances, etc. – we must go much further with communication as a leader. If we lose communication with our team we lose our connection with our team, and if we lose our connection with the team – we've lost the team. Fact!

Good communication can be classed as an art, but a lot of leaders forget its importance and that different methods do achieve remarkably different results. These days, we have electronic communication at our easy disposal and here we have a relatively convenient and powerful set of tools, such as email or recorded video, to get the message across to the masses or to different parts of the globe with incredible speed.

In the workplace these do help in relaying messages across organisations quickly, and for mass communication it serves its purpose. But these methods have one important shortfall: they don't allow for proper dialogue and also the message being received can be misinterpreted. And even when we do use electronic communication such as video or phone conferencing that allows dialogue, it can take away the intimacy to convey the right messages or to fully appreciate the message being received, especially in a group setting.

There is nothing more frustrating than when you are trying to convey an important message or creative intent, and are confined to a video conference – when you know that if you were face to face the whole thing would be far easier and more transparent.

In order to exchange the right messages with a purpose of building trust we need conversation. Good open conversation. And ideally this is face to face, as only 7 per cent of our communication is through words and 38 per cent is through our voice (including tone and inflection). The remaining 55 per cent is non-verbal, through our body language. Nonetheless, good high-level dialogue can actually change the way the brain operates – and the way someone thinks.

Anyone that has attended a good counselling or coaching session will tell you that they can walk away from these sorts of conversations and can literally transform the way they see the world! Their mood has been boosted, and the mental knots that may have tangled their thinking previously have amazingly become undone.

Our inner conversations

Now, I appreciate that we are not all trained counsellors or coaches, but as a responsible self-leader recognising the importance of good conversation is a must. Even when it comes to self-talk and our inner conversations, we feed our own minds every day. It can be easy for us to slip more negative statements into self-talk or mental chatter and fill our minds with the reasons why we can't do something, or why we will never achieve this or that.

Rather, use self-talk to your advantage. If you catch yourself doing it – stop! Take control over it. Then ensure that you remain acutely observant of your self-awareness, as negative self-talk can dampen your moods. Work to replace these more negative comments with more positive ones until you create the habit of filling your mind with good positive statements.

If you are too emotionally clouded, then distract yourself somehow. Play a sport, go for a run or even clean your apartment or house – as a start. Anything really. Physical activity is a wonderful distractor when you feel you can't escape the internal chatter. Just, get away from the negative talk you fill your head with. Begin to think positive, and then *feel positive*!

Conversational intelligence

Beyond our own self-talk are the conversations we have with our team members. One basic fundamental mistake I have seen leaders make is to forget that conversation is two-way. This may strike you as an obvious statement, but I've seen this mistake being made time and time again: the leader simply does not listen.

He or she talks, but they simply – don't listen. Also, when they don't understand, they don't enquire.

This 'my way or the highway' attitude, where the leader won't digest and respond to what is being said, will only lead to mistrust and a mental gap being built between you as the leader and your team members. And there really is no need to go there.

To grow the conversation, we need to employ good conversational intelligence; this can really grow and nurture the relationships of whole teams and even companies. This is where we step up our conversations as leaders to such a level whereby asking searching questions makes a real impact on your team members by getting them to think and also have you exploring the situation at hand. And where we also create a shared vision of success.

This shared vision is not done with predictive presumption at the result we wish to see or perceive to be the answer. But for something much more dynamic that we need, and what Judith E. Glaser calls in her book *Conversational Intelligence: How great leaders build trust and get extraordinary results* (Bibliomotion, Inc., 2004) essentially using share and discover type exchanges. Here she introduces the concept of game-changing conversations that move people in a whole new way, thus allowing you and your team to co-create together and benefit massively. In her book she describes three different levels of conversation:

Level 1 – Transactional

Conversations often categorised as 'Tell and Ask', where people are just exchanging information, updates and facts.

Level 2 – Positional

These conversations are categorised by 'Advocate and Inquire', i.e. I am advocating for what I want (not just telling you) and I am enquiring about your beliefs so I can influence you with my view.

Level 3 – Transformational

Transformational conversations are marked by 'Share and Discover' interaction dynamics. When I share first, my brain receives a cue that I will be vulnerable with you and that I will open up my inner thoughts, ideas and feelings[51]. With this type of conversation we co-create in this way and find that together we achieve a richer shared success. Typically, these powerful exchanges will far outweigh any preconceived notions. Therefore, these share and discover exchanges ought to be explored and practised to bring about the best in you and your team.

Let transformational conversations flow

This co-creating cannot be achieved with a pre-planned agenda on how things will play out, or worse still trying to manipulate the conversation to what you want to hear. It's through a degree of managed exploration that we really find out the issues or the true status of any situation. Even in whiteboarding sessions where we are brainstorming for improvements to a position we are in, what we ought to be doing is really trying to understand the 'true' status without anyone feeling the need to go into a protective or defensive mode in order for them to preserve their position, whatever that may be.

By genuinely working together, by being transparent and honest, we build the rapport and trust with our team members that is so healthy in the longer run for all parties involved. This is a terribly important approach to help to forge relationships during and beyond the difficult situations that can arise in the workplace, in our everyday relationships and well beyond.

*'The single biggest problem in communication
is the illusion that it has taken place.'*

George Bernard Shaw

CULTURE, LEADERSHIP STYLE AND THE SITUATION

When leading others, we must adapt to what is transpiring around us. Just as we adapt to the varying situations that happen throughout the day, and as a result behave in different ways with different people, leadership of others is the same. There are various styles of leadership that are taught and can be found in books today. Personally, I warm to the emotional leadership styles that are addressed by Goleman, Boyatzis and McKee in the book *Primal Leadership* – learning to lead with emotional intelligence. (Harvard Business Review Press, 2004)

Here there are six styles introduced. Four of these styles are called: Visionary, Coaching, Affiliative and Democratic. These leadership styles create a resonance that boosts performance. The last two are: Pacesetting and Commanding. However, leadership styles should be applied with caution. These styles draw on aspects of emotional intelligence, discussed in chapter three, Emotional Mastery.

1. Visionary

The visionary leader articulates where a group is going, but not how it gets there – setting people free to innovate, experiment and take calculated risks. Inspirational leadership is the emotional intelligence competence that most strongly undergirds the visionary style. Transparency, another emotional intelligence competency, is also crucial. If a leader's vision is disingenuous, people sense it. The emotional intelligence competency that matters most to a visionary leader however, is empathy. The ability to sense what others feel and understand their perspectives helps a leader articulate a truly inspirational vision.

2. Coaching

The coaching style is really the art of the one-on-one. Coaches help people identify the team member's unique strengths and weaknesses, tying those to their personal and career aspirations. Effective coaching exemplifies the emotional intelligence competency of developing others, which lets a leader act as a counsellor.

3. Affiliative

The affiliative style of leadership represents the collaborative competency in action. An affiliative leader is most concerned with promoting harmony and fostering friendly interactions. When leaders are being affiliative, they focus on the emotional needs of workers, using empathy. Many leaders who use the affiliative approach combine it with the visionary approach. Visionary leaders state a mission, set standards, and let people know whether their work is furthering the group goals. Ally that with the caring approach of the affiliative leader and you have a potent combination.

4. Democratic

A democratic leader builds on a triad of emotional intelligence abilities: teamwork and collaboration, conflict management and influence. Democratic leaders are great listeners and true collaborators. They know how to quell conflict and create harmony in teams and with individuals. Empathy also plays a role and a democratic approach works best as a leader when you are unsure what direction to take and need ideas from able employees.

5. Pacesetting

Pacesetting as a leadership style must be applied sparingly, restricted to settings where it truly works. Common wisdom holds that pacesetting is admirable. The leader holds and exemplifies high standards for performance. They are obsessive about doing things better and faster, quickly pinpointing poor performers.

Unfortunately, applied excessively, pacesetting can backfire and lead to low morale as workers think they are being pushed too hard or that the leader doesn't trust them to get their job done. The emotional intelligence foundation of a pacesetter is the drive to achieve through improved performance and the initiative to seize opportunities. But a pacesetter who lacks empathy can easily be blinded to the pain of those who achieve what the leader demands.

Pacesetting works best when combined with the passion of the visionary style and the team building of the affiliate style.

6. Commanding

The command leader demands immediate compliance with orders but doesn't bother to explain the reasons. If subordinates fail to follow orders, these leaders resort to threats. They also seek tight control and monitoring. An effective execution of the commanding style draws on three emotional intelligence competencies: influence, achievement and initiative. In addition, self-awareness, emotional self-control and empathy are crucial to keep the commanding style from going off track.

Of all the leadership styles, the commanding approach is the least effective. Consider what the style does to an organisation's climate. Given that emotional contagion spreads most readily from the top down, an intimidating, cold leader contaminates everyone's mood. Such a leader erodes people's spirits and the pride and satisfaction they take in their work. The commanding style works in limited circumstances, and only when used judiciously. [1]

For example, I have used the commanding style of leadership, and seen this style used, whilst serving in the armed forces in genuine emergency situations. When you have to ensure that personnel and equipment are in the right place at the right time, it's the only style that will help everyone through the crisis. Once the crisis is over, this style of leadership is no longer appropriate.

We all have a natural leadership style that feels right and we typically employ it when needed as we normally go into autopilot in situations we find ourselves in. Indeed, when I spent time working alongside the NHS in the UK, I found that the ex-frontline nursing staff seconded to our project used an 'affiliative' style of leadership, and they tended to always adopt this caring approach. Whereas I can't imagine you will see this style of leadership on the floor of the stockroom that often – if at all.

Therefore, the environment and culture that you work in, to an extent, will dictate the style of leadership you will be allowed to get away with. And with the expression 'you will be allowed to get away with', I mean that even though you can consciously choose to alter your style of leadership, the culture of the organisation, and even the country you are in, will all play a factor in to what degree people will accept a new leadership style.

For example, you could choose to employ a more pace-setting style. However, if you employ this new leadership style and deviate wildly from what people are used to, or if you mistake the genuine need for its appropriate use, your team members will mentally rebel and therefore this leadership style will backfire.

As an example, if a team are worn down and exhausted due to being overworked, they will be in survival mode. So primitive instincts will take over their thoughts and actions. They will hear but not listen and ultimately not follow through on any requests, or if they do, they will make a poor job of it at best. Therefore, if you paceset too much – your team will switch off! I've personally seen this happen and been subjected to it on several occasions. Being mindful and observant of the situation at hand and how the team or team member is coping with it plays a major role in the leadership style that you should apply.

Don't get yourself into the mindset that you or your situation is somehow different and the warning in the example above does not apply to you – as you will only be fooling yourself. After all, we are dealing with people, and when we are genuinely worn down our bodies and our minds are in need of rest and recuperation. And as a leader you have the responsibility to recognise this and manage yourself and your emotions first.

Adapt your behaviour and change your leadership style. Relax, and calm the tempo down to suit the new situation. If any leader flogs a team that is tired and in need of rest by a continued pace-setting style of leadership, and don't take any responsibility for the situation by employing some remedial action, then they should seriously consider their position as a leader. It's that simple.

This is coupled with the fact that a leadership style must feel natural to you, meaning that you can't readily employ something that feels new, strange or awkward to you. If so, there is a genuine possibility you will come across as clumsy and overly nervous, and that will unnerve your team members. This is not good for morale.

Rather, if you are looking to develop other leadership styles, it is useful to consciously choose to adapt your current style and try out other styles gradually, and in safe working situations. Then do this until you feel more confident with them. Ensure that if you do, however, you are working within the constraints of the culture you are in. For example, company, country, etc., and maintain a good awareness of both how you act and how others are responding to you.

Stay consciously aware of their responses to your altered behaviours, but don't overanalyse. If we overanalyse, we lose our ability to act quickly in situations. It's good to experiment with short episodes of a new leadership style until you feel more confident to employ a new style for longer periods in a more dynamic setting, in the heat of everyday working life. But most importantly don't hold back from experimenting with new styles. To be a great leader you really need an arsenal of different styles at the ready for the different situations that arise within your day. Believe you me, they will be needed.

So, if we draw all these elements together, we need to be able to take account of a triad of elements:

- The culture you are leading in.
- The leadership styles that you feel more confident with.
- The situation you find yourself in.

But most importantly I need to stress something that I noted in the last paragraph: we do need to call on different leadership styles, as the one thing that never stays the same is the situation at hand.

We live in a dynamic world and our organisations and our teams face new situations every day, and to adopt one leadership approach all of the time – simply never works! We need to remain dynamic also. By switching leadership when necessary, and mixing this with leading from the front, middle and from behind where necessary, will give you maximum flexibility to move your team in different situations well.

'Leaders must be close enough to relate to others,
but far enough ahead to motivate them.'

John C. Maxwell

DON'T MAKE THE MISTAKE OF HOLLOW LEADERSHIP

I once did some work for a client on a project for a large corporate IT solutions company, and at the same time I was chosen to play a role for a bid team for another area of the organisation on a project to support the UK police force. I've been involved with several bids over the years in one guise or another, and for those of you that have never been involved in one, it can be a frantic few weeks, months or even years of pulling the pieces together to attempt to successfully win a new contract. It's vital of course for organisations to win at least some bids, in order to survive. Even so, sometimes they spread themselves too thinly, to a tipping point, to win them all.

Well, several others and I attended a kick-off meeting for this new bid, which consisted of us remaining seated through a presentation of a set of slides, which lasted approximately two hours. Now, most of us in the room were already working flat-out full-time on other project work, but we were requested to attend. And so the timing of this bid wasn't perfect by any stretch. And even though the intention was that we would swap across to the bid team full-time, we were all feeling a little overwhelmed by the prospect of this fairly aggressive-looking piece of work.

Still, irrespective of any demands we had on our plates – for the many reasons explained to us – we were still depended upon to put a strong proposal together. Therefore, they required everyone in that room to put in some considerable effort to make this 'must-win' piece of work take off. Okay, so if this was the case, where was the inspiration? Where was the fuel to motivate us, to get our juices flowing?

I sat and watched, and waited.

Towards the end of the meeting, there was some shuffling around of paper and slides and then someone left the room to bring in a more senior figure. He was there to give us the motivational talk, to inspire us in order to kick off this aggressive bid with a bang! To dig deep down and into our hearts and stimulate those motivational juices inside.

Well, his talk lasted around five minutes and it couldn't have inspired anything or anyone. With one hand on the door handle most of the time during his talk, he looked as if he had just popped in on his way to the kitchen to make a coffee for a quick chat. But, hold on, this project was important! A must-win! This was going to be an aggressive bid and we were up against several other strong competitors to win this work. Surely, we needed the visionary talk! Surely, we needed to have our hearts lifted and our minds inspired. Surely?

We needed to get emotionally engaged deep into the heart of our mission. After all, there were some key people in the room. And this was our big chance!

But frankly his talk was weak and rather lacklustre. His words were bland and dull, and I was convinced his head was already in another room on his next important thing. His address didn't reach anyone's ankles never mind our hearts and minds. So, I will always remember that talk for a classic case of – what not to do – to inspire a team to reach their goal!

As a consequence, I could feel the cold air of disappointment in the room. He made one fundamental mistake that a leader can make with this kind of talk. His biggest failure…. In fact, the major thing he couldn't be bothered to do…. *He hadn't even taken the time to inspire himself.*

Please, never fall into the trap as a leader to think that you can simply turn the handle to inspire your team. This never, ever works. You must at all times believe in the mission first; if you don't your team will work this out. In fact, they will smell it – a ruddy mile away.

CHANGE, OBSTACLES, CURVEBALLS AND US

One of the biggest and most challenging differences you will face as the leader of others, as opposed to being a self-leading team member, is that it's your responsibility to move obstacles out of the way of individuals on your team, and to get them back on track and reset the direction as quickly as possible. No one likes abrupt change, but change, obstacles or those unforeseen curveballs, especially in the workplace, are bound to happen at some point. The biggest challenge for you will be – with an almost certain promise – that the timing will be far from convenient. This is Sod's Law at work, and you won't be the first to think this and not the last either.

However, you need take immediate action to remove the problem from your team; it is your responsibility after all, and as leaders we must accept these inconveniences and annoyances with as least resistance as possible. I firmly believe, having been subjected to many curveballs during my life and my career that were out of my control, quick acceptance of the change is key! The alternative only prolongs the agony and prevents problem-solving of the issue at hand.

Breakdown the barriers

Today the world can be a complex place and some of us work in incredibly challenging environments. Although as a leader we need a clear view of what our team are up to on their tasks, some leaders in today's complex business environments will lack the understanding of their team member's individual assignments. Nonetheless, in order to help get your team members quickly back on track as a result of a derailment, you need to be able to appreciate their individual assignments and the issues they are suffering from due to the problem they now face.

One great way to do this is to create a mental model of the landscape that each member of your team is working on. This is best done in advance of any issues that may arise, as when problems throw themselves to the fore, you should automatically switch to solution mode. However, for you to create the best mental model of what your team are doing, you need to be in assessment mode, where there is the time available to make an intelligent and appreciative assessment of their work.

The creation of this mental model is not about planning, but it's closely related, and is best developed through one-to-one transformational conversation. Maybe whiteboarding your team members' tasks or spending time with them at their desks discussing their work. Whatever it takes to create an appreciation of their particular task at the highest level possible for you to form a mental picture of their work in hand.

One point to note is that this shouldn't be done from the perspective of 'I don't know what you are doing, so please describe this to me', but rather, 'as a leader in order for us to succeed together, I need the best understanding of your assignments as possible'. You don't need to say this, of course – but think it and act on this intention.

When this is carried out for your direct reports, you both will gain a better understanding of their tasks, and potentially their obstacles and dependencies. And after having spent enough time with each individual member you will gain a good insight into what they are doing, with a view of trying to see their challenges from their perspective – and not yours. From my experience in doing this, you may be surprised at the outcome you receive.

A new world will open up in front of your eyes. And you are likely to see and potentially solve issues for them on the spot. As a result, your relationship will only grow stronger through an increased level of trust.

But one thing is for certain, as a leader you will be in a stronger position for having completed a mental-modelling task such as this. This last point is critically important, as some leaders can make the mistake of being dogmatic and can fall foul of shortsighted thinking, i.e. they don't think of the end goal enough and they certainly don't have a mental picture of the team's assignments. However, an assessment done well, and with every team member using good transformational conversation, will help you create that 3-D unbiased view of the landscape that your team are working in. Doing this can only add to you and your team's success, whatever is thrown your way.

'The art of life is a constant readjustment to our surroundings.'

Kakuzo Okakura

NOW, OVER TO YOU

The art of leadership is an extension of leading yourself. And this means building and applying your self-leadership skills to yourself before you embark on leading others. Aspects such as self-discipline, relationship building and ethical decision-making are of crucial importance. And to ask these of yourself, before you can ask it of another, is the thing to do for the benefit of all.

When we lead, we lead by example. This ought to shine through from you at all times, and more so when things don't go to plan.

Therefore, will you ask anything of your team tomorrow, in a different way than you did before? Will you approach the delivery of tasks, maintain communication and continue to build the relationship, and create the desire in them to push on, more rationally?

Leading others is a gift. Not everyone will want to take on this task, but we all can learn to lead if we wish to. Leaders are made and not born, irrespective of what you may hear.

Take the time to sit back and consider your team members. What are the striking aspects of their personalities? What essential skills do they bring to the fore that help the team at large? What are their peculiarities? And what are the things they need to build on, where transformation conversations and boosting morale – through active engagement – will help to bring about incredible change in what they offer?

And also, how can you work with your team in a higher capacity than you have to date – to bring out the best in them? Maybe you don't know them well enough to answer these questions. If not, then there is no better time to start than now.

As leaders, we should always bear in mind that some will want to follow just as much as you want to lead. To aid this, inspire them, motivate them, get them to picture the mission as if it had already happened; and roll with the punches when they arrive.

Beware of hollow leadership, and never manage your team in the false belief that it will always be the answer to reaching the team's goal. While to manage is essential, to lead is to stimulate and to lift. To have your team seeing beyond the current horizon to the end objective, such that they will help you – and themselves – to create something marvellous. This is something that will help them grow and become something truly inspirational. It's now over you to go the extra mile and make your leadership count.

PERSONAL CONTRIBUTION
DEREK TAYLOR: IT MANAGER

A Reflective Look at Leadership and Self-leadership

I have spent forty-plus years in the IT industry as a software developer and tester, for businesses ranging from small (second-hand car dealer software) to larger and more complex systems (military command on control and air traffic control). For most of the last twenty-five years I have been in the more senior roles leading teams up to twenty people and at times had to coordinate bigger groups during activities that demanded it (resourcing operational tests in an air traffic control environment, for example).

I have been reflecting on a number of my latter roles looking after teams responsible for testing operational systems that are in service and the development of systems that are to replace existing operational systems.

Areas I consider important that are desirable in relation to self-leadership when leading others are:

- Communication
- Decision-making
- Active listening
- Bigger-picture thinking
- Making others succeed, but failing yourself
- Some general points...

Communication

Communication with a team takes many forms and is the key to everything you do and this should be combined with an honest and a happy approach. Speak to people and share information with the team verbally, electronically and physically.

When presenting information (plans, goals, process, etc.) in a meeting, engage the audience, share ownership and running of the meeting with others. This will ensure that everyone is engaged. Understand your different types of audience and reflect the level of communication to suit.

Decision-making

Believe in yourself, no really believe in yourself as there will be times that you will sometimes doubt yourself. The biggest differentiator is you and you had better believe it!

You need expertise, but will have to realise that you cannot know it all. Then, as a leader it is paramount to develop the decision-making skills to handle working in an environment where everyone knows more than you, but you are the one left to make that final decision. How do you acquire the decision-making skill? Well, personally, at meetings, I watch people all the time (tone of voice, facial expression, how polite and firm they are, etc.) and when I have been in interesting and difficult situations, noted on how the key points were handled and then reflected on them after the meeting.

So always be ready to make the decision because when you do, it will feel good to know that everyone will go away with a positive outcome (they may not agree, people appreciate a decision rather than no decision).

Finally, always support the team decisions. And if someone makes an error the leader has to share that responsibility and help direct the correction of that decision, and the items that are to be learned from the situation and actions to take forward.

Active listening

My experience in this area is that leaders and managers do not actively listen to people and often interrupt others. You have to realise that information or an answer you are after could be embedded in a short story with a long introduction!

A part of really listening that should be avoided is getting competitive – where people seem to match for match experiences that just sound like they are in competition with the person they are listening to. Learn to work in examples that are similar but are positive to the discussion.

So, listen, always listen. This is a buzz word/phrase, but do 'actively listen' to the person speaking to you.

Bigger-picture thinking

It is important and indeed essential to look at the bigger picture at work. This is a skill that can be used both at work and in your own personal life, so this should be a skill that is developed early on in your self-development. In today's service-oriented approach, you may think that this is outside of my area of knowledge, but the principle is still the same. If you do not understand what your end user wants and the ins and outs that support the wider picture then you may fail to understand someone's problem/need.

When people observe good examples of leadership they begin to use that person as an example in conversations. This builds up the confidence in that person and allows them, if they so wish, to use those work-developed skills outside of the workplace. This in turn will bring exposure to leadership in different personal situations that can help develop your overall leadership portfolio.

Making others succeed but failing yourself

I have always worked to help my team succeed and have discovered that I can successfully lead others and ensure the people they are leading reach their goals but cannot always address self-leadership in the same manner. So it is important to look at and develop your own self-leadership skills. Ensure you have clear goals and the ability to focus on your tasks.

One key aspect is not to allow yourself to fail by helping others succeed. This is a normal trap to get into, which means you have to realise that you have to say no at times in order to effectively deliver your own objectives. This means taking a step back, giving more control, and allowing others to develop and deliver under their own control with boundaries set by you.

Build up both your leadership and other skills. You may not be able to answer all the detailed questions, but a good understanding and the ability to direct others to a possible answer is key.

Some general points...

Leadership is not one model fits all and never changes. There are certain leadership skills and styles that are stock items and certain ones that will be added and used depending on the situations you encounter under your leadership.

The way to handle people is ever evolving as any company changes to adapt to a dynamic world, and mature company people (I do not necessarily mean older people) and working practices are slowly or rapidly consumed by new, repackaged and potential fast-change approaches.

Give praise and accept it positively. If you are given praise from the team, do not shrug it off and/or dismiss it. I find that when receiving praise it is a positive confirmation that I am achieving what I have set out to do as a leader, and as a leader it is your responsibility to give praise where it is due to others in the team. This helps to build confidence, and helps to connect you all.

Understand that as a leader you can join in but at times you are the one people will turn to and hence you will need to switch to a professional/good buddy approach to reflect the situation, from informal meetings to formal appraisals.

Remember, that one day a person that you had in your team may cross your path later in both of your careers and maybe equal or further up the ladder than you. So do not just see them as the young shy individual they might have been, because they could now be the CEO of a company you find yourself in. Actively acknowledge their career progression.

Chapter 7

Serving Others

'Never look down on anybody unless you're helping him up.'

Jesse Jackson

Up until now, in the other six chapters in this book, I have addressed some fundamental principles of self-leadership. These provide a mainstay for surviving and thriving out there in the real world, both at work and in life generally. Some of the critical aspects covered are: to know yourself through greater self-awareness; to take responsibility for your actions; to gain greater control over emotions, such that these aspects of your personality are serving you.

These steps all go towards greater self-leadership; there is no doubt! Though stating that, there is a final topic that creates a different kind of strength in us and which is an element essential for both our personal and our spiritual growth. And this last step is to provide a service to others. To take the gaze away from you and on to those around you, or those in need of support.

A simple example of this is to provide a little extra love for your family, friends and even work colleagues, through more compassion. If you genuinely express compassion, and by this I mean from the heart, you will be surprised at the difference to your self-esteem, and you as a person, as a result. A small effort towards serving another will reward you in ways you never thought possible.

And if you extend this act to make serving others your pursuit in life, you will become profoundly fulfilled.

To 'serve others' through acts of providing care, helpfulness, support, compassion or benevolence, when conducted through kindness, is virtuous. To carry out acts of altruism, whether simple things or not, do as much for the recipient as the giver; even if the giver feels no gratification whatsoever. But irrespective of this, if there is an element of enjoyment or not, when serving another is done with genuine thoughtfulness, it confirms what it is to be useful in life.

It's painful but correct to say that the world has enough takers. Those with empty promises, those that wish to line their own pockets, fill up their self-esteem tanks, to take and tread over those less fortunate than themselves. So for heaven's sake, don't count yourself as one of them! When you treat others with a servile mentality, you'll be surprised at how welcome you will be received. How you will brighten up the day of another, and fill yourself with gratification as you see how you have benefited them.

The power to serve another generates tremendous energy in life at large. The strength to serve manifests itself in a whole variety of ways and serving others is done by people in all walks of life and different circumstances. Some of us will grow up with a want to serve others, in that it will be our chosen career path. Others may stumble upon the need to help another through circumstance or a wish to choose to act with a more 'serving' mindset. In addition to this they may even belong to an organisation that embraces the concept of *Servant Leadership* in its leadership culture. This approach turns traditional leadership models on their head; whereby the primary goal of the leader is to serve whereby organisations can thrive as a result.

Nevertheless, it is one of the noblest actions anyone can undertake. Done with honesty and integrity, it provides you, the giver, with a wealth of benefits that we will explore. That may strike you as surprising if you haven't had the opportunity to serve consciously before.

From my own experience, the first time I was fully aware that I was witnessing an act of genuine heartfelt service was when my wife, Jane, was giving birth to our second child. You will remember the difficult story of our first born, Maria, back in chapter three. And in conversation, the midwife told me that midwifery was all she wanted to do as a career, she had yearned to do it from an early age.

We came to discuss this as Jane, who was deep in labour and had been for some considerable time, was currently asleep with exhaustion, and I had become fascinated at the care and attention the midwife was giving her. For it had been a genuinely tiresome day, whereby at one point, a whole medical team swarmed around my wife as they struggled to find our baby's heartbeat. This over-whelming event being a dramatic side effect of the fact that the medical team had induced the birth due to earlier complications.

Although the pandemonium had settled down at this point in the evening, Jane was still suffering somewhat. After having been given an epidural for the pain, which hadn't fully taken, it was now close to midnight, and it had been a painfully long and tiring day.

She now lay relatively still but was still in some pain, and slipped in an out of awareness; yet being attended to by the midwife. And as I sat on the broad windowsill of the labour room late into the evening, I simply watched as the midwife took care of her with the utmost warmth and kindness. It was if Jane was her closest sister. I was indeed taken aback by her compassion. In all, she tended to her for several hours, and as far as I can remember it was the first time I had witnessed another person with a real, deep need to care for another that they did not know. I was touched deeply as a result. And the experience has stayed with me ever since.

While I can't remember every little detail that happened that evening, what I do recall is that the experience somewhat humbled me. And that memory is just as vivid in my mind as the birth of my son, which happened in the early hours of that Monday morning.

The midwife even came in early for her next shift, later that day, especially to see Lewis; his eyes now full of bright wonder. The young baby that she had helped tirelessly into this world, only a few hours before, just looked content. I concluded, through my discussions with the midwife during the previous evening, and witnessing the kindness she displayed, she would probably have turned up for her shift unpaid. She knew Jane had had a really rough day, and I'm convinced that she wanted to see the birth through, and was doing everything she could to make sure things went smoothly.

Apart from the overriding joy of having a second child, this was my prevailing memory over the course of my wife's last few hours of labour. How could someone be so committed to supporting another? And to care for someone else with such thoughtfulness? To be so attentive. Yes, it was her job to provide midwifery, but this was a prime example of one human reaching out beyond themselves, and supporting another being through skill, diligence and love. Also, to take responsibility for two other people. And then work conscientiously and attentively, leading herself to a successful outcome on the back of what had been a somewhat eventful and challenging day for all.

INNER GROWTH AND SERVICE

The topic of self-leadership is mostly concentrated on the self, as the very nature of the title demonstrates. To practise the art of self-leadership, however, does mean you interact with others – it has to. And we do this every day. Although you can view self-leadership as a fairly self-centric subject.

In moving on to a topic that primarily addresses what we do for someone else, we need to be able to balance what relevance this has on our leadership. The leadership of me.

Here we need to address the subject that encompasses our need to connect with others and to contribute beyond ourselves – taking the focus off us, for a period, and on to someone else, or a group of people. When you get down to the utter foundation of what life is all about –

life is really to create meaning. And meaning does not come from what you get; it comes from what you give. Ultimately it's not what you get that will make you happy in the long term, but rather who you become and what you contribute[52]. What's more, this happiness is one of the most incredible benefits that we can gain from serving. Which only goes to enliven our soul and feed our emotional well-being.

Contribution beyond ourselves can touch someone's life in a way that improves it for the better. Where you are directly serving another and can hopefully see the whites of their eyes, know them, or have a genuine heartfelt interest in their plight – it will make a real difference to you. Fundamentally, the more human the contact, the more your personal growth and the bigger the emotional impression it will have on you as a result of helping them in some way.

SERVING OTHERS AND SOCIAL MEDIA

It's sad that with the rise in technology and its faster pace, society is changing and adapting in a negative way. It can be argued that we are, on the whole, less likely to contribute to others than say a generation ago. An example would be the rise in the use of social media, where some may wrongly mistake this detached form of connection as a form of contribution beyond themselves in some way. And as such, are happy to sit behind their keyboard for hours on end, stuffing data into the ether. In that by telling others how they like their favourite breakfast, or by pushing home on to their audience who their favourite sport's team is, they are somehow shaping their opinion – through the effect they believe it has on others. Little do they realise, this personal, opinionated form of advertising is only a craving for significance and can prevent people from having personal and healthy social contact.

The only examples of how you can use social media to contribute beyond yourself are to create an authentic connection to lift another's spirits or to pass on genuinely 'useful' or 'vital' information to society en mass, or through the ability it gives you to make an online donation to a charity.

While technology such as this has its place as a method of online escapism and remote connection, real personal human contribution beyond ourselves is only possible through a hands-on approach. These more face-to-face situations are where you can make the most significant difference in various ways such as volunteering, caring and support.

SOME REAL BENEFITS OF SERVING OTHERS

Serving in these ways provides massive benefits to both parties. For just you alone, supporting others will give a greater sense of well-being and inner contentment. It will grow your self-confidence and help to raise your self-esteem. The more closely you are heart aligned with how you are serving another with genuine kindness, the greater the personal benefits you will feel.

Just to reflect on some statistics in the field of volunteering alone in the UK, the report 'A National Survey into Volunteering' conducted by NVCO (National Council for Voluntary Organisations), on January 2019, stated: 'Around two-thirds of volunteers (68%) agreed their volunteering had helped them feel less isolated', and 'over three-quarters (77%) of volunteers agreed that volunteering had improved their mental health and well-being'[53].

In addition to the above, giving and helping are wired into us, and our brains typically reward us with feelings of joy and satisfaction. How many times have people said that doing things to help others 'just feels good', or that 'I get as much out of it as they do'. Research by three National Health Institutions in the USA worked on a collaborative project titled 'Cognitive and Emotional Health Project – the Healthy Brain'. The goal was to uncover the neurology of unselfish actions that reach out beyond kin to strangers. Nineteen subjects were each given money and a list of causes to which they might contribute. Functional magnetic resonance imaging revealed that making a donation activated the mesolimbic pathway, the brain's reward centre, which is responsible for dopamine-mediated euphoria[54]. When people do 'unto others' in kindness, it lights up the primitive part of the brain that also lets us experience joy. This is good news: even contemplating doing good for others goes with, rather than against, a big portion of the grain of human nature[55].

We can see from the above results that a form of contribution beyond yourself can provide you with real personal benefits. It merely gives your life a real lift. These figures demonstrate a validation of the positive individual outcomes that serving others can bring about. In addition to these more physiological and emotional benefits, serving others only goes to grow the spiritual side of our well-being. There are no religious connotations in the use of this term here; it is identifying that our soul is lifted through acts of kindness. This spiritual side is our 'inner peace', calmness and sense of connectedness that we can experience inside us, which are the more subtle aspects of our nature that each of us holds.

When we reach beyond ourselves and see and feel the impact that we have had on another, it provides us with spiritual growth and allows us to appreciate all that is good within. Ultimately, when we serve another in some way, we are having an impact on humanity at large, and then we are in a position to sense this spiritual benefit. When we do, we realise that we are connected to a much higher force than ourselves. And this helps to bring about a – much – greater meaning to life.

'Life is not meaningful... unless it is serving an end beyond itself; unless it is of value to someone else.'

Abraham Joshua Heschel

SELFISHNESS VERSUS SELFLESSNESS

Leading ourselves and serving others brings about a question of how much we concentrate on ourselves, in balance with the effort and time we spend on another. I have already addressed some of the benefits to us of service to another; the aim of this is to support the cause, not only to help the recipient but also the giver. This all gives rise to needing a balance, a sliding scale if you will, of what we can reasonably do for another while we ensure we are looking after ourselves, and vice versa.

This topic touches on the subject our sense of identity, or our ego, which I touched on previously. And how selfish and selfless we are, and how we ought to be able to strike a balance with our ego.

Consider this – you were not born with any possessions. So, you had nothing from day one. Then as life moves on, we all begin to accumulate possessions, and our ego begins to grow. This growth seems to be natural for us in that the ego is not something you ask for, or even apply for; it just becomes. However, it can prevent us from being able to see beyond ourselves in order to lay our eyes on another to provide some degree of kindness or caring.

I had a direct experience of this myself when my daughter was born, and she came home with us. She must have been only a week or two old, and I was sitting on the edge of the bed with her, having just fed her.

Then, while I was trying to work out if she was still hungry, and I had her sat on my lap, holding her head and shoulders – she was suddenly sick! I instantly put her down on the bed; carefully, I may add. But I was completely covered in what I'd just fed her and was far more worried about that. It instantly reminded me of the television character Dr Who, where the Tardis has more on the inside than you can see from the outside. There was milk everywhere. I was in complete shock as I could not work out where all the milk had come from, and I was sadly focused entirely on myself.

However, I was promptly scolded at the time, by my wife, for paying little attention to our baby, being more worried about me; and of course, she was entirely correct. This interruption awoke me, and in that moment I was utterly self-centred and acutely selfish. It left a real mark on me that I remember vividly to this day over twenty years later. On that occasion, my ego got in the way – and I learned a valuable lesson!

That experience is a simple example of the fact that unless we become observant or self-aware of our actions, our ego will remain in a prime position to govern a lot of our more self-centred or self-important behaviours in life. Ego if you consider it, is evident in people you cross, and again, is a natural growth as part of our make-up as it is our sense of identity. Overall, the ego is a complex construct that we all have and something with which we can identify.

However, in the context of serving others, we need to be self-aware that our ego can quickly get out of hand in that we become hugely egotistic: the ability for someone to have an inflated opinion of themselves. Therefore, we have to maintain our self-awareness and be mindful of ego, our sense of ourselves.

When it does get out of hand, ego defines ambition as striving to be better than everyone else, winning at all costs, accumulating more stuff, and being seen by others as brilliantly successful. Ego needs us to reject any idea of being connected in oneness to all that exists in the world. We must instead prove our alignment with ambition by having lofty goals and objectives[56]. The bigger the goals we have for ourselves, the more we accumulate and the more status we acquire. Then with our big goals and plans for our lives, the more we become aware of what we are missing. This loop will carry on to the point where we end up in a self-perpetuating cycle; unless we can escape the clutches of being egotistical, that is.

On the other hand, if we develop our ego, through techniques such as meditation, it slowly begins to evolve. Our sense of individuality grows to expand to those around us, so no longer are we just focused on 'I'; rather we bring the world around us and other people into our sense of identity. So, we have less of a boundary between us and the world around us. We, in this sense, can appreciate that connectedness with others and the world around us.

This expanded sense of identification is not ego-defining ambition, a small and concentrated ego focused on the self, which at the extreme is pitiful and pathetic. Rather, it is an ego raised to a new state of consciousness to include others, thus being more selfless, less judgemental, more caring.

For example, in recent times there has been some flooding in the UK due to the sheer amount of rainfall we have had. The other day I watched a video clip of a passer-by who swam into deep flowing water to save a lady, who had been in the water for hours, trapped. This man risked his life for another human being – who was a complete stranger to him. And there is simply no way that everyone would be prepared to even contemplate this heroic action. He had no special equipment with him, and was wearing just his ordinary clothes. But this is a simple example of where the ego has been raised to a state where it helps us look less into our ourselves, and more at those around us.

Essentially, as ego evolves the boundary between us and the world, and those around us, lessens. We are by nature, more selfless. And to serve others, ultimately strongly supports our journey to become fulfilled.

A need to create balance

On the subject of selfishness – and to flip everything on its head slightly – we also have to bear in mind that selfishness is part of our biology. When you eat because you are hungry, you are being selfish, and when you want to hide out of the rain, this again is a selfish act. And if we wish to work late to complete a task and will be late home, despite putting our partner out, this too is being selfish.

People are driven by pain and pleasure and therefore we need to look after ourselves, to care for ourselves, to do what we believe is in our best interest. Which, to a degree, is being selfish, but we need to do it, as we are human. But we need to create a balance. Therefore we ought to be careful of the amount that we do for others so that it's not to the detriment of ourselves. That is not to say that we don't do it; rather, we must be careful to balance what we do to take care of our needs against the needs of others.

However, to prevent our behaviour from being driven off course by our ego, we need to observe our behaviour. Be mindful of your actions around others, reflect and ask yourself if you are inspired by accumulating too much stuff, such as cars, jewellery or money. Are you solely wanting to grow your empire purely for the emotional kick that it will give you, meaning there is no practical reason for doing so? If so, then there is a possibility you are being too selfish. And if you believe you might be, the best course of action is to observe and reflect on your behaviour. Genuinely ask yourself whether you are content with how you act. Does it make you feel satisfied?

If you take the time to contemplate the questions, and not pay lip service to them, then there is only one way forward: to make progress towards creating a life driven less by ego.

INDEPENDENCE AND DEPENDENCE

When you stand back and reflect, there are two qualities or factors involved in moving you forward so that you can have a meaningful life. These two factors are independence and dependence. Independence is our ability to get things done by ourselves, and dependence, the degree by which we need, or reply upon, assistance, or help, or encouragement, to get those same things done. Let's face it we are all somewhere on that spectrum, between independence and dependence for a whole variety of different needs. That is, we all need help with something in life. Even the most successful person you know requires some degree of assistance; it's a given. They simply cannot do everything by themselves!

Ultimately, we need to bear in mind that we all depend on others to a greater or lesser extent; we required considerable intervention and assistance as newborns. To accept it allows us to take responsibility for our future selves.

This critical point, for our consideration, is that the older our bodies grow then the needier they become; and when the time comes, we will need to reach out to others for their help, care, support and acts of selflessness. It is worthwhile reflecting on the point being raised here. As at some point, there will be a need for you to consider your own situation. There will come the point where your needs will impact others, or you will become dependent upon them in the future.

This particular point being discussed, is not meant to sound gloomy or downhearted, just realistic. But in turn what may be the consequences, for those that you may know who have not reached out through stubbornness, pride or a false sense of independence but do need the support? Maybe, there is someone that you know that can do with help right now but who does not have the emotional intelligence or depth of courage to ask for it?

If we reflect on this point it allows us to take a wider perspective on our lives fully, and helps to force the fact that the act of selflessness is an essential factor in serving others. Not only will the act of being selfless, when genuine and from the heart, help to lessen the influence of our ego, but due to the law of cause and effect, or karma, it will come back to us in ways that we never expected.

Our fleeting independent or semi-independent years will rely on much more support the older we get – as we did when we were infants. Maybe not exceptionally so, as there are semi-independent people that are into their ripe old age, but they all require more support than they did when they were in their youth – that is a fact. Hence, make a conscious choice and choose to be selfless at times – acting from the heart.

The more you apply the act of selflessness, then the easier it will become, until one day it becomes a habit, and the more you will gain as a result. It may not happen immediately, but it will come back to you in ways you never expected.

A selfless act will be in direct conflict with the ego but will grow our self-leadership toolset as well as our spiritual awareness. We must nonetheless remain selfish to an extent to protect our self-worth in life and not to be taken advantage of; this is an essential and relevant point. But creating balance and acting selflessly and genuinely, when appropriate, is such a noble act. If practised often, it will become a habit, which I hope you will employ and also enjoy.

'Every action generates a force of energy that returns to us in like kind . . . what we sow is what we reap. And when we choose actions that bring happiness and success to others, the fruit of our Karma is happiness and success. Karma is the eternal assertion of human freedom . . . Our thoughts, our words, and deeds are the threads of the net which we throw around ourselves.'

Swami Vivekananda

SERVING OTHERS, WITH THE END IN MIND

If there is one thing, people in the modern age are now becoming guilty of it's steering away from the fact that no one gets out of this life alive. We all must die, pass on from this existence, depart this mortal plane – whichever phrase feels more comfortable to describe what may feel an uncomfortable subject. This topic is not meant in any way to sound miserable or melancholy; it's merely a fact of life.

It is a reminder of a point which I believe will help reinforce my topic here – in that if we reflect on our mortality, and if we do this deeply enough such that it makes an emotional mark, this reflection allows us to look at life differently.

While writing this chapter, an ex-colleague of mine passed away, and it forced me to reflect on my own life – quite profoundly. I worked alongside him for over two years but knew him for much longer, and in all, I got to know him well. He died comparably young of a serious form of cancer – and I genuinely miss him being around.

Though I knew his condition was terminal, because of the therapy he was put on things at one point looked more promising for him. In the end, he took a turn for the worse, and he did pass away rather suddenly. The bizarre thing was that we were in communication four days before, and there was no way of predicting what would happen. And in all, it both made me consider what my relationship was like with him before he passed away, and it was an abrupt reminder of my own mortality.

And I do believe some considered contemplation on our own dying is healthy in only that it can take our gaze away from ourselves and onto the wonders of the world around us, and arguably more importantly, towards our relationships with others. Why? Because our relationships are the life-blood of life. Our relationships help to create and mould us as people, and hopefully for the better.

We start in life by building relationships with our parents and this blossoms into many hundreds, if not thousands, of relationships throughout our lives; our relationships affect us enormously. And when we are close to parting this life and reflect on our years, our close relationships with others provide us with some of our most beautiful memories. So, a natural extension of this is to consider what we've done for others while we were able.

But to return to the subject of death, we all must go, we all die at some point and, more than this, we can take nothing with us from this life. If you look around at everything you have accumulated in your life thus far and consider all you have, when you pass on from your being none of it goes with you; you leave all of it behind.

That point may be difficult for you to swallow, but then again, at the same time it is cruelly self-evident.

I'm sure you may wish to provide for your children or dependents, or even give a portion of your estate to charity when you pass on, and these are ethical and responsible wishes. Yet, if we reflect on the fact that we can't take anything with us when we die, this should help put things into perspective if we ever find ourselves guilty of caring a little less for others than we probably should. Because once we have enough, without being greedy, maybe some of what we have can be given away?

There are always needy people around who don't have enough to get by on in life. You only need to look into the shopping malls late at night in most major cities to see this first hand, to see those living rough on the streets. This sight of those living in this way should help sober the selfish out there.

Regrets and relationships

However, if we consider our existence a little further, we are suffering from a situation in that the first world has become a society that, to an extent, is ignoring the fact that we die. Maybe this is because we are living longer. Better healthcare, new treatments like antibiotics, kidney dialysis and early chemotherapy, better nutrition, immunisation programmes and other developments radically changed people's experience of illness and offered hope of cure, or at least postponement of dying[57]. This fact has triggered a mind-shift away from expecting to die and towards looking for a cure; therefore, when death does happen, it is more of a shock for the bereaved. The fact that in everyday life we are less accustomed to the dying process of others means that some of us are living a delusion that we will always be here, as if life will go on for ever, but this is of course not true.

If you take the opportunity to imagine that you are in your final hours looking back on life and reflecting on what you may have done differently, like the rest of us, you would have a list of things that could have been different. And that is very normal. I don't believe for one single moment anyone leaves this plane with a clean sheet; hindsight is a truly wonderful thing.

But wouldn't it be ideal not to have end-of-life regrets? And while regrets are self-indulgent and typically people do tend to have them when we reflect on our lives, it is wise to consider what regrets we may have in years to come now, to see if we can make amends from this point forward. And so, in the context of this 'step' of self-leadership, if we were looking back on our life, would we wonder if there was any more we could have done for others if we were able to? To be less selfish, less self-indulgent. To never have to look back and say, 'I wish I would have done "this" or "that" to help another in some way.'

I am not stating in any way that there is a need for us to spend all our available time to serve others; that would be simply absurd. I'm merely pointing out that there is more peace of mind that can be found when we have a bigger driver in our life other than ourselves. Again, this is an important element of our inner growth, as humans on this planet, so it is worthwhile considering the points made here.

We are all connected, and therefore it makes sense to extend help to another, where we can. To take our eyes away from the mirror and to focus on someone else. Commonly referred to as the golden rule, a great principle applies in life: 'Do unto others as you would have them do unto you.' If you take the time to follow that simple approach in life, you can never go far wrong.

If you can imagine humanity is a tree, then every individual on the planet are all branches from that same tree. Our intelligence connects us. It provides us with a way for us to communicate with each other fundamentally. We are all linked. We all come from the same source and have a relationship with one another that has much more in common than you may initially know.

Take, for example, the solid bond that a mother has for a child, especially when first born; this connection is tangible and robust but has come out of nowhere, born of human nature and nothing else. However, this relationship can't stay this way for ever. People must strive, grow and move on, and this means that the bond must loosen, but it never dies. Well, this bond – this connection – is an extreme example of the relationship that we all have with each other, we are all parts of one sum. Therefore, it makes sense that we have a vested interest in our inner growth to serve another where we can. If nothing else, it makes us feel good, it gets our juices going, and that good feeling inside us – counts.

'Helping one person might not change the world,
but it could change the world for one person.'

Anonymous

AMBITION, GRATITUDE AND HUMILITY

Bill Gates, who founded Microsoft, and was reputed at one point to be the richest man in the world, is now a superb ambassador in respect of serving others. Bill, with his wife Melinda, founded the Bill & Melinda Gates Foundation back in 2000, and this institute is reported to be the largest foundation in the world. The organisation serves the whole world and regularly collaborates with non-profit organisations to alleviate the world's most pressing concerns, such as HIV/AIDS. Its healthcare budget alone exceeds that of the World Health Organisation (WHO)[58].

So, while I understand that Bill does like to keep himself busy by nature, you may wonder why he doesn't sit back on his wealth and do very little? Instead, he assists others less fortunate around the globe. He has invested a lot of his time and tens of billions of US dollars in the foundation.

And whereas you may consider he has the money to do this, that is not the point. The point is that the venture that Bill is in with his wife clearly must provide them with a level of internal satisfaction and a new life purpose. Directing their focus and attention towards philanthropic ventures, to help those less fortunate than themselves, must give them an immense thrill. It's a positively tremendous act when you consider it.

Bill and Melinda are examples of several successful people across the globe, who you would initially consider would always choose to strive for greater success throughout their career, but for who there appears to be a tipping point. A point where it is not about them any more; it's not about gaining more wealth, or having more material possessions: it's about serving others in some way. Bill and Melinda Gates would appear to have transcended the drive for the self; in some higher sense of purpose, they've reached a turning point and look to others to support.

And so, why do some of us in life turn our attention to a greater purpose than ourselves when we have achieved a certain level of attainment? You might say without thinking about it too much that it's a way of spending money, or maybe it's to be seen by others as performing a good deed, so there's a degree of vanity involved. And while arguably I'm sure there is an element of truth in both of these points for some, on the whole, it's not about that. There must be a more significant realisation, a sense of awareness that it is not just about them or their achievements any more.

Well, I believe what has been achieved by these people is a real sense of both gratitude and humility that has been generated by a level of success. They have lowered their sense of importance; they have seen beyond themselves and are feeling a genuine need to reach out to serve another, and remain grateful for the privilege. Both gratitude and humility being two marks of a great leader.

Gratitude concerning others in life allows us to remain grateful for what we achieve, accomplish or even are. To have relationships with others, to be grateful to be in the company of those that you want to, and to enjoy their presence. And then to be genuinely thankful for the experience and the joy and contentment it brings.

You can spend fifteen minutes with someone and genuinely engage with them, and build up more rapport with that person than you would build up in a day if less interested, less engaged. Besides, being humble allows us to stay low in life and to be strong, according to Dr Wayne Dyer who was a renowned author and speaker in the fields of self-development and spiritual growth puts it, 'the sea is one of the strongest forces in the world all the rivers and streams flow into the sea. The sea does nothing but lays low. It stays humble. By staying low, you remain strong and allow things to happen, to come to you.'

Some of the best leaders in the world practice humility and assist others. Allow yourself to have a vested interest in those you choose to help, really listen to their plight deeply to gain a fuller appreciation of where they are at, and you will then put yourself in the best position, and the best mindset, to help them.

If you stay humble when helping or assisting another and genuinely learn to understand their difficulty, it puts you in a much better position to serve. Whether this is your chosen career or merely the understanding that you give another through conversation to remain humble but strong allows you to connect with others in ways that the ego prevents.

You don't need to wait for success to reflect on how you help another along in life. Even if you serve occasionally in some way, you will find an inner growth that is much bigger than ambition alone can bring. You will have self-led yourself to become a better person for it, I guarantee it.

There is nothing wrong with ambition, or at least there is nothing wrong with being ambitious as long as it serves the greater good. Ambition is traditionally likened to activity, and it creates, innovates, causes development, and on a personal note, it matures our internal growth through the challenge!

Ambitious people can make the seemingly impossible possible with the right vision, determination and tenacity, not forgetting the small matter of funding. And while on the flip side activities such as solitude and meditation in the pursuit of inner peace and enlightenment may be considered ambitious goals, in themselves they perhaps reject the notion of ambition. But ambition driven by the ego to the detriment of others is intoxicating and causes damage to someone somewhere along its path, and thus should be avoided at all costs.

That is an important point to remember when leading yourself – you must be able to appreciate the impact of your actions on others. It is a fundamental element of your emotional intelligence to be able to recognise the result of your actions on others, but ambition driven too hard will prevent you from being aware of your impact. It will cloud your vision, you remain singularly focused, as your actions are driven by hormones such as testosterone and dopamine.

But most of us in business and life with a more determined personality type have experienced ambition at one point or another, and most of this is healthy ambition. There is a desire to achieve and to create. However, when purpose becomes all about status, rank, or money and serves no practical means other than how it makes someone feel, then they have to take a good long hard look in the mirror and self-reflect on whom they have become. Whom have they grown into, and consider what genuinely matters in their life and actions. And then question where their steps will take them, to what end? What are the repercussions?

True nobility is not about being better than anyone else; it is about being better than the person you once were – this is the mark of a great self-leader.

*'You can easily judge the character of a man
by how he treats those who can do nothing for him.'*

Malcolm Forbes

NOW, OVER TO YOU

This last chapter is asking you to be more attentive to others while still keeping yourself in mind. The reasons? Well, we are all part of humanity, and the final step towards our self-leadership bow is to accept this as truth – and take action. And this, in turn, will return a mutual benefit to both whom you serve and you.

Again, there must be a balance. We need to balance selfishness and selflessness. Selfishness is an instinct, in that we need to be selfish to live. However, we will never achieve any real level of satisfaction if we are entirely selfish. Some component of our nature must remain selfless if we want to achieve happiness and be completely satisfied. We will never gain fulfilment through possessions alone.

To see if you believe that you live with the right balance of serving yourself and serving others, you need to consider your life and your relationships – and how you serve others today. Then reflect and consider whether you need to change this. A great way to do this is by drawing a picture, where you are in the middle, and then start to identify the relationships that you have with others in your life. This relationship diagram can start with immediate family, and work out to distant family, friends and work colleagues, or even clients. And then can end up at groups or parties of people you don't know. This could be those you raise charitable money for or groups you may volunteer for, or similar.

Then move on to asking yourself, honestly, if you are content with your contribution to each. If you are genuinely satisfied with your outcome, then fine. But where you find a gap, where you believe you can serve more, explore in what ways that could be.

It would be best if you did not ask the question, 'What must I do?', to prevent thinking of how others might respond, or to prevent feelings of guilt. Instead, the question you should pose to yourself is, 'Do I have the genuine opportunity to serve, which I will feel comfortable with, now and later in life?' And this can be in a small way – a word of encouragement, a card – or a hefty dose of love and benevolence.

To be able to serve others is a superb human characteristic; it also serves you in that it makes you a complete person, a more noble character. To serve another will enhance your self-leadership skills as you grow and flourish in moral value and nobility as a result.

PERSONAL CONTRIBUTION
PAUL NEW: PHYSIOTHERAPIST

My great mistake

My name is Paul New, and I'm a physiotherapist. When I look back over my working life, I realise that I have spent almost my entire time serving other people. I left physio school, like nearly all physios do, honestly believing that the skills and techniques I had learned at university would make people better – a naïve belief that I was the fix, that I healed the injured! But this thought, that perhaps happens because, as a newly qualified healthcare professional, you have nothing else, is a common misperception. You have no clinical mileage yet, just untested theory and no practical knowledge or experience in the craft of delivering therapy.

That thought usually lasts until the day you make a great mistake! A mistake that suddenly shatters your perception of the world of scientific truths. Which up until this point was held as absolute, and forever after this point the world is never the same again.

My great mistake came on a hectic day of back-to-back patients. With the usual hustle and bustle of helping people on and off the treatment couch, shoehorns, pullovers and left-behind walking sticks, which are all part of a busy day in clinic. I was treating a poor man who struggled in with a painful, hot and swollen knee, and I decided to try and help alleviate his symptoms with some ultrasound treatment. After it was complete, the patient miraculously jumped up off the couch and thanked me profusely, as his knee felt much better. I escorted him to the door, we exchanged a handshake, and I left as the successful therapist and returned to the room to write notes – then spotted the plug on the wall was off! The machine was off! No ultrasound had been given; I had performed a sham treatment! It was a great mistake – but the guy was better for not being given any ultrasound whatsoever!

This misconception again is a common experience in therapy, and it makes you suddenly snap to attention wide-eyed. You ask yourself, 'What the hell just happened there?' I helped someone without doing what I thought I did. And that's the point!

To me, every clinical consultation is a small self-leadership challenge. Where you need to lead a patient towards a recovery, support through a problem, help to achieve a goal and encourage towards a new beginning or a different future. That requires self-leadership but not in the way that one might intuitively think. Nobody will engage with therapy if they are ordered to follow instructions or shouted at for not doing the exercises they have been set. So, what is to be done then, if we want a successful outcome?

In physiotherapy, patients are led back to health by being supported, listen to, cared for, encouraged, advised and served by their therapy team. We serve our customer base, we support them, not cure them, and to do that we have to care. It takes an open-minded attitude to listen attentively to the needs of others, to be compassionate to their experiences and to act with the correct responsibility to bring out the best in them. To put their needs before ours, before theory, before clinical rules and evidence-based algorithms. The more I worked on my own self-leadership (listening skills are vital in clinical practice), the more I understood the impact that problems had on the lives of my patients. The better grasp I had of their experiences, the better decisions I made and the better results I achieved.

My great mistake taught me that caring and serving is just as important as all the clinical theory-based treatments. Studying can guide you, but if you don't get the balance right, none of the theory will work anyway.

You don't have to have all the answers to lead a recovery process or a team, but you do have to serve others! You do have to emotionally really be there; you do have to empathise, to listen, to care and indeed be there for other people in the team. To give confidence to people, to get others to try, to help people to be better, to flourish and to find fulfilment, you must first serve them. And I think this holds true as a universal truth. The question must always be, 'What I can do to help this person achieve their aims?' To me, that's all part of my self-leadership, but it's different from what I originally thought it was.

Afterword

Build A Better Tomorrow

Thank you for sharing this journey of the *7 Steps to Successful Self-Leadership* with me. You will have now discovered that these steps are primarily born out of a substantial amount of real-world experience – experience enriched with original stories, learned lessons, trial and error, contributions and research. I did not know that any of my life experiences or what I observed in others would one day be accumulated to form a book. But I absolutely felt in the back of my mind, given my journey thus far, this book was in me. I feel thrilled you've got to this point.

Self-leadership is all about taking responsibility to do the right thing in order to thrive – hence the book title. Even though, as we all know, that life will have the canny knack of creating challenges along our journey. However, if we make it our goal to make the best choices possible, then, step-by-step, we can at least advance in the right direction towards a better future.

I wholeheartedly believe from my own experiences in my self-leadership – and those I have led, trained and consulted with – that these seven steps are the fundamental building blocks to becoming a more rounded individual, and to thrive in work and life. In the real world.

I also genuinely hope that you can benefit from this book and gain everything that I intended from it. To self-lead, grow and change is not always easy, and significant change does not happen overnight. But in addition to that, sometimes we are too close to ourselves to see that change is happening and that our character has grown and adapted. Self-leading can be a little deceiving in this sense, we can't always see our growth first hand. But by leading ourselves, we are naturally ever-evolving, and always moving forward. Never overlook this important point, always remain mindful of your growth.

If you encounter a setback, please don't become discouraged by this. Challenges all are part and parcel of the rich tapestry of the building of a more solid leader and more capable person overall. Pick yourself up, as tomorrow is another day. Roll with the punches and keep the momentum going. This is the stuff of life and you need to move and work with what is present and now.

The next steps for you are to ensure that you have undertaken the actions in the 'Now, over to you' sections at the end of each chapter. Don't give yourself the excuse to miss them out – this is not self-leadership. Live in the arena of life, and don't shy away from it.

I wrote this book to help you, but you can always seek me out to serve in some way at www.georgewilkinson.co, so never feel you are on your own out there. Either way, good luck!

Now, over to you – go lead yourself, and others today – to build a better tomorrow.

Acknowledgements

I have to start by thanking my superb wife, Jane. From reading the early drafts and giving me some challenging but highly useful advice, so I could edit, she was as important to this book getting done as I was. Thank you so much. Also, a heartfelt thanks go to *all* my immediate family for being patient with me through the efforts of writing this book; without whose understanding it would never have been possible.

In no way would this book even be written if it wasn't for a deep conversation that I had with a true gent Jon Cassell back in 2009, who was the one that planted a seed in my mind; that over time grew into this book. A highly evolved individual, who has a wizard's mind. Also to Danny Dobson an outstanding Peak Performance Consultant and Executive Coach, and whose wise and inspiring guidance created my direction, and kept me going in the darker days of my writing. I would also like to thank Steve Williams a world authority in paediatrics and craniopathy, who paid an interest and shared the lessons he'd learned along his own author's journey. That interest made me adapt my strategy where I reached the end as a result.

I would like to thank all of my contributors to each chapter: Bill Webster, for being the first to agree to one, and who kept me excited every time I spoke to him. For Diane and Megan, whose contribution I received one Sunday stopped me in my tracks, and frankly inspired me to complete the book. To Jon Cassell, mentioned above, who simply had to help since he unknowingly inspired the idea behind this book. To Clive Smith, a fellow author for listening to the progress I was making and passively holding me to account. To Robert Rogers, for inspiring me in life in general and for providing such a swift response to a contribution to my request. To the extent that it created even more momentum in me. To Derek Taylor, who in the past I have had the absolute pleasure of working alongside - and I know his words count. To Paul New, who was a late but important contributor, but whose words wonderfully complemented the last chapter.

To those who helped me on the journey to improve this work, which included my Beta readers and those who performed additional content reviews: Garry Craig, Alan Handley, Paul New, Deb Seal and Marian Way. I'd also like to thank all of those who provided professional support, guidance and inspiration, which included all the team at RedDoor particularly Clare Christian and Heather Boisseau for having the faith in the idea for *Thrive* and for bringing it into being. To Megan Sheer for being patient with me in the development of my drawings. To Adam Thorpe (The Brand Chap) for the development of my book cover and his understanding. My editors and proofreader who helped bring the final work to life: Martine Chapman, Nicky Gyopari and Kathy Steer.

To all the individuals I have had the opportunity in my journey to lead, be led by, or watch their leadership from a distance. You inspired me to lead myself and to lead and serve others to a greater extent, and for being the foundation for *Thrive*.

A final thanks to those wonderful and larger than life characters that I have met and worked alongside in my journey to get to this book, in my personal life and through in my time in the armed services and beyond; there are too many to mention. Those that were teaching me the hard lessons and experiences of life, where some I have shared in this book. When neither they, nor I, knew those lessons would ever go down on paper. Life is somewhat strange the way it all works out.

Notes

CHAPTER 1 – ACHIEVING SUCCESS

1. Chamine, S (2012). *Positive Intelligence.* (2016 Edition ed.). Austin Tx: Green leaf Book Group Press.

2. Kristin neff, C. c2020. Self-Compassion website. [Online]. [02 March 2019]. Available from: https://self-compassion.org/what-self-compassion-is-not-2/

CHAPTER 2 – PERSEVERANCE

3. Robbins, T. 2014. Entrepreneur Europe website. [Online]. [08 December 2019]. Available from: https://www.entrepreneur.com/article/240441

4. Schunk, D. H. 2001. Self-regulation Through Goal Setting. ERIC/CASS Digest ED 462671, US Department of Education, Office of Educational Research and Improvement

5. Bolt, U. 2013. ITV website. [Online]. [19 September 2019]. Available from: https://www.itv.com/news/update/2013-09-19/usain-bolt-setting-goals-is-the-key-to-my-success/

6. Fuller, R. 2019. BBC website. [Online]. [16 August 2019]. Available from: https://www.bbc.co.uk/sport/tennis/49367223

7. Gallup Inc. (2017). *State of the Global Workplace.* New York: Gallup Press.

8. Thomas, C.P. 2013. Harvard Business Review website. [Online]. [14th July 2018]. Available from: https://hbr.org/2013/04/does-money-really-affect-motiv

9. Thomas, C.P. 2013. Harvard Business Review website. [Online]. [14th July 2018]. Available from: https://hbr.org/2013/04/does-money-really-affect-motiv

10. Alchoholorg. c2020. American Addiction Centres website. [Online]. [18 July 2018]. Available from: https://www.alcohol.org/alcoholics-anonymous/step-1/

11. Hague, T. (2018). *Perseverance: the seven skills you need to survive, thrive, and accomplish more than you ever imagined.* Canada: Viking.

12. Roman, S. (2011). *Living with Purpose: Keys to Personal Power and Spiritual Transformation.* California: New World Library.

13. Pettinger, T. 13 February 2008. Biography Online website. [Online]. [28 February 2020]. Available from: https://www.biographyonline.net/politicians/nelson-mandela.html

14. Csikszentmihalyi, M. (2002). *Flow: The classic work on how to achieve happiness.* : Harper and Row.

15. Csikszentmihalyi, M. (2002). *Flow: The classic work on how to achieve happiness.* : Harper and Row.

CHAPTER 3 – EMOTIONAL MASTERY

16. Lexicocom. 2020. Lexico website. [Online]. [03 January 2019]. Available from: https://en.oxforddictionaries.com/definition/emotion

17. Goleman, D.R.C. (1996). *Emotional Intelligence: Why it can matter more than IQ.* London: Bloomsbury.

18. Richman, L. Kubzansky, L. & Maselko, J. 2005. Positive Emotion and Health: Going Beyond the Negative. ResearchGate. 24(4), pp. 422–429.

19. Yoo SS, Gujar N. Hu P., Jolesz F.A., Walker M.P. The human emotional brain without sleep—a prefrontal amygdala disconnect. Curr Biol. 2007;17(20):R877-R878. doi:10.1016/j.cub.2007.08.007

20. Bradberry, T. c2020. TalentSmart website. [Online]. [2 March 2019]. Available from: http://www.talentsmart.com/articles/11-Habits-of-Supremely-Happy-People-2147446655-p-1.html

21. Roenthal, N.E. (2011). *Transcendence – Healing and Transformation through Transcendental Meditation.* New York: Tarcher.

22. Tmhomecom. 2015. Transcendental Meditation home website. [Online]. [10th August 2018]. Available from: https://tmhome.com/benefits/generating-happiness-positive-emotions-and-well-being-with-meditation/

23. Lynch, D (2016). Catching The Big Fish. USA: Penguin Random House USA.

24. Dobelli, R. (2014). *The Art of Thinking Clearly*. London: Sceptre.

25. Robbins, T. (1992). *Awaken the Giant Within: How to Take Immediate Control of Your Mental, Emotional, Physical and Financial Life*. London: Simon and Schuster Ltd

26. Nhs. c2020. NHS UK website. [Online]. [7 April 2018]. Available from: https://www.nhs.uk/Conditions/stress-anxiety-depression/Pages/mental-benefits-of-exercise.aspx

27. White, D. c2018. PsychCentral website. [Online]. [10 November 18]. Available from: https://psychcentral.com/lib/improving-your-emotional-health-through-healthier-eating/

28. Goleman, D. Boyatzis, R. & Mckee, A. (2004). *Primal Leadership: Learning to Lead with Emotional Intelligence*. USA: Harvard Business Review Press.

29. Goleman, D. Boyatzis, R. & Mckee, A. (2004). *Primal Leadership: Learning to Lead with Emotional Intelligence*. USA: Harvard Business Review Press.

30. Maier, S. (2019). *100 Great Mindset Changing Ideas (The 100 Great Ideas Series)*. Singapore: Marshall Cavendish International (Asia) Pte Ltd.

31. Bradberry, T. & Greaves, J. (2009). Emotional Intelligence 20. San Diego: Talent Smart.

CHAPTE XR 4 – EMBRACING FAILURE

32. Becker-phelps, L. 2016. Psychology Today website. [Online]. [20 July 2019]. Available from: https://www.psychologytoday.com/us/blog/making-change/201611/what-do-when-you-feel-failure

33. Roosevelt, T. 2010. Leadership Now website. [Online]. [14 June 2019]. Available from:https://www.leadershipnow.com/leadingblog/2010/04/theodore_roosevelts_the_man_in.html

34. *Very Good Lives*: Copyright © J.K. Rowling 2008.

35. Wikipediaorg. c2020. Wikipedia website. [Online]. [7 February 2020]. Available from: https://en.wikipedia.org/wiki/Harry_Potter

36. Schwartz, T., Gomes, J. & Mccarthy, C. (2010). *Be Excellent at Anything*. New York: Free Press.

37. Morrish, J.K. c2020. Management Today website. [Online]. [4 July 2019]. Available from: https://www.managementtoday.co.uk/does-word-resilience-from/any-other-business/article/1401232

38. Chopra, D. (1989). *Quantum Healing: Exploring the Frontiers of Mind/Body Medicine*. New York: Bantam New Age.

CHAPTER 5 – DECISION-MAKING

39. Osman, M. 2015. The Psychological Society website. [Online]. [14 April 2019]. Available from: https://thepsychologist.bps.org.uk/volume-28/february-2015/does-our-unconscious-rule

40. Chang, R. 2014. Tedx website. [Online]. [18 June 2018]. Available from: https://www.ted.com/talks/ruth_chang_how_to_make_hard_choices?language=en

41. Way, M. (2013). *Clean Approaches for Coaches: How to create conditions for change*. Fareham, England: Clean Publishing.

42. Neal, L. Spetzler, C. 2017. Harvard Business Review website. [Online]. [02 May 2020]. Available from: https://hbr.org/2015/05/an-organization-wide-approach-to-good-decision-making

43. Goleman, D. Boyatzis, R. & Mckee, A. (2004). *Primal Leadership: Learning to Lead with Emotional Intelligence*. USA: Harvard Business Review Press.

44. Shpancer, N. 2010. Psychology Today website. [Online]. [30 May 2019]. Available from: https://www.psychologytoday.com/gb/blog/insight-therapy/201010/action-creates-emotion

45. Myatt, M. 2012. Forbes website. [Online]. [16 May 2019]. Available from: https://www.forbes.com/sites/mikemyatt/2012/03/28/6-tips-for-making-better-decisions/#2ceb5a6634dc

46. Kahneman, D. (2011). *Thinking Fast and Slow*. Great Britain: Penguin Books.

47. Boyes, A. 2020. Harvard Business Review website. [Online]. [3 May 2020]. Available from: https://hbr.org/2020/03/dont-let-perfection-be-the-enemy-of-productivity

CHAPTER 6 – LEADERSHIP OF OTHERS

48. Corp, L. 2018. Biography Your Dictionary website. [Online]. [26 April 2020]. Available from: https://biography.yourdictionary.com/articles/martin-luther-kings-vision-change-world.html

49. History com editors. 2020. History website. [Online]. [26 April 2020]. Available from: https://www.history.com/topics/black-history/civil-rights-act

50. Maccoby, A. 2004. Harvard Business Review website. [Online]. 11 August 2018]. Available from: https://hbr.org/2004/09/why-people-follow-the-leader-the-power-of-transference

51. Glaser, J.E. (2014). *Conversational Intelligence: How Great Leaders Build Trust and Get Extraordinary Results*. New York: Bibliomotion Inc.

52. Robbins, T. 2014. Entrepreneur website. [Online]. [19 October 2018]. Available from: https://www.entrepreneur.com/article/240441

CHAPTER 7 – SERVING OTHERS

53. Mcgarvey, A. et al (2019). Time Well Spent: A National on the Volunteer Experience. Great Britain: NVCO.

54. Post, S. (2011). *The Hidden Gifts of Helping*. United States of America: Josey-Bass.

55. Post, S. (2011). *The Hidden Gifts of Helping*. United States of America: Josey-Bass.

56. Dyer, W. (2010). *The Shift: Taking Your Life from Ambition to Meaning*. United States of America: Hay House.

57. Mannix , K. (2017). *With the end in Mind: How to Live and Die Well*. London: William Collins.

58. Chepkemoi, J.E. 2017. World Atlas website. [Online]. [19 October 2019]. Available from: https://www.worldatlas.com/articles/which-are-the-wealthiest-charitable-foundations-worldwide.html

About the Author

George Wilkinson moved away from Edinburgh, his city of birth, to join the British Royal Navy and left having served during the Gulf war in 91. He subsequently spent almost three decades working with leading organisations such as SKY, Hewlett Packard, Fujitsu, and the NHS. Here he performed strategic leadership, consulting and training roles, and now works with a variety of clients to help teams and individuals harness their real potential.

Find out more about RedDoor
Press and sign up to our
newsletter to hear about our
latest releases, author events,
exciting **competitions**
and more at

reddoorpress.co.uk

YOU CAN ALSO FOLLOW US:

 @RedDoorBooks

 Facebook.com/RedDoorPress

 @RedDoorBooks